Lecture Notes in Computer Science 11772

More information about this series at http://www.springer.com/series/7407

Qi Zhang · Xiangwen Liao ·
Zhaochun Ren (Eds.)

Information Retrieval

25th China Conference, CCIR 2019
Fuzhou, China, September 20–22, 2019
Proceedings

 Springer

Editors
Qi Zhang
Fudan University
Shanghai, China

Xiangwen Liao
Fuzhou University
Fuzhou, China

Zhaochun Ren
Shandong University
Qingdao, China

ISSN 0302-9743   ISSN 1611-3349 (electronic)
Lecture Notes in Computer Science
ISBN 978-3-030-31623-5   ISBN 978-3-030-31624-2 (eBook)
https://doi.org/10.1007/978-3-030-31624-2

LNCS Sublibrary: SL1 – Theoretical Computer Science and General Issues

This Springer imprint is published by the registered company Springer Nature Switzerland AG
The registered company address is: Gewerbestrasse 11, 6330 Cham, Switzerland

Preface

The 2019 China Conference on Information Retrieval (CCIR 2019), co-organized by the Chinese Information Processing Society of China (CIPS) and the Chinese Computer Federation (CCF), was the 25th installment of the conference series. The conference was hosted by Fuzhou University in Fuzhou, Fujian, China, during September 20–22, 2019.

The annual CCIR conference serves as the major forum for researchers and practitioners from both China and other Asian countries/regions to share their ideas, present new research results, and demonstrate new systems and techniques in the broad field of information retrieval (IR). Since CCIR 2017, the conference has enjoyed contributions spanning the theory and application of IR, both in English and Chinese.

This year we received 90 submissions from both China and other Asian countries, among which 13 were English papers and 34 were Chinese ones. Each submission was carefully reviewed by at least three domain experts, and the Program Committee (PC) chairs made the final decision. The final English program of CCIR 2019 featured 13 papers.

CCIR 2019 included abundant academic activities. Besides keynote speeches delivered by world-renowned scientists from China and abroad, as well as traditional paper presentation sessions and poster sessions, we also hosted doctoral mentoring forums, a young scientist forum, an evaluation workshop, and tutorials on frontier research topics. We also invited authors in related international conferences (such as SIGIR, WWW, WSDM, CIKM) to share their research results as well.

CCIR 2019 featured four keynote speeches by Khalid Al-Kofahi (Reuters Thomson), Yi Zhang (University of California, Santa Cruz), Jirong Wen (Renmin University of China), and Zhi Geng (Peking University).

The conference and program chairs of CCIR 2019 extend their sincere gratitude to all authors and contributors to this year's conference. We are also grateful to the PC members for their reviewing effort, which guaranteed that CCIR 2019 could feature a quality program of original and innovative research in IR. Special thanks go to our sponsors for their generosity: Elens, Dworld AI Tech, Huawei, Baidu, CIPOL, and Sogou. We also thank Springer for supporting the best paper award of CCIR 2019.

August 2019

Chengxiang Zhai
Yiqun Liu
Qi Zhang
Xiangwen Liao
Zhaochun Ren

Organization

Steering Committee

Shuo Bai	Shanghai Stock Exchange, China
Xueqi Cheng	Institute of Computing Technology, Chinese Academy of Sciences, China
Shoubin Dong	EastChina University of Science and Technology, China
Xiaoming Li	Beijing University, China
Hongfei Lin	Dalian University of Technology, China
Ting Liu	Harbin Institute of Technology, China
Jun Ma	Shandong University, China
Shaoping Ma	Tsinghua University, China
Shuicai Shi	Beijing TRS Information Technology Co., Ltd, China
Mingwen Wang	Jiangxi Normal University, China

Conference General Chairs

Chengxiang Zhai	University of Illinois Urbana-Champaign, USA
Yiqun Liu	Tsinghua University, China

Program Committee Chairs

Qi Zhang	Fudan University, China
Xiangwen Liao	Fuzhou University, China

Youth Forum Chairs

Rui Yan	Peking University, China
Minlie Huang	Tsinghua University, China

CCIR Cup Chair

Tong Ruan	East China University of Science and Technology, China

Proceedings Chair

Zhaochun Ren	Shandong University, China

Publicity Chair

Peng Zhang   Tianjin University, China

Sponsorship Chair

Zhicheng Dou   Renmin University of China, China

Local Chair

Yunbing Wu   Fuzhou University, China

Treasury Chair

Xiaoyan Yu   Fuzhou University, China

Program Committee

Shuo Bai   Wanxiang Blockchain Labs, China
Xueqi Cheng   Institute of Computing Technology, Chinese Academy
                               of Sciences, China
Fei Cai   National University of Defense Technology, China
Dongfeng Cai   Shenyang Aerospace University, China
Zhumin Chen   Shandong University, China
Yi Chang   Jilin University, China
Yajun Du   Xihua University, China
Shoubin Dong   South China University of Technology, China
Zhicheng Dou   Renmin University of China, China
Shicong Feng   Beijing Siming Software System Co., Ltd, China
Jiafeng Guo   Institute of Computing Technology, Chinese Academy
                               of Sciences, China
Xuanxuan Huang   Fudan University, China
Yu Hong   Suzhou University, China
Minlie Huang   Tsinghua University, China
Zhongyuan Han   Heilongjiang Institute of Technology, China
Donghong Ji   Wuhan University, China
Tieyan Liu   Microsoft Asia Research Institute, China
Yiqun Liu   Tsinghua University, China
Ting Liu   Harbin Institute of Technology, China
Hang Li   Toutiao AI Lab, China
Hongfei Lin   Dalian University of Technology, China
Yue Liu   Institute of Computing Technology, Chinese Academy
                               of Sciences, China
Ru Li   Shanxi University, China
Xun Liang   Renmin University of China, China

Yanyan Lan	Institute of Computing Technology, Chinese Academy of Sciences, China
Yuan Lin	Dalian University of Technology, China
Guoliang Li	Tsinghua University, China
Chenliang Li	Wuhan University, China
Kang Liu	Institute of Automation, Chinese Academy of Sciences, China
Xiangwen Liao	Fuzhou University, China
Peiyu Liu	Shandong Normal University, China
Jianming Lv	South China University of Technology, China
Shaoping Ma	Tsinghua University, China
Jun Ma	Shandong University, China
Bing Qin	Harbin Institute of Technology, China
Hongfei Yan	Peking University, China
Liyun Ru	Beijing Sogou Technology Development Co., Ltd, China
Tong Ruan	East China University of Science and Technology, China
Zhaochun Ren	Shandong University, China
Shuicai Shi	Beijing TRS Information Technology Co., Ltd, China
Bin Sun	Peking University, China
Le Sun	Institute of Software, Chinese Academy of Sciences, China
Dawei Song	Tianjin University, China
Huawei Shen	Institute of Computing Technology, Chinese Academy of Sciences, China
Deyi Xiong	Suzhou University, China
Xuemeng Song	Shandong University, China
Jie Tang	Tsinghua University, China
Songbo Tan	Tongbao Fortune Beijing Science and Technology Co., Ltd, China
Jirong Wen	Renmin University of China, China
Xiaochuan Wang	Sohu, China
Bin Wang	Institute of Computing Technology, Chinese Academy of Sciences, China
Haifeng Wang	Baidu, China
Hongjun Wang	Beijing TRS Information Technology Co., Ltd, China
Mingwen Wang	Jiangxi Normal University, China
Ting Wang	National University of Defense Technology, China
Lihong Wang	National Computer Network and Information Security Management Center, China
Suge Wang	Shanxi University, China
Xiaojun Wang	Peking University, China
Zhengtao Yu	Kunming University of Science and Technology, China
Tong Xiao	Northeastern University, China

Contents

Social Computing

Query Processing and Retrieval

Mining User Profiles from Query Log

Minlong Peng[1,2], Jun Zhao[1,2], Qi Zhang[1,2(✉)], Tao Gui[1,2], Xuanjing Huang[1,2], and Jinlan Fu[1,2]

[1] Shanghai Key Laboratory of Intelligent Information Processing, Fudan University, Shanghai, China
{mlpeng16,zhaoj19,qz,tgui16,xjhuang,fujl16}@fudan.edu.cn
[2] School of Computer Science, Fudan University, 825 Zhangheng Road, Shanghai, China

Abstract. This paper introduces a novel method for mining user profiles (e.g., age, gender) using the query log in a search engine. The proposed method combines the advantage of the neural network for representation learning and that of the topic model for interpretability. This is achieved by plugging a parametric Gaussian mixture distribution layer into the neural network. Specifically, it first uses the popular convolution neural network to model the query content, generating a dense vector presentation for each query. Based on this representation, it infers the searching topic of the query, by fitting a Gaussian mixture distribution, and obtains the query topic distribution. Then, it deduces the distribution of topics that the user cares about by aggregating the query topic distribution of all the queries of the user. Profile prediction is performed based on the resulting user topic distribution. We evaluated this framework using a real search engine data set, which contains 40,000 labeled users with age, gender, and education level profiles. The experiment results demonstrated the effectiveness of our proposed model.

Keywords: Query log · User profile · Neural network · Topic model

1 Introduction

Along with the rapid development of the World Wide Web, search engines have become increasingly important for users to obtain information from the continually growing resources on the internet. To improve the user experience and satisfy the requirements of different users, a variety of methods have been proposed to incorporate the profiles of users when providing search services such as personalized search [12], query expansion [2]. It is no doubt that users with different profiles will search for different web pages even with the same query. With this consideration, the explicit customization method that asks users to fill in their personal information during registration has been widely used by many web sites to personalize the layout and content of the web site. However, this

---

The authors wish to thank the anonymous reviewers for their helpful comments.

Q. Zhang et al. (Eds.): CCIR 2019, LNCS 11772, pp. 3–15, 2019.
https://doi.org/10.1007/978-3-030-31624-2_1

method can become time consuming and introduce a burden to users, making them unwilling to do this. Users usually prefer easier methods. Therefore, it is necessary to automatically mine user profiles from their search behaviors.

In this work, we aimed to automatically mine user profiles from the query log. This was based on the assumption that different users with different profiles may have different interests and accordingly different search behaviors. Therefore, the contents of their queries should be statistically different. And different from previous published works, which extracted the user profiles in a unsupervised manner, we manually labeled some profiles of the user and treated this as a multi-task classification task. To perform this task, we proposed a novel neural topic network (NTN). It combines the advantage of the neural network for feature presentation and that of the topic model for interpretability. Specifically, it uses the *one-layer convolution network* [6] to automatically extract feature representation of queries. Based on this representation, it infers which topic the query is generated from. By aggregating all of the queries of a user, it further infers which topics the user cares more about and generates the topic distribution of each user with a Gaussian mixture model (GMM). The experimental results on a dataset with 40,000 labeled users and three profiles (i.e., age, gender, and education level) provided by the Sogou search engine demonstrated the effectiveness of the proposed model. An analysis of the generated user topic distribution proved that this distribution can indeed reflect the different interests of users with different profiles.

In summary, the main contributions of this works include: (i) We explore a method to mine user profiles from the query log in the search engine. (ii) To perform this task, we propose a novel neural topic network, which combines the advantage of the neural network for feature presentation and that of the topic model for interpretability, by plugging a parametric Gaussian mixture distribution layer into the neural network. (iii) The proposed model outperforms all of the compared methods for all three user profiles. Further analysis on the user topic distribution shows impressive results.

2   Related Work

In the last few years, the need for Web search service to automatically adapt to their users has been recognized by many search engines such as Baidu[1] and Google. And there have been several prior attempts to personalize Web search. Some studies have proposed methods to automatically extract profiles of user from their search behaviors [3]. These systems mainly differ in the type of data used to create the user profile. [11] built a profile by analyzing the Web pages visited by the user as they browsed. [16] used the bookmarks of users for this purpose. And [15] used the queries and search results as the information source. These works usually extracted a user profile in an unsupervised manner, which represented the user profile by a list of concepts of interest [15] or a bookmark-like list of pages.

---

[1] http://www.baidu.com.

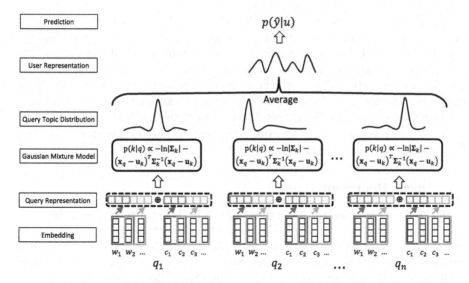

Fig. 1. General architecture of the proposed model. Query representation is obtained from both its character sequence and segmented word sequence using convolution neural networks. A following GMM layer then maps the query representation into a topic distribution, which is then aggregated with an average pooling mechanism to generate the topic distribution of a user with n queries.

Gaussian Mixture Topic Models. A Gaussian mixture model is a probabilistic model that assumes that all the data points are generated from a mixture of a finite number of Gaussian distributions with unknown parameters. One can think of mixture models as generalizing k-means clustering to incorporate information about the covariance structure of the data as well as the centers of the latent Gaussians. [13] applied this model to the low-dimensional semantic vector space represented by dense word vectors to extract the latent topic distribution of short texts. Compared to conventional topic modelling schemes such as probabilistic latent semantic analysis (pLSA) [5] and latent Dirichlet allocation (LDA) [1], which requires the aggregation of short messages to avoid data sparsity of word co-occurrence patterns in short documents, this framework works on large amounts of raw short texts.

3   Approach

We consider the following problem setting. There are n_l manually labeled search engine users L_u and n_u unlabeled users U_u. Every user u has searched a set of queries $Q_u = \{q_1, \cdots, q_{|Q_u|}\}$, where $|Q_u|$ is the set size. And every query consists of a sequence of characters $q = [c_1, \cdots, c_n]$. The goal of this task is to learn classifiers to distinguish the profiles of the unlabeled users based on their corresponding queries.

In this work, we performed this task with a neural topic network, which combined the representation learning of neural network with the topic learning of a GMM topic model. Figure 1 depicts the general architecture of this framework. It first extracts the vector representation of each query of the user with a convolution neural network on both the word level and character level. Based on this representation, it deduces the topic the query searching for with a Gaussian mixture model. By aggregating this distribution of the whole queries of the user with a average pooling, it obtains the user presentation in topic space. And the final prediction is performed based on this user presentation.

3.1   Query Representation

In this work, we propose to model the query on both the character and word levels. On the character level, we directly model the character sequence of queries to obtain their vector representations. For this purpose, we apply the *one-layer convolution network*. It is a variant of the traditional convolution network proposed by Kim et al. [6]. Specifically, let $c_i \in R^{k_c}$ be the k_c-dimensional character vector, corresponding to the ith character in the query. A query of length n (padded if necessary) is represented as follows:

$$\mathbf{q} = \begin{bmatrix} \mathbf{c}_1, \cdots, \mathbf{c}_n \end{bmatrix}$$

The *one-layer convolution neural network* takes the dot product of the filter $\mathbf{m} \in R^{k_m \times h}$ with each h-gram in $\mathbf{q}$ to obtain sequence $\mathbf{s}$, as follows:

$$s_i = f(\mathbf{m}, \cdot, \mathbf{q}_{i:i+h-1} + b). \tag{1}$$

Here, $b \in R$ is a bias term, and f is a non-linear function (e.g., tanh). This filter is applied to each possible window of characters in the sequence $\{q_{1:h}, \cdots, q_{n-h+1:n}\}$ to produce a feature map:

$$\mathbf{s} = [s_1, \cdots, s_{n-h+1}]$$

To address the problem of various query lengths, it then applies a max-overtime pooling operation over the feature map and takes the maximum value $\hat{s} = \max(\mathbf{s})$ as the feature corresponding to this particular filter. The aim of this operation is to capture the most relevant h-gram feature, i.e., the one with the highest value. By extending the operation to multiple filters with various window sizes, it obtains multiple features:

$$\mathbf{x}_c = \begin{bmatrix} \max(\mathbf{s}^1) \cdots \max(\mathbf{s}^d), \end{bmatrix} \tag{2}$$

where d is the filter number. These features form the representation of $\mathbf{q}$ on the character level. On the word level, we first segment the character sequence of the query into words using the Jieba[2] Chinese word segmenter. We argue that this will introduce the prior knowledge of Chinese reading habit, encoded within

---

[2] https://github.com/fxsjy/jieba/.

the word segmenter. Then, similar to the processing on the character level, we apply the *one-layer convolution neural network* to the resulting word sequence and obtain the corresponding query presentation on the word level $\mathbf{x}_w$. The final representation of query $\mathbf{q}$ consists of the combination of $\mathbf{x}_c$ and $\mathbf{x}_w$:

$$\mathbf{x}_q = [\mathbf{x}_c \oplus \mathbf{x}_w],$$

where $\oplus$ denotes the concatenation operation.

3.2 User Representation

In this section, we describe the method used to construct the user presentation with the obtained query representation $\mathbf{x}_q$. To this end, we propose to model the semantic vector representation of users using a soft version of the GMM, whose components capture the notion of latent topics[3]. Our conjecture is that the Gaussian mixture model can learn the latent topics by clustering over the distributed representation of each query. Each topic cluster chooses its related queries with its cluster center and variance matrix. This is somehow like the attention mechanism in neural machine translation, which generates attention over queries for each topic. And the informative and uninformative queries are separated into different topic clusters.

Formally, if we choose to model a user with K topics, we need to estimate μ_k, Σ_k, $p(k|\mathbf{q}) \; \forall \; k \in K$, $q \in Q_u$, namely the means, covariances, and mixture weights. Given a query q and its representation $\mathbf{x}_q$, the probability of q being of the topic k is defined as follows:

$$p(k|q) = \frac{\exp\left(-\ln|\Sigma_k| - (\mathbf{x}_q - \mu_k)^T \Sigma_k^{-1}(\mathbf{x}_q - \mu_k)\right)}{\sum_{i=1}^{K} \exp\left(-\ln|\Sigma_i| - (\mathbf{x}_q - \mu_i)^T \Sigma_i^{-1}(\mathbf{x}_q - \mu_i)\right)}.$$

Here $|\Sigma_k|$ denotes the determinant of matrix Σ_k and Σ_k^{-1} is its inverse. To encourage every query to be of only one topic, we additionally minimize the entropy of $p(k|q)$ during the training process, with the loss defined as follows:

$$\mathcal{L}_{ent} = \frac{1}{|V_q|} \sum_{q \in V_q} \sum_{k \in K} -p(k|q) \log p(k|q), \tag{3}$$

where V_q denotes the training query set. After that, we aggregate the query topic distribution of all the queries of the user and obtain the topic distribution for the user:

$$\mathbf{p}(\cdot|u) = \frac{1}{|Q_u|} \sum_{q \in Q_u} \mathbf{p}(\cdot|q), \tag{4}$$

where $|Q_u|$ is the number of searched queries of user u and $\mathbf{p}(\cdot|q) = [q(k = 1|q), \cdots, p(k = K|q)]$. We use this distribution as the user presentation, i.e., $\mathbf{x}_u = \mathbf{p}(\cdot|u)$.

---

[3] We refer to the latent multinomial variables in the GMM as topics, so as to exploit query-oriented intuitions, but we make no epidemiological claims regarding these latent variables beyond their utility in representing probability distributions on queries.

4   Model Initialization

4.1   Embedding Initialization

In neural network learning, it is a popular practice to train word or character representations with a language model on large unlabeled datasets to initialize the corresponding embeddings in the task-specific neural network models. For character embeddings, we trained a recurrent neural network based language model [9] on the character sequence $[c_1, \cdots c_n]$ of each query:

$$p(c_1, \cdots, c_n) = \prod_{t=1}^{n} p(c_t|c_{<t}), \tag{5}$$

where $c_{<t}$ refers to the character sequence before time step t. To estimate this generation probability, we applied the long-short term memory network (LSTM) [4]. For word embeddings, we use the continuous bag-of-words language model [8] on the segmented words of each query. Compared to the recurrent based language model, this is more robust to the segmentation errors. Formally, it treats every query as a window and constrains words within a query to be close in the embedding space.

4.2   Topic Initialization

The goal of topic initialization is to initialize the user representation x_u, generated with our GMM topic model. Generally speaking, we first train an unsupervised topic model, obtaining a topic distribution θ_u for the user u. Then, we train the GMM topic model to fit this topic distribution on the loss $\mathcal{L}_{topic}$, as follows:

$$\mathcal{L}_{topic} = \frac{1}{n_l + n_u} \sum_{u \in L_u \cup N_u} ||x_u - \theta_u||^2.$$

After that, we train the GMM topic model on the classification loss. In this work, we apply the unsupervised LDA topic model for this purpose. However, LDA is conventionally applied to documents that are typically at least a few hundred of words, while queries are usually closer to several words. To address this issue, following the work of Weng et al. [18], we aggregate all of the segmented queries of a user u into a document d_u and apply the LDA to this aggregated document.

Formally, an user is associated with a multinomial distribution θ_u over T topics. Each topic is associated with a multinomial distribution ϕ over words. θ_u and ϕ have Dirichlet prior with hyper-parameters α and β respectively. For each word in the aggregated document d_u, a topic z is sampled from the multinomial distribution θ_u associated with the document, and a word w from the multinomial distribution ϕ associated with topic z is consequently sampled. This generative process is repeated N_{d_u} times to form document d_u, where N_{d_u} is the total number of words in d_u. For model inference, we use Gibbs sampling [10] to estimate the document (user) topic distributions θ_u.

5   Model Learning

We perform profile prediction with a softmax non-linear layer, taking $\mathbf{x}_u$ as the input:

$$p(\hat{y}|u) = \frac{\exp(\mathbf{v}_{\hat{y}}^T \mathbf{x}_u + b_{\hat{y}})}{\sum_{y' \in V_y} \exp(\mathbf{v}_{y'}^T \mathbf{x}_u + b_{y'})}. \tag{6}$$

Here, $\mathbf{v}_{\hat{y}}$ is a trainable vector corresponding to the label $\hat{y}$, and $b_{\hat{y}}$ is bias term. V_y refers to the unique label set. The prediction loss is defined as follows:

$$\mathcal{L} = - \sum_{u \in L_u} \log p(\hat{y} = y|u), \tag{7}$$

where y is the object label of user u for the given profile.

5.1   Addressing Label Noise

During the analysis of 1000 randomly sampled labeled users, we found that only about 85% of the users were definitely labeled for the age profile, while the labels of the rest of users were disputable. With this observation, we proposed to inject some noise into the labels. However, instead of assigning a small uniform probability $\frac{\epsilon}{L}$ to the non-object labels, where L is the number of unique labels [14], we tried to utilize the rational relationship between labels. As the age labeling is a partition of consecutive ages, it is reasonable to assume that it is more likely the labeling noise of a given label comes from its adjacent labels. Based on this assumption, for the age and education profiles, we propose the following label noise injection mechanism. Formally, we convert the one-hot label into a multinomial distribution as follows:

$$q(\hat{y} = i|u) = \frac{\exp(-|i - y|)}{\sum_{j=1}^{6} \exp(-|j - y|)I(j \neq y)} \epsilon$$
$$+ I(i = y)(1 - \epsilon), \tag{8}$$

where y is the object label, ϵ is a hyper-parameter controlling the noise magnitude, and $I(\cdot)$ is an indicator function. This means when given label is closer to the object one in the label space, there if greater probability that the user should be labeled with this label.

5.2   Multi-task Learning

It has been proven in many works [?,?,?] that multi-task learning can improve system performance, especially when tasks are closely related. With this consideration and the reasonable assumption that there is some inherent relationship between user profiles, we applied a multi-task learning framework to predict

Table 1. Statistics of different profiles in the dataset. Here, the age is measured by year, i.e., 0–18 denotes 0–18 years old.

Age		Education		Gender	
Description	# of Example	Description	# of Example	Description	# of Example
Unknown	486	Unknown	3,366	Unknown	782
0–18	15,954	Doctor	140	Male	22,766
19–23	10,492	Master	242	Female	16,452
24–30	7,374	Undergraduate	7,638		
31–40	4,354	High school	11,154		
41–50	1,140	Middle school	15,234		
>51	200	Primary school	2,226		

different user profiles simultaneously. Specifically, we make all of the profile prediction tasks share the parameters of the *one-layer convolution network*, character embeddings, and word embeddings. Other components are task-specific. The final loss of the system is accordingly defined as follows:

$$\mathcal{L}(\boldsymbol{\Phi}) = \sum_t \alpha_t \mathcal{L}_t(\boldsymbol{\Phi}_s, \boldsymbol{\Phi}_t) + \beta \mathcal{L}_{ent}, \tag{9}$$

where $\boldsymbol{\Phi}_s$ denotes the shared parameters, $\boldsymbol{\Phi}_t$ denotes the task specific parameters of task t, and α_t is the hyper-parameter weighting the loss of task t.

6   Experiment Setup

6.1   Dataset

The proposed model was evaluated on the query logs of the Sogou search engine. It contains 40,000 labelled users and 200,000 unlabeled users. From the labeled dataset, we split off 20,000 users as the training set, with the remaining 20,000 users forming the testing set. Each user has three type of profiles, i.e., age, gender, and education level. The statistics of these three profiles are listed in Table 1.

6.2   Compared Methods

We first compared the proposed model with several baseline methods:

- **MF**: This model predicts the profile that occurs most frequently in the training dataset. It sets the bottom line for the other compared methods.
- **NB**: Naive Bayes is implemented with the bag-of-word features extracted from the aggregated user queries d_u.

- **KNN**: This model uses the k-nearest neighbors algorithm [7] to perform this task. It represents a user as an N-dimensional vector of items. For the prediction of a given user, it first selects n of the most similar users from the labeled data set with the cosine similarity. It then assigns the most frequent profiles within these similar users to the given user.
- **SVM**: This is an L2-regularized linear support vector machine. It mixes up segmented queries of each user and obtains an N-dimensional word tf-idf vector. It applies a one-vs-all setting for the multi-class classification.
- **LDA**: In this model, we perform the prediction with a logistic repression model on the topic distribution θ_u extracted with the LDA [1] model.

Then, we performed an ablation study on each component of the proposed model. To this end, we implemented the following variants of the proposed model:

- **NTN-CE**: This variant removes the query embedding on the character level. In other words, the dense query representation is only extracted from the segmented word sequence.
- **NTN-WE**: This variant removes the query embedding on the word level. That is to say, the dense query representation is only extracted from the character sequence.
- **NTN-GMM**: This variant performs average pooling over the queries of a single user to obtain his/her vector presentation, instead of modelling the topic distribution of the user with a GMM model.
- **NTN-LM**: This variant does not train the language model to initialize the character and word embeddings. Instead, it initializes the character and word embeddings randomly from a uniform distribution $[-0.1, 0.1]$.
- **NTN-LDA**: This variant does not pre-train the GMM topic model.
- **NTN-LN**: This variant does not inject any noise into the label.
- **NTN-MT**: This variant does not perform multi-task learning. Instead, it trains task by task for different profiles.

6.3 Implementation Details

All of the models were trained on the training dataset and tested on the testing dataset described in the Dataset section without any further processing. For the proposed model and its variants, we set the dimensions of the character embeddings and word embeddings to 50 and 100, respectively. For the *one-layer convolution network*, we applied 50 filters for each n-gram size $\in \{2, 3, 4\}$ to the character sequence and applied 100 filters for each n-gram size $\in \{1, 2\}$ to the segmented word sequence. Topic number K was set to 100. The label noise level ϵ was set to 0.15 for the age profile and 0.1 for the education profile. Dropout with a keeping probability of 0.5 was applied to the character embeddings and word embeddings. For training, we used the RmsProp [17] step rule with the learning rate set to 0.005.

6.4   Evaluation Metric

For the evaluation, we apply the accuracy measurement metric for each task.
And the average accuracy on the three tasks is applied to measure the overall
performance:

$$\overline{P} = \frac{P_a + P_g + P_e}{3} \tag{10}$$

where P_a, P_g, and P_e is the accuracy on the age, gender, and education profiles,
respectively.

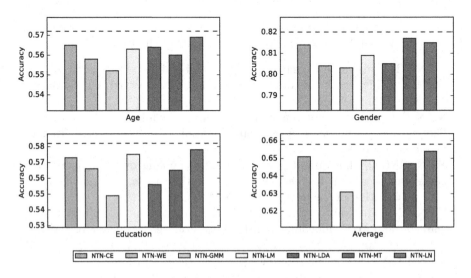

Fig. 2. Ablation study on each component of the proposed model. Each bar corresponds
to a variant of the proposed model with one component removed. The dotted line refers
to the performance of our proposed model with all of the components.

Table 2. Comparison between the proposed model and several baseline methods.

Model	Age	Gender	Education	Average
MF	0.398	0.578	0.408	0.461
NB	0.450	0.728	0.384	0.521
KNN	0.462	0.731	0.402	0.532
SVM	0.540	0.782	0.524	0.615
LDA	0.532	0.795	0.552	0.627
NTN	**0.572**	**0.815**	**0.580**	**0.656**

6.5   Results and Discussion

We first give comparisons between the proposed model and baselines. Table 2 lists the performances of these models on the three profiles. We can first observe that our proposed model (NTN) consistently outperforms the compared methods for all three profiles. On the average accuracy of the three profiles, our proposed model achieved about 3% absolute improvement over the most comparative LDA model.

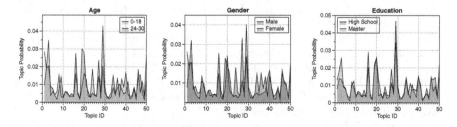

Fig. 3. Average topic distribution $\mathbf{x}_u$, extracted with the GMM topic model, of users with different profiles. For display reasons, we only show the results of the 0–18 and 24–30 year old users for the age profile. And for the education profile, we only show the results of high school students and masters. Values of the x-axis denote the topic ids.

We next give the results of our ablation study on each component of the proposed model. Figure 2 shows the results of the comparison between the proposed model and its variants. We first focus on the average performance of these models, as depicted in the bottom right picture. From this picture, we can see that the GMM topic model layer has the greatest influence on the proposed model. Once we have removed this component and performed mean-over-query pooling to obtain the user presentation, the absolute accuracy drops by 2.7%. The second sensitive component is the initialization of the user topic distribution with an unsupervised LDA model. It contributes about 1.6% absolute accuracy to the proposed model. This proves the feasibility of initializing the embedded GMM layer with an unsupervised topic model. Another important component of the proposed model is the word level query presentation, which also contributes about 1.6% absolute accuracy. This shows that it is necessary to segment a query into a word sequence and the informativeness of the prior knowledge within the Chinese word segmenter. Besides, we have previously argued that there is some segmentation noise within the segmenter. This was proven by the result of the NTN-CE model, in which the absolute accuracy dropped by approximately 0.7% compared to that of our proposed model.

7   Conclusions

In this paper, we addressed the task of mining the age, gender, and education level of users using their query logs. To perform this task, we proposed a novel neural topic model, which used a neural network to extract feature presentation of the query and a GMM topic model to model the topic distribution searched by the user. We evaluated the proposed model on a real search engine dataset, which contains 40,000 labeled users and 200,000 unlabeled users. Experimental results demonstrated the effectiveness of our model.

References

1. Blei, D.M., Ng, A.Y., Jordan, M.I.: Latent dirichlet allocation. J. Mach. Learn. Res. **3**(Jan), 993–1022 (2003)
2. Chirita, P.A., Firan, C.S., Nejdl, W.: Personalized query expansion for the web. In: Proceedings of the 30th Annual International ACM SIGIR Conference on Research and Development in Information Retrieval, pp. 7–14. ACM (2007)
3. Golemati, M., Katifori, A., Vassilakis, C., Lepouras, G., Halatsis, C.: Creating an ontology for the user profile: method and applications. In: Proceedings of the First RCIS Conference, No. 2007, pp. 407–412 (2007)
4. Hochreiter, S., Schmidhuber, J.: Long short-term memory. Neural Comput. **9**(8), 1735–1780 (1997)
5. Hofmann, T.: Probabilistic latent semantic indexing. In: Proceedings of the 22nd Annual International ACM SIGIR Conference on Research and Development in Information Retrieval, pp. 50–57. ACM (1999)
6. Kim, Y.: Convolutional neural networks for sentence classification. arXiv preprint arXiv:1408.5882 (2014)
7. Larose, D.T.: K-nearest neighbor algorithm. In: Discovering Knowledge in Data: An Introduction to Data Mining, pp. 90–106 (2005)
8. Mikolov, T., Chen, K., Corrado, G., Dean, J.: Efficient estimation of word representations in vector space. arXiv preprint arXiv:1301.3781 (2013)
9. Mikolov, T., Karafiát, M., Burget, L., Cernockỳ, J., Khudanpur, S.: Recurrent neural network based language model. In: Interspeech, vol. 2, p. 3 (2010)
10. Porteous, I., Newman, D., Ihler, A., Asuncion, A., Smyth, P., Welling, M.: Fast collapsed GIBBS sampling for latent dirichlet allocation. In: Proceedings of the 14th ACM SIGKDD International Conference on Knowledge Discovery and Data Mining, pp. 569–577. ACM (2008)
11. Pretschner, A., Gauch, S.: Ontology based personalized search. In: 11th IEEE International Conference on Tools with Artificial Intelligence, 1999. Proceedings, pp. 391–398. IEEE (1999)
12. Shen, X., Tan, B., Zhai, C.: Implicit user Modeling for Personalized Search. In: Proceedings of the 14th ACM International Conference on Information and Knowledge Management, pp. 824–831. ACM (2005)
13. Sridhar, V.K.R.: Unsupervised topic modeling for short texts using distributed representations of words. In: VS@ HLT-NAACL, pp. 192–200 (2015)
14. Szegedy, C., Vanhoucke, V., Ioffe, S., Shlens, J., Wojna, Z.: Rethinking the inception architecture for computer vision. arXiv preprint arXiv:1512.00567 (2015)
15. Tanudjaja, F., Mui, L.: Persona: A contextualized and personalized web search. In: Proceedings of the 35th Annual Hawaii International Conference on System Sciences, 2002. HICSS, pp. 1232–1240. IEEE (2002)
16. Thomas, C.G., Fischer, G.: Using agents to personalize the web. In: Proceedings of the 2nd International Conference on Intelligent User Interfaces, pp. 53–60. ACM (1997)

17. Tieleman, T., Hinton, G.: Divide the gradient by a running average of its recent magnitude. Lecture 6.5-rmsprop: COURSERA: Neural Netw. Mach. Learn. **4**(2), 26–31 (2012)
18. Weng, J., Lim, E.P., Jiang, J., He, Q.: Twitterrank: finding topic-sensitive influential twitterers. In: Proceedings of the third ACM International Conference on Web Search and Data Mining, pp. 261–270. ACM (2010)

A User Effort Measurement for Query Selection

Shusi Yu[1(✉)], Ting Jin[2], Zhefu Shi[1], Jing Li[1], and Jin Pan[1]

[1] Coupang Corporation, Jinke Road 2889, Shanghai, China
{shusi.yu,jeffzs,ryan.li,jin.pan}@coupang.com
[2] Hainan University, Renmin Road 58, Haikou, China
tingj@fudan.edu.cn

Abstract. User effort is an important measurement of search quality. It strongly affects user experience and finally, affects conversion. There are measurements about user effort in search. However, they all take only query result browsing efforts into account. Few of them measures the effort of query selection, or the effort to choose a suitable query. This paper shows that query selection effort is a significant part of overall user effort, almost as important as browsing effort. This paper further introduces an entropy-like effort measurement approach for query selection. Statistic and simulation results strongly indicate that our measurement reflects real user effort better.

Keywords: User effort · Search quality · Query selection

1 Introduction

User effort is an important measurement of search quality. It strongly affects user experience and finally, affects conversion. There are measurements about query result browsing efforts. For example, [14] and [12] quantify user effort by the number of items user browsed. However, to the extent of our knowledge, few of them measures the effort of query selection, or the effort to choose a suitable query. Ignoring query selection effort will leads to some ridiculous inferences. For example, obviously users are going to minimize their query effort to find the item they will purchase. But if we ignore query selection effort, statistics of query-purchases show that more effort per purchase for a certain query, more items are purchased for that query.

For example, we consider query "Slippers" and its sub-query "Women's Slippers". For the former query, users browse 25.19 items averagely to find the desired one. For the latter, only 11.64 items. If item browsing effort is the only effort, the former is much less efficient than the latter. Since users tend to minimum their effort, users shall use "Women's Slippers" much more frequently and

This paper is supported by National Nature Science Foundation of China (61562020, 61862021) and Hainan Provincial Natural Science Foundation of China (618QN217).

Q. Zhang et al. (Eds.): CCIR 2019, LNCS 11772, pp. 16–25, 2019.
https://doi.org/10.1007/978-3-030-31624-2_2

covert much more items in the query. However, the fact is exactly opposite. User convert 300% more items in the former than the latter. Furthermore, more than 30% items can be discovered in "Women's Slippers" is also converted in "Slippers". That means users choose a less efficient query while they have a "better" way. This is not likely happen unless choosing a query itself takes effort.

This paper introduces an entropy-like effort measurement approach for query selection. The idea is inspired by researches in linguistics. They indicate that mental lexicon is tree-like so that overall word selection effort can be measured by word entropy. In the proposing approach, query selection effort is measured by query entropy. Probability for each query is measured as the proportion of purchases of this query against global purchases. Query selection effort of an individual query is the negative logarithm of query probability. Total query selection effort is a query probability weighted summarization of individual query selection efforts, or entropy of all queries.

Statistics shows that query selection effort is a big part of total effort and can be measured by our approach. It shows that total user effort per purchase, including query selection effort and item browsing effort, is roughly equal for all queries. Higher query selection effort introduces lower browsing effort. The results indicate that overall user effort is already minimized. We further show some examples that how using sub-queries trades query selection effort for item browsing effort. We also launch a user effort minimizing simulation. The simulation shows that minimizing both query selection effort and item browsing effort results a power law distribution of # relevant items for each query. The distribution is very similar to its real world correspondence. On the contrary, if we ignore query selection effort, the simulation results a uniform distribution. The simulation provides further evidences of the effectiveness of our approach.

Contributions of this paper is enumerated as follows:

1. A unique measurement, probably the first quantified measurement for query selection in information retrieval.
2. Simulation and statistic results to evaluate the approach.
3. A possible explanation for power law distributions in information retrieval.

2   Related Works

User effort measurement is an important aspect of information retrieval researches. [6,8] shows a strong correlation between user effort and final profit of e-commerce business. There are several approaches measuring user effort. [14] measures user effort by counting items browsed before a relevant item. [12] further takes ranking weights into consideration when there are multiple relevant items and relevance levels. However, most of them discuss about measuring item browsing efforts. To the extent of our knowledge, few discussion exists about query selection efforts.

Query selection effort is the effort users contribute to discover a proper query. A proper query means less browsing effort to discover the required items [13]. In other words, users may contribute query selection efforts to save item browsing efforts. In a long run, summation of the two kinds of efforts shall remain in a stable minimum way [2]. If we discuss the problem in a computer science prospect, the effort to discover a query depends on the organization structure of the lexicons storing all queries. Although the lexicon structure in brain is not a settled problem of science, there are researches indicate that mental lexicon structure is roughly a tree [4,5,7,15]. Therefore query selection effort on a tree is negative logarithm. Other researches in linguistics [3] also indicate that the effort to select a word from mental lexicon is negative logarithm.

There are many power laws in information retrieval. For example, [10] shows that term frequency, document length, query frequency, query length follow power law. [1,9] further contributes models to fit the power law of query length. However, none of them provides explanation of the power law. Previous researches [11] explain power law usually takes a complex network approach. However, the approach is not suitable for information retrieval since there is no network or organisation in search. [3] introduces a minimum effort to explain the power law which sounds to be reasonable here.

3   User Effort Measurement

Query selection effort: Innovation of measuring query selection effort assumes that mental lexicon of queries is roughly a tree [4,5]. In a tree, the effort to visit a query q_i is approximately $-log(p_i)$, where p_i is the probability of q_i. That means a more probable query is more likely to be closer to root, and to be visited with less effort. With this measurement of a single query, we measure total query selection effort by the entropy of queries. Considering a set of queries $\{q_1, q_2, ..., q_n\}$. The probability of corresponding queries is $\{p_1, p_2, ..., p_n\}$. Therefore total effort E of query selection is:

$$E_{QS} = \sum_{i=1}^{n} -p_i * log(p_i) \tag{1}$$

Item browsing effort measurement: We follow [14] to measure item browsing effort. The measurement is a probability weighted summation of query result items being browsed. For a certain query q_i, we have query result item list $c_1, c_2, ..., c_m$, corresponding item ranks and probabilities. For a certain item c_j, browsing effort is its rank weighted by its probability, formally $prob(c_j) * rank(c_j)$. Therefore total item browsing effort is:

$$E_{IB} = \sum_{i=1}^{n}\sum_{j=1}^{m} prob(c_j) * rank(c_j) \tag{2}$$

Total effort, consists of query selection effort and browsing effort, is shown as follows. Where λ is the weight of two kinds of efforts.

$$E = \lambda E_{QS} + (1 - \lambda)E_{IB} \tag{3}$$

4   Statistical Results

This Section illustrates user effort distribution of all queries in our measurement (considering both query selection effort and item browsing effort) and previous measurements(considering only item browsing effort). Data from 2019-q1 of Coupang purchase. Figure 1 shows user effort of [14]'s approach all queries as points. In this case we choose only queries with more than 10 purchases. Here we can see larger effort means more purchase. This is completely against commonsense.

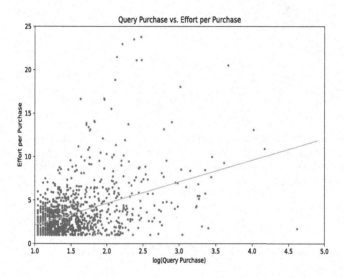

Fig. 1. Each point in the figure is a query. Query Purchase is purchase amount of the query. Effort per Purchase is the average effort consumed per purchase for the query. The light blue line is the regression curve of queries. The figure uses effort measurement of previous approach. (Color figure online)

Figure 2 shows user effort measured by our approach. Here λ is set to 0.5. We can see that the result is more reasonable. Total effort remains the same when query-purchase increases. This means our effort measurement is better than previous ones since we get more reasonable result. The result also indicates that overall user effort is already minimized for most queries.

Figure 3 shows a negative correlation between query selection effort and item browsing effort. The result indicates that total effort to discover an item is statistically a constant. More query selection effort means less item browsing effort, and vise versa.

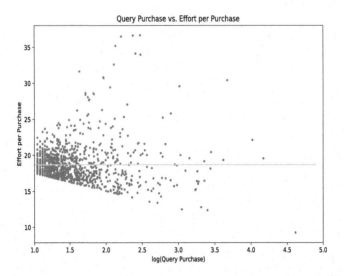

Fig. 2. Each point in the figure is a query. Query Purchase is purchase amount of the query. Effort per Purchase is average effort consumed per purchase for the query. The light blue line is the regression curve of queries. The figure uses OUR effort measurement. (Color figure online)

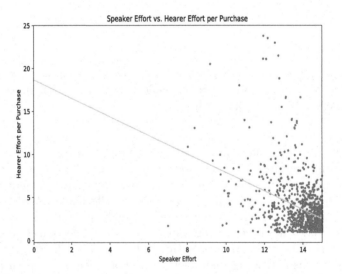

Fig. 3. Each point in the figure is a query. The Figure shows a negative-correlation between two kinds of efforts. The light blue line is the regression curve of queries. (Color figure online)

5   Descriptive Examples

Table 1. "Slippers" and its sub-queries

Query	Old effort	% items in super-query	New effort
Slippers	25.19	–	33.55
Women's Slippers	11.64	43.12%	31.87
Mule Slippers	13.47	40.09%	33.54
Crox Slippers	11.07	28.75%	29.28
Women office slippers	10.31	33.31%	29.21
Adidas Slippers	10.01	41.23%	30.93
Indoor Slippers	9.17	29.52%	32.87

Involuntarily, if there are different queries retrieving the same item, users will choose the least effort query. However, if we consider only item browsing effort, we will find that many items are retrieved by different queries with different efforts. For example, Table 1 shows query "Slippers" and its sub-queries. We can see that "Slippers" and its sub-queries share a big part of common items. For example, "Women's Slippers" shares 43.12% common items with its super query, while there is a significant item browsing effort difference between them. 11.64 vs. 25.19, more than double. When we also consider query selection effort, total user effort to discover an item is almost the same for the queries which can approach to same items (Table 2).

Tables 1 and 3 shows user effort of query "Sneakers" and "Ramen". We can see that "Sneakers" and "Ramen" are similar to "Slippers". Queries and its sub-queries consume roughly the same amount of user effort. When users choose to

Table 2. "Sneakers" and its sub-queries

Query	Old effort	% items in super-query	New effort
Sneakers	7.07	–	38.63
Women sneakers	10.98	26.75%	37.88
Girl sneakers	14.65	33.84%	31.85

Table 3. "Ramen" and its sub-queries

Query	Old effort	% items in super-query	New effort
Ramen	9.69	–	35.71
Shin Ramen	8.25	26.75%	33.81
Cup ramen	6.98	26.75%	34.96

use sub-queries, they trade query selection effort for item browsing effort. These examples lead to the same conclusion as Sect. 4 in a detailed perspective.

6   Simulation Results

The simulation is going to approach minimum user effort by tuning the number of items relevant to a query. Using our measurement, the simulation results in a power law query-#relevant distribution, very close to real world distribution. Using measurements considering only item browsing effort result in a uniform distribution, far from real world distribution.

Obviously, users want to minimum their effort to find their desired items. If item browsing effort is the only effort for users, users are going to use queries as precise as possible and minimize the number of items relevant to every query. This is a uniform distribution of query-#relevant items. However, it is not the truth. Our observations and former researches show that query-relevance distribution follows a power law.

[3] presents an explanation of power law in word frequency for natural languages. He assumes that total effort of a natural language system consists of language speakers effort and hearer effort. Speaker effort is the entropy of word probabilities. If a single word dominates the language, that is, all objects described by the language are represented by the same word, speaker contributes least effort. Hearer effort is the word probability weighted summation of object-probability entropies. If every single item is represented by individual word, hearer contributes least effort. A simulation which minimizing total effort of speaker and hearer results to a power law distribution of word-object.

In this section we launch a similar simulation of minimizing effort. Assume we have n queries and m items in the simulation. A $n \times m$ matrix R stores the relevance between queries and items. If q_i is relevant to c_j, cell $R_{i,j}$ is 1, otherwise is 0. We initialize R with random 0 or 1 and minimize total effort by random tuning. First we measure total effort of R. Then we randomly choose a cell of R and reverse its value. If the tuning decreases total effort, we keep the value. If not, we restore it. The tuning keeps on going until no effort decrease can be observed.

Two effort measurement is simulated in the section. Our approach and [14]'s approach. Query-relevant-item distribution of our effort measurement is illustrated in Fig. 4. Simulation result shows that our query-relevant-item distribution well fits real world query-relevant-item distribution. On the contrary, query-relevant-item distribution of [14]'s effort measurement is a uniform distribution, far from real world distribution.

Furthermore, [1] shows that many distributions in search follow power law. Figure 5 is the log-log curve of real world query-relevant-item distribution of top 1000 queries. The curve shows that real world query-relevant-item distribution also follows power law. Since our simulation perfectly fits real world curve, the result indicates that the effort minimizing approach can be a serious theoretical account of the power laws in search.

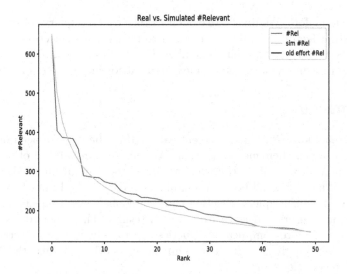

Fig. 4. Real vs Simulated #Relevant Item per Query

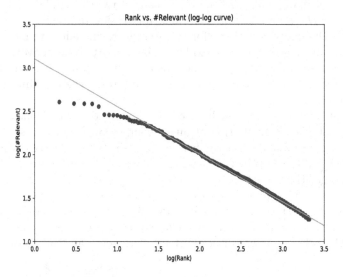

Fig. 5. Rank vs. #Relevant Item, log-log curve

The result provides more evidence that query selection effort counts and our measurement is the correct one for query selection effort.

7   Conclusion

This paper contributes an approach to measure user effort of query selection. We argue that current user effort measurements is not complete since they ignore query selection effort. We illustrate evidences to show that query selection effort is an important factor of total user effort. Introducing query selection effort leads to more reasonable query-purchase number. Furthermore, we also show that our entropy-like measurement is a good measurement for query selection effort.

8   Discussion

The query selection effort measurement we used maybe not the accurate effort users used to index their mental lexicon. We measure probability of queries by their frequency in Coupang. However, according to general knowledge, actual probability of a query shall be the probability used globally. In our future work, we shall try measuring query selection effort by global term frequency.

Furthermore, users can learn from search results. Their mental lexicon can grow longer and more complicated. Queries can take less query selection effort when users get familiar with them. Our future work will take the learning progress into consideration.

The paper discovers a minimum effort approach to explain why purchase-rank curve is a power law. The approach can be used to explain other power law in search. The power law of click-rank, impression-rank curves can also be explained by the query-selection effort vs. item browsing effort framework. The power law of query length can be explained by a effort trade between adding a new word and foreseen more browsing. Also, previous researches find that top and tail queries follow different power law. Future researches can find why they are different.

The result of this paper can be used to measure the effectiveness of query completion. The key contribution of query completion is saving user effort by guessing which query the user actually select. This paper introduces an approach to quantify the effort saved by the suggestion. This can lead to more precise query completion algorithms.

Furthermore, this paper leads to an approach to measure how much does user effort worth. Intuitively, users can trade effort for purchase cost. If they can discover a suitable top item, maybe they do not bother to browse tail ones. This is how SEM works. A precise user effort measurement can lead to future SEM researches.

References

1. Arampatzis, A., Kamps, J.: A study of query length. In: Proceedings of the 31st Annual International ACM SIGIR Conference on Research and Development in Information Retrieval, pp. 811–812. SIGIR 2008, ACM, New York (2008). https:// doi.org/10.1145/1390334.1390517, https://doi.acm.org/10.1145/1390334.1390517
2. Azzopardi, L.: Query side evaluation: an empirical analysis of effectiveness and effort. In: Proceedings of the 32nd International ACM SIGIR Conference on Research and Development in Information Retrieval. SIGIR 2009, pp. 556–563. ACM, New York (2009). https://doi.org/10.1145/1571941.1572037, https://doi. acm.org/10.1145/1571941.1572037

3. Cancho, R.F.I., Solé, R.V.: Least effort and the origins of scaling in human language. Proc. Nat. Acad. Sci. **100**(3), 788–791 (2003). https://doi.org/10.1073/pnas.0335980100. https://www.pnas.org/content/100/3/788
4. Elman, J.L.: An alternative view of the mental lexicon. In: Trends in Cognitive Sciences, pp. 301–306 (2004)
5. Fay, D., Cutler, A.: Malapropisms and the structure of the mental lexicon. Linguist. Inquiry **8**(3), 505–520 (1977). http://www.jstor.org/stable/4177997
6. Ferro, N., Silvello, G., Keskustalo, H., Pirkola, A., Järvelin, K.: The twist measure for IR evaluation: taking user's effort into account. JASIST **67**, 620–648 (2016)
7. Kempen, G., Vosse, T.: Incremental syntactic tree formation in human sentence processing, a cognitive architecture based on activation decay and simulated annealing. In: Sharkey, N. (ed.) Connectionist Natural Language Processing: Readings from Connection Science, pp. 83–100. Springer, Dordrecht (1992). https://doi.org/10.1007/978-94-011-2624-3_5
8. Long, C., Wong, R.C.W., Wei, V.J.: Profit maximization with sufficient customer satisfactions. ACM Trans. Knowl. Discov. Data **12**(2), 19:1–19:34 (2018). https://doi.org/10.1145/3110216. https://doi.acm.org/10.1145/3110216
9. Lv, Y.: A study of query length heuristics in information retrieval. In: Proceedings of the 24th ACM International on Conference on Information and Knowledge Management. CIKM 2015, pp. 1747–1750. ACM, New York (2015). https://doi.org/10.1145/2806416.2806592, https://doi.acm.org/10.1145/2806416.2806592
10. Petersen, C., Simonsen, J.G., Lioma, C.: Power law distributions in information retrieval. ACM Trans. Inf. Syst. **34**(2), 8:1–8:37 (2016). https://doi.org/10.1145/2816815. https://doi.acm.org/10.1145/2816815
11. Peterson, J., Dixit, P.D., Dill, K.A.: A maximum entropy framework for nonexponential distributions. Proc. Nat. Acad. Sci. **110**(51), 20380–20385 (2013). https://doi.org/10.1073/pnas.1320578110. https://www.pnas.org/content/110/51/20380
12. de Vries, A.P., Kazai, G., Lalmas, M.: Tolerance to irrelevance: a user-effort oriented evaluation of retrieval systems without predefined retrieval unit. In: Coupling Approaches, Coupling Media and Coupling Languages for Information Retrieval, pp. 463–473. RIAO 2004, Le Centre de Hautes Etudes Internationales D'Informatique Documentaire, Paris, France, France (2004). http://dl.acm.org/citation.cfm?id=2816272.2816314
13. Wu, P., Wen, J.R., Liu, H., Ma, W.Y.: Query selection techniques for efficient crawling of structured web sources. In: Proceedings of the 22nd International Conference on Data Engineering. ICDE 2006, p. 47. IEEE Computer Society, Washington, DC (2006). https://doi.org/10.1109/ICDE.2006.124
14. Yilmaz, E., Verma, M., Craswell, N., Radlinski, F., Bailey, P.: Relevance and effort: an analysis of document utility. In: Proceedings of the 23rd ACM International Conference on Conference on Information and Knowledge Management. CIKM 2014, pp. 91–100. ACM, New York (2014). https://doi.org/10.1145/2661829.2661953
15. Youn, H., et al.: On the universal structure of human lexical semantics. Proc. Nat. Acad. Sci. **113**(7), 1766–1771 (2016). https://doi.org/10.1073/pnas.1520752113. https://www.pnas.org/content/113/7/1766

Temporal Smoothing: Discriminatively Incorporating Various Temporal Profiles of Queries

Wang Pengming$^{(\boxtimes)}$, Chen Qing, and Wang Bin

College of Information Engineering, East China Jiaotong University,
Changbei Open and Developing District, Nanchang 330013, China
zhangwuji115@163.com, 80925699@qq.com, wangbin11@xiaomi.com

Abstract. Document smoothing has been shown to play a critical role to deal with the zero probability problems in the query likelihood retrieval model. Unlike traditional approaches using the same corpus language model for every document, the mainstream of the current methods introduce an additional smoothing item that can reflect the content of each document. However, these methods would either ignore the temporal characteristics of queries, or handle temporal factors in a multi-step process that cannot be explained in an unified solution, which rules out many potentially good alternatives. We instead propose a novel method, called *temporal smoothing*, which can alleviate the above problems. In particular, by using the overall temporal distribution of documents to smooth the temporal profile of a given query, the estimated temporal query model can be used in query likelihood retrieval model as an unified solution. Empirical evaluations based on a collection of Twitter documents and some standard benchmarks demonstrate the effectiveness of the proposed *temporal smoothing* mechanism in the retrieval task.

Keywords: Temporal feature · Smoothing ·
Query likelihood retrieval model

1 Introduction

Query likelihood retrieval model [1], in which document model θ_d would models what kind of queries would be posed by users who like document d. According to the Maximum Likelihood Estimator (MLE), we have:

$$p_{ml}(w|\theta_d) = \frac{c(w,d)}{\sum_{w \in V} c(w,d)} = \frac{c(w,d)}{|d|}. \tag{1}$$

where $c(w,d)$ is the count of word w in d and $|d|$ is the length of d, or total number of words in d.

W. Pengming—PhD, Lecturer, major research covers information retrieval, machine learning, etc.

© Springer Nature Switzerland AG 2019
Q. Zhang et al. (Eds.): CCIR 2019, LNCS 11772, pp. 26–38, 2019.
https://doi.org/10.1007/978-3-030-31624-2_3

Table 1. Comparison of various document smoothing approaches for different smoothing items used by them. We argue that the smoothing items used in traditional methods is intuitively not optimal since we essentially assume that all the unseen words in different documents would have similar probabilities; while the two middle kinds of improvements still have several issues in the practice. The new *temporal smoothing* method will alleviate these problems.

	Smoothing item (*reference language model*)
traditional methods	Only *basic* (item): the corpus language model
document-dependent smoothing methods	*basic* + an item reflecting the content of each document
time-sensitive smoothing methods	*basic* + some time factors
this work: temporal smoothing	a fusion of *basic* item and temporal profiles of queries

One problem with this ML estimator is that an unseen word in document d would get a zero probability, making all queries containing an unseen word have zero probability for the entire query $p(q|\theta_d)$. Therefore, smoothing has been introduced to solve that zero probability problem, and it plays a similar role to term weighting in traditional *tf-idf* model [2], which has been shown to play a critical role in the query likelihood retrieval model.

Table 1 provides a comparison of various document smoothing approaches.

The simplest way to smooth documents is additive smoothing [3], in which each word, including an unseen word, has got a small amount of extra count. Instead, the probability of an unseen word is generally assumed to be proportional to the probability of the word given by a *reference language model*. In particular, the maximum likelihood estimate can be interpolated with the reference language model θ_r with a fixed or unfixed coefficient λ to control the amount of smoothing:

$$p_{QL}(w|\hat{\theta}_d) = (1 - \lambda)p_{ml}(w|\theta_d) + \lambda p(w|\theta_r). \qquad (2)$$

A natural choice of the reference language model would be the language model estimated based on the entire document collection, called background language model, since intuitively it reflects the general word frequencies in the collection. We refer to this kind of document smoothing methods as "*traditional methods*", among which stand out Jelinek-Mercer smoothing [4] with a fixed smoothing coefficient, and Dirichlet prior smoothing [5], Absolute Discounting smoothing [6] with an unfixed smoothing coefficient.

However, smoothing every document with the same corpus language model is intuitively not optimal since we essentially assume that all the unseen words in different documents would have similar probabilities [7]. Take the query "*women's day*" shown in Fig. 1b for example, the probability of word "*celebrate*" appeared in the documents before March 8th may well not be the same as that after March 8th, because the latter would likely target another festival.

To our best knowledge, there are two main lines of research to improve the smoothing techniques. Based on the investigation and analysis to these two lines of research (Sect. 2), we go further to develop a novel method, called *temporal smoothing*, on a firm basis:

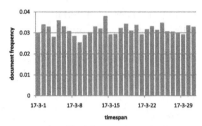

(a) temporal profile of the query ""weather forecast""

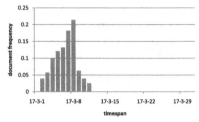

(b) temporal profile of the query "women's day"

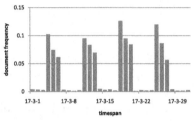

(c) temporal profile of the query "go to church"

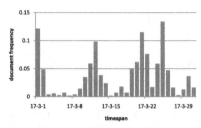

(d) temporal profile of the query "market promotion"

Fig. 1. Temporal profiles of several representative queries. The datasets used for drawing is crawled from Twitter during the time period from March 1st, 2017 to March 31st, 2017. The graph's horizontal axis shows the timespans split by days, and the vertical axis shows normalized document frequency based on the number of documents containing query keywords per timespan. The temporal profiles of these four queries show different patterns of none peak, one peak, more than one regular peak, or more than one irregular peak, respectively. These trends will be clearer as the time period enlarged.

- Based on the analysis of the temporal profiles of various queries (Sect. 3.1), adopting a variance of relevance modeling solution to model the period of time relevant to a given query, call "temporal query model", and presenting the problem of zero probability in temporal profiles of queries (Sect. 3.2).
- To solve the problem of zero probability above, we use the overall temporal distribution of documents in our collection, called "background temporal model", to smooth the temporal query model (Sect. 3.3).
- By integrating the smoothed temporal query model into query likelihood retrieval model, proposing an unified solution (Sect. 3.4), which can capture the temporal characteristics of queries and get significantly better performance than all standard benchmarks in the retrieval task (Sect. 4).

2   Related Work

As depicted in Table 1, the new *temporal smoothing* method is inspired by two lines of research: **document-dependent smoothing methods** introducing some document dependent strategies into smoothing, but not take account of the temporal characteristics of queries, which may undermine their smoothing effectiveness; and *time-sensitive smoothing methods* taking some temporal factors into account, but typically in a multi-step process that cannot be explained in an unified solution.

2.1   Document-Dependent Smoothing Methods

One way to improve the smoothing techniques is to introduce document dependent smoothing that can reflect the content of the document, for example by representing documents and queries in a latent topic space and estimating the generation probability accordingly.

These methods can typically be formalized as an interpolation form:

$$p(w|d) = (1 - \alpha)p_{QL}(w|d) + \alpha p_{DD}(w|d). \tag{3}$$

where $p_{QL}(w|d)$ and $p_{DD}(w|d)$ represent the word probability estimated with basic query likelihood model and a specific document-dependent strategy respectively. α is the parameter that controls the weights of these two interpolation terms.

Specifically, by incorporating topic level estimation into language model approaches, previous works such as the cluster-based retrieval model [8] and the LDA-based retrieval model [9] have obtained consistent improvements over the basic language models. Nonetheless, the learning cost (of topic models) is expensive on a large corpus.

Recently, Goyal et al. [10] propose a neighborhood based document smoothing model by exploiting lexical association between terms, but they make drastic revision on the traditional smoothing functions as well. Ai et al. [11] study how to effectively use the paragraph vector (PV) model in the language model framework to improve ad-hoc retrieval, and incorporate the language estimation of the distributed bag of words version of PV (PV-DBOW) into the query likelihood model as a document dependent smoothing technique. This method, however, is essentially a topic enhanced language model, which still needs extra learning cost.

PV-DBOW smoothing method can be regarded as the state-of-the-art method of its kind, and is adopted as one standard benchmark for this paper.

Note that the temporal characteristics of queries are not considered in this kind of methods; however, the temporal characteristics have obvious influences for document smoothing. Returning to our example query *"women's day"*, imagine that there are two documents whose content are identical, of course, they would be considered as the same in document-dependent smoothing methods. However, if one document published before March 8th, while the other one published after March 8th, the generation probabilities of them should intuitively be not the same.

2.2   Time-Sensitive Smoothing Methods

Recently, numerous works [12,13] are interested in describing the temporal nature of a query using a probability distribution over time, and this distribution is typically referred as a *"temporal profile"* of the query [14].

Based on a TREC corpora in which each document is annotated with a timestamp corresponding to the date the document was published, Jones and Diaz [14] suggest to count documents containing the query words, and assign weight to each day on the basis of that count. Our *temporal smoothing* method adopts and extends that idea.

Efron and Golovchinsky [15] propose an extension of the query likelihood model that considered not only when a document was published but also the relationship between the publication time and the query. They also proposed temporally informed smoothing, so that older documents that are further from the target time associated with the query are smoothed more aggressively. However, what they overlook is that not all the queries are recency-based queries.

Because term distributions in microblog services exhibit unique characteristics, Metzler et al. [16] argue that smoothing the general English language model is necessary to dampen the effect of over-weighting very rare terms, and propose a novel temporal query expansion (TDE) technique based on the temporal co-occurrence of terms. In particular, given keyword query q, they first automatically retrieve a set of N timespans for which the query keywords were most heavily discussed. For each pseudo-relevant timespan, a burstiness score is computed for all of the terms that occur in messages posted during the timespan. The burstiness score is meant to quantify how trending a term is during the timespan. Thus, if the query is being heavily discussed during the timespan and some term is also trending during the timespan, then the term may be related to the query. Seo et al. [17] observed similar results with traditional pseudo-relevance feedback techniques.

In contrast to traditional smoothing methods, time-sensitive smoothing methods have obtained consistent improvements by introducing various different temporal factors, yet, in spite of this, these methods almost have to work in a multiple-step mode, for example, TDE needs an additional step for the pseudo-relevant timespan feedback, which cannot be explained in an unified solution. In this work, we try to find an unified solution along the ideas of making use of temporal factors.

In this paper, TDE is adopted as another standard benchmark as the representative of its kind.

3   Temporal Smoothing

The basic idea of *Temporal Smoothing* is the following: we try to introduce a timespan variable t into query likelihood retrieval model. Formally, when a query q appears, we would first estimate the probability distribution of relevant document in each timespan, and then estimate the probability of target document generated from each timespan. Thus, the probability of generating a specific document d would be:

$$
\begin{aligned}
p(d|q) &= \sum_{t \in T} p(d, t|q) \\
&= \sum_{t \in T} p(d|t, q) p(t|q).
\end{aligned}
\tag{4}
$$

where T represents the whole time period of documents, which consists of all the timespans; the first factor in this summation, $p(d|t)$, represents the probability of target document d generated from a specific timespan t with respect to the given query q, while the second factor in the summation, $p(t|q)$, is merely the *temporal profile* of the given query q. The work in this paper focuses on the second factor.

3.1   Temporal Profile

We are interested in describing the temporal nature of a query using a probability distribution over timespans.

In Fig. 1 we see simple probability distributions over days for some typical queries *"weather forecast"*, *"women's day"*, *"go to church"*, and *"market promotion"* in a corpus of documents crawled from Twitter during the time period from March 1st, 2017 to March 31st, 2017. From this figure, we can see that the temporal profiles of these four queries show different distribution patters respectively, in particular, there is no obvious peak in the document distribution for query *"weather forecast"*, query *"women's day"* show only one peak, and the remaining two queries both reveal more than one peaks, however, the peaks in query *"go to church"* is orderly, while the peaks in query *"market promotion"* is irregular. These trends will be clearer as the time period enlarged.

Following previous works [14], we refer to these distributions as *temporal profiles* of the queries. Our goal is to model the temporal profile of a given query.

3.2   Temporal Query Model

Given the document collection with time-stamps, one way to build the temporal profile of a given query would be to count documents containing the query keywords, and then assign weight to each day on the basis of that count. Formally, we would like to estimate the distribution $p(t|q)$ where t can be any granularity of timespan, in this paper the granularity is set as the day scale. However, this information is not present in the query.

We adopt a variant of relevance modeling solution [18] to this estimation problem. Formally, our *temporal query model* is initially defined as:

$$
\tilde{p}(t|q) = \frac{1}{\left| \hat{R} \right|} \sum_{d \in \hat{R}} \tilde{p}(t|d).
\tag{5}
$$

where $\hat{R}$ is the set of documents that containing the query keywords. The factor in this summation represents the temporal information we have about the document. In our corpus, each document contains a unique timestamp, so this factor can reduce to a dirac delta on timespans,

$$\tilde{p}(t|d) = \begin{cases} 1 & \text{if } t \text{ is equal to the document date, } t_d \\ 0 & \text{otherwise} \end{cases} \tag{6}$$

However, as shown in Fig. 1, there is a great deal of timespans with zero probability in temporal profiles of some queries, making all documents contained in these timespans would have zero probability for the corresponding query. This is clearly undesirable. Intuitively, no documents appearing may due to holidays, other news events gaining precedence, or vagaries about publication times near midnight, or across different timespans. It may still be reasonable to assume that a day is relevant to a query, if adjacent days are relevant to the query. Therefore, the problem we have to solve is to smooth $\tilde{p}(t|q)$, so that we do not assign zero probability to any timespan.

3.3   Temporal Smoothing by Using Background Temporal Model

In analogy to using the background language model to smooth documents, we use the overall temporal distribution of documents in our collection, called "*background temporal model*", to smooth the original temporal query model.

Independent of the query we are modeling, the background temporal model can provide useful information about the general characteristics of term frequency and document frequency over days. Formally, the *background temporal model* is defined as:

$$\tilde{p}(t|C) = \frac{1}{|C|} \sum_{d \in C} \tilde{p}(t|d). \tag{7}$$

where C is the set of all documents in the collection.

Then, the estimate of temporal query model, i.e., *temporal smoothing*, can be linearly interpolated with this background model such that:

$$p_{ts}(t|q) = \beta\tilde{p}(t|q) + (1 - \beta)\tilde{p}(t|C). \tag{8}$$

where β is a smoothing parameter, which can be set as a fixed value or a unfixed value. For efficiency, we set that parameter to a fixed value in this paper, while the setting of unfixed value would be left to our future works.

3.4   An Unified Solution

So far, with above temporal smoothing method, the second factor of the summation in Eq. 4, $p_{ts}(t|q)$, is obtained. As for the first factor of the summation, $p(d|t,q)$, there may be many solution choices. In this paper, we choose to use the general unigram language model estimated based on the documents from the specific timespan, which we denote as θ_t.

As a consequence, the object item $p(d|t, q)$ can be solved as:

$$p(d|t, q) = p(d|\theta_t)$$
$$= \prod_{w \in V_t} p(w|\theta_t)^{c(w,d)}. \tag{9}$$

where V_t represents the vocabulary built based on the documents in timespan t. The full details of *statistic language model* can refer to this article [7].

Taking these derivations together, Eq. 4 can then be written as an unified solution:

$$p(d|q) = \sum_{t \in T} p(d|t, q)p(t|q)$$
$$= \sum_{t \in T} p(d|\theta_t)p_{ts}(t|q) \tag{10}$$
$$= \sum_{t \in T} \left\{ \prod_{w \in V_t} p(w|\theta_t)^{c(w,d)} \right\} \{ \beta \tilde{p}(t|q) + (1 - \beta) \tilde{p}(t|C) \}.$$

where the smoothing parameter β is the only super-parameter need to be adjusted, and we will investigate its importance in the experimental part of this paper.

4   Experiment and Evaluation

This section describes our empirical evaluation of the proposed *temporal smoothing* method.

4.1   Corpus

Our document collection consists of data that we collected from Twitter using their Streaming API[1]. The API delivers a continuous 1% random sample of public Twitter messages (also called "tweets"). Our evaluation makes use of data collected between March 1st, 2017 and March 31st, 2017. After eliminating all non-English tweets, our corpus consists of 32,661,843 English tweets, which corresponds to roughly 1,000,000 tweets per day. Although this only represents a 1% sample of all tweets, we believe that the corpus is sizable enough to demonstrate the utility of our proposed approach.

4.2   Queries

To evaluate our new method, we prepared a list of 4 typical queries whose temporal profiles differ significantly from each other, as depicted in Fig. 1. The temporal profiles of these queries have substantially different characteristics, such as the

---

[1] Available at http://dev.twitter.com/pages/streaming_api/.

document frequency in single timespan, popularity, etc. For example, there is no obvious peak in the document distribution for query *"weather forecast"*, query *"women's day"* show only one peak, and the remaining two queries both reveal more than one peaks, however, the peaks in query *"go to church"* is orderly, while the peaks in query *"market promotion"* is irregular. These trends will be clearer as the time period enlarged.

4.3   Temporal Smoothing Result

To evaluate the quality of a particular configuration of our new *temporal smoothing* method, we run the temporal smoothing task described in the previous section with 10 set of smoothing parameter β in Eq. 8, the range of values allowed

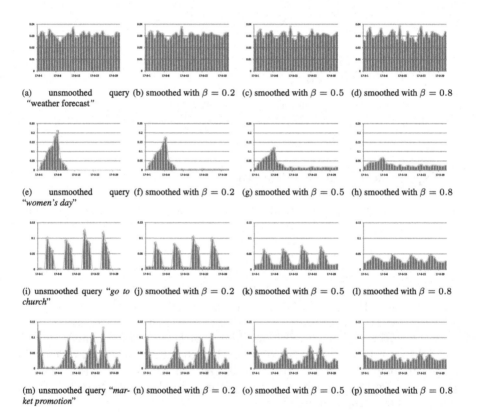

(a)   unsmoothed   query (b) smoothed with $\beta = 0.2$ (c) smoothed with $\beta = 0.5$ (d) smoothed with $\beta = 0.8$
"weather forecast"

(e)   unsmoothed   query (f) smoothed with $\beta = 0.2$ (g) smoothed with $\beta = 0.5$ (h) smoothed with $\beta = 0.8$
"women's day"

(i) unsmoothed query *"go to* (j) smoothed with $\beta = 0.2$ (k) smoothed with $\beta = 0.5$ (l) smoothed with $\beta = 0.8$
church"

(m) unsmoothed query *"mar-* (n) smoothed with $\beta = 0.2$ (o) smoothed with $\beta = 0.5$ (p) smoothed with $\beta = 0.8$
ket promotion"

Fig. 2. Temporal Smoothing effects on several representative queries with different levels of smoothing. From this figure, we find that the temporal profiles of query *"weather forecast"* are almost constant, regardless of level of temporal smoothing, however, the smoothing effects on another three queries are evident. Furthermore, changes in the temporal profiles of query *"market promotion"* are the greatest, and it is actually easy to understand because the peaks in this query are irregular while tending to be smoothed as the smoothing parameter grows.

Table 2. The comparison of retrieval performance between *temporal smoothing* method with different levels of smoothing and comparison methods described in Sect. 2. Overall, the new *temporal smoothing* methods with some specific value of smoothing parameter consistently surpass all comparison approaches for all queries, and the improvement is statistically significant in most cases.

Methods		Queries				MAP
		weather forest	women's day	go to church	market promotion	
		$AP = (P@10 + P@20 + P@30)/3$				
non-smoothing method		0.3711	0.4003	0.3610	0.3716	0.3760
traditional methods (Dirichlet prior smoothing)		0.4447	0.4243	0.4010	0.3985	0.4171
document-dependent smoothing methods (PV-DBOW smoothing)		0.4860	0.4720	0.4333	0.4112	0.4506
time-sensitive smoothing methods (TDE smoothing)		0.4565	0.4464	0.4046	0.4040	0.4279
temporal smoothing methods	$\beta = 0.0$	0.4046	0.4158	0.3728	0.3854	0.3947
	$\beta = 0.1$	0.4381	0.4419	0.4021	0.3887	0.4177
	$\beta = 0.2$	0.4496	0.4494	0.4132	0.4005	0.4282
	$\beta = 0.3$	0.4629	0.4694	0.4297	0.4050	0.4417
	$\beta = 0.4$	0.4685	0.4726	0.4381	0.4197	0.4497
	$\beta = 0.5$	0.4782	**0.4977***	**0.4798***	**0.4254**	**0.4703***
	$\beta = 0.6$	**0.4941**	0.4802	0.4494	0.4184	0.4605
	$\beta = 0.7$	0.4691	0.4624	0.4188	0.4076	0.4395
	$\beta = 0.8$	0.4646	0.4383	0.4017	0.3863	0.4227
	$\beta = 0.9$	0.4359	0.4177	0.3809	0.3814	0.4040
	$\beta = 1.0$	0.3990	0.4034	0.3703	0.3812	0.3885

*The improvement is statistically significant at the level of 0.05 according to the Wilcoxon signed rank test.

for β is from 0 to 1, and the step-size is set to 0.1. Intuitively, when $\beta = 0$, we end up with no temporal smoothing, while setting $\beta = 1$ would essentially ignore the original document distribution and completely reset the query temporal model to the temporal profile estimated based on the entire document collection.

Figure 2 plots the temporal profiles of above 4 queries with different values of smoothing parameter β. For the limitation of thesis, we only show 4 subfloats for each query. From this figure, we find that the temporal profiles of query "*weather forecast*" are almost constant, regardless of level of temporal smoothing, however, the smoothing effects on another three queries are evident.

Furthermore, note that two timespans with same probability value $\tilde{p}(t|q)$ in the unsmoothed temporal profile of a given query, might obtain different probability value $p_{ts}(t|q)$ after some level of temporal smoothing. Notable examples are the zero-probability timespans in the unsmoothed temporal profile of query "*women's day*", not only do them all obtain non-zero probabilities, but some differences exist between their probabilities. This again attributes to the fact that two identical documents in different timespans might have different generative probabilities.

As for whether the *temporal smoothing* method can improve the resulting performance of retrieval task, we have taken further actions to study that problem.

4.4   Retrieval Result

To provide a high-quality evaluation setting, we firstly use pooling technique to builds a collection of candidate relevant-documents based on top 100 documents obtained by all approaches mentioned in this paper, and then, leverage CrowdFlower[2], a popular crowdsourcing platform, to annotate the candidate documents with their relevant levels on a scale of 0 to 5. The final label of each candidate document is used as a gold standard. Table 2 reports the performance of our *Temporal Smoothing* approach against some comparison methods described in Sect. 2, measured by AP and MAP ($N = 10, 20, 30$).

Overall, of the existing standard benchmarks, PV-DBOW smoothing method [11] is a better one; in the meanwhile, we notice that the new *temporal smoothing* methods with some specific value of smoothing parameter β are consistently surpass all comparison approaches for all queries, and the improvement is statistically significant in most cases, indicating that when choosing a good smoothing parameter, the new *temporal smoothing* method can play well for the retrieval task.

We further note that the retrieval performance is very sensitive to the value of smoothing parameter β. In particular, when parameter value varying from 0 to 1, the retrieval performance appears an obvious fluctuation, within this the point of best performance occurs around $\beta = 0.6$.

On the other hand, we note that the improvements of retrieval performance based on the new *temporal smoothing* method are not the same for different queries. Although intuitively the cause might be the wide discrepancy among their temporal profiles, it still needs confirming and supporting by more systematical analyses.

4.5   Analysing and Evaluating

Intuitively, there is close correlation between the impacts of the new *temporal smoothing* method on retrieval performance for different queries, and the temporal profiles of these queries.

Note that the overall temporal distribution of documents in our collection, i.e., background temporal model, is invariant. Therefore, as the increase of smoothing parameter β, the estimated temporal query model would deviate from its original temporal profile, and draw closer to background temporal model.

From Fig. 2, we can see that at high smoothing level, the estimated temporal query models of *"women's day"* and *"go to church"* appear obvious deviation; at the same time, as depicted in Table 2, the retrieval performance for these two queries was significantly improved after temporal smoothed. As for the other

---

[2] http://www.crowdflower.com/.

two queries, although the promotion of retrieval performance is not significant, the new *temporal smoothing* method still has obtained some profiles.

5   Conclusions and Future Work

In this paper, we propose a novel document smoothing method, call *temporal smoothing*, which combines the temporal profiles of queries with the basic smoothing item in query likelihood retrieval model, and ultimately get an unified solution. Empirical evaluations based on a collection of Twitter documents and some standard benchmarks, the new *temporal smoothing* methods with some specific value of smoothing parameter are consistently surpass all comparison approaches for all queries, and the improvement is statistically significant in most cases.

Note, however, that this is just a small pilot study with a small-scale corpus and only four queries, the elementary experiment results shown above should be confirmed on the basis of large scale label corpus.

Acknowledgments. This work is supported by the National Natural Science Foundation of China (61572494, 61462027), the fund project of Jiangxi Province Education Office (GJJ170418, GJJ180315) and Jiangxi University Humanities and Social Science Project (SZZX16013).

References

1. Ponte, J.M., Croft, W.B.: A language modeling approach to information retrieval. In: Proceedings of the 21st Annual International ACM SIGIR Conference on Research and Development in Information Retrieval, pp. 275–281. ACM (1998)
2. Salton, G., Wong, A., Yang, C.-S.: A vector space model for automatic indexing. Commun. ACM **18**(11), 613–620 (1975)
3. Chen, S.F., Goodman, J.: An empirical study of smoothing techniques for language modeling. In: Proceedings of the 34th Annual Meeting on Association for Computational Linguistics, pp. 310–318. Association for Computational Linguistics (1996)
4. Jelinek, F.: Interpolated estimation of markov source parameters from sparse data. In: Proceedings of the Workshop on Pattern Recognition in Practice (1980)
5. Zhai, C., Lafferty, J.: A study of smoothing methods for language models applied to ad hoc information retrieval. In: International ACM SIGIR Conference on Research and Development in Information Retrieval, pp. 334–342 (2001)
6. Ney, H., Essen, U., Kneser, R.: On structuring probabilistic dependences in stochastic language modelling. Comput. Speech Lang. **8**(1), 1–38 (1994)
7. Zhai, C.: Statistical language models for information retrieval. Synth. Lect. Hum. Lang. Technol. **1**(1), 1–141 (2008)
8. Liu, X., Croft, W.B.: Cluster-based retrieval using language models. In: Proceedings of the 27th Annual International ACM SIGIR Conference on Research and Development in Information Retrieval, pp. 186–193. ACM (2004)
9. Wei, X., Croft, W.B.: Lda-based document models for ad-hoc retrieval. In: Proceedings of the 29th annual International ACM SIGIR Conference on Research and Development in Information Retrieval, pp. 178–185. ACM (2006)

10. Goyal, P., Behera, L., McGinnity, T.M.: A novel neighborhood based document smoothing model for information retrieval. Inf. Retrieval **16**(3), 391–425 (2013)
11. Ai, Q., Yang, L., Guo, J., Croft, W.B.: Improving language estimation with the paragraph vector model for ad-hoc retrieval. In: Proceedings of the 39th International ACM SIGIR Conference on Research and Development in Information Retrieval, pp. 869–872. ACM (2016)
12. Gupta, D., Berberich, K.: Diversifying search results using time. In: Ferro, N., et al. (eds.) ECIR 2016. LNCS, vol. 9626, pp. 789–795. Springer, Cham (2016). https://doi.org/10.1007/978-3-319-30671-1_69
13. Spitz, A., Gertz, M.: Terms over load: leveraging named entities for cross-document extraction and summarization of events. In: Proceedings of the 39th International ACM SIGIR Conference on Research and Development in Information Retrieval, pp. 503–512. ACM (2016)
14. Jones, R., Diaz, F.: Temporal profiles of queries. ACM Trans. Inf. Syst. (TOIS) **25**(3), 14 (2007)
15. Efron, M., Golovchinsky, G.: Estimation methods for ranking recent information. In: Proceedings of the 34th International ACM SIGIR Conference on Research and Development in Information Retrieval, pp. 495–504. ACM (2011)
16. Metzler, D., Cai, C., Hovy, E.: Structured event retrieval over microblog archives. In: Proceedings of the 2012 Conference of the North American Chapter of the Association for Computational Linguistics: Human Language Technologies, pp. 646–655. Association for Computational Linguistics (2012)
17. Seo, J., Croft, W.B.: Geometric representations for multiple documents. In: Proceedings of the 33rd International ACM SIGIR Conference on Research and Development in Information Retrieval, pp. 251–258. ACM (2010)
18. Lavrenko, V., Croft, W.B.: Relevance based language models. In: Proceedings of the 24th Annual International ACM SIGIR Conference on Research and Development in Information Retrieval, pp. 120–127. ACM (2001)

Investigating Query Reformulation Behavior of Search Users

Jia Chen, Jiaxin Mao, Yiqun Liu$^{(\boxtimes)}$, Min Zhang, and Shaoping Ma

Department of Computer Science and Technology, Institute for Artificial Intelligence,
Beijing National Research Center for Information Science and Technology,
Tsinghua University, Beijing 100084, China
chenjia0831@gmail.com, maojiaxin@gmail.com,
{yiqunliu,z-m,msp}@tsinghua.edu.cn

Abstract. Search engine users usually strive to reformulate their queries in the search process to gain useful information. It is hard for search engines to understand users' search intents and return appropriate results if they submit improper or ambiguous queries. Therefore, query reformulation is a bottleneck issue in the usability of search engines. Modern search engines normally provide users with some query suggestions for references. To help users to better learn their information needs, it is of vital importance to investigate users' reformulation behaviors thoroughly. In this paper, we conduct a detailed investigation of users' session-level reformulation behavior on a large-scale session dataset and discover some interesting findings that previous work may not notice before: (1) Intent ambiguity may be the direct cause of long sessions rather than the complexity of users' information needs; (2) Both the added and the deleted terms in a reformulation step can be influenced by the clicked results to a greater extent than the skipped ones; (3) Users' specification actions are more likely to be inspired by the result snippets or the landing pages, while the generalization behaviors are impacted largely by the result titles. We further discuss some concerns about the existing query suggestion task and give some suggestions on the potential research questions for future work. We hope that this work could provide assistance for the researchers who are interested in the relative domain.

Keywords: Query suggestion · Query reformulation ·
User behavior analysis

1 Introduction

With the rapid development of Web search techniques, people are becoming increasingly dependent on search engines to solve problems these days. However, it seems users tend to submit short and ambiguous queries [11] which are

This work is supported by Natural Science Foundation of China (Grant No. 61622208, 61532011, 61672311) and National Key Basic Research Program (2015CB358700). This research is partly supported by the Tsinghua-Sogou Tiangong Institute for Intelligent Computing.

© Springer Nature Switzerland AG 2019
Q. Zhang et al. (Eds.): CCIR 2019, LNCS 11772, pp. 39–51, 2019.
https://doi.org/10.1007/978-3-030-31624-2_4

too vague to be fully understood by search engines. This makes query formulation a bottleneck issue in the usability of search engines [9]. Sometimes the users may endeavor several search rounds to reformulate their queries until they find some relevant results that fulfill their information needs. To ease the users' burden, modern commercial search engines usually provide query suggestions for them to better acknowledge their search tasks and express their queries more clearly. The previous work [12] has shown that appropriate query suggestions can significantly improve users' search satisfaction, especially for those navigational queries. Therefore, it is of vital importance to improve the query suggestion performance in commercial search engines.

To better understand users' search intents and model their information needs, session context information such as previous queries and click-through data have been employed by numerous approaches for query suggestion. Many of them make good use of the "wisdom of crowds" to mine the relations and similarities between queries. Some methods extract the query co-occurrences in the search log or apply Markov models to learn the query connections [2,13]. They assume that the most frequent follow-up queries for the current one are more likely to be submitted by users in the next. These methods are simple and achieve good performances sometimes, but may also suffer from the data sparsity problem (e.g. query suggestion for long-tailed queries). To tackle this obstacle, some researchers attempt to incorporate statistical features or clickthrough information into their models to learn better user reformulation behaviors. Jiang et al. [3] conduct a detailed analysis on a search log and extract some features to learn user reformulation behavior through some learning-to-rank algorithms. With the emergence of deep neural networks, more work focus on employing Recurrent Neural Networks (RNNs) to model users' sequential intra-session behaviors. For instance, Li et al. [8] propose a hierarchical attention network that applies the attention mechanism at both word- and session-level for context-aware query suggestion. Jiang at el. [7] first incorporate the embeddings learned from a session-flow graph into a reformulation inference network to predict the reformulation embedding for the next query.

Although these methods have achieved exciting performances in terms of predicting the next query within a search session, it is still unclear whether they can enhance users' search processes. In fact, to which extent they can help users to better, faster complete their search tasks still remains to be investigated so far. Moreover, existing evaluation approaches have their own limitations. Most studies aim to improve the rank of the next query in the candidate sets. However, one question is why should we boost the priority of this query even if it does not articulately express the user's search intent? Also, some other concerns should be taken into consideration. For example, there are a number of similar queries in the candidate list, but we only take one of them as our intended query and ignore the semantic similarities. Then the one-hit metrics such as MRR@k, SR@k or MISS@k may not accurately evaluate the suggestion performance under this circumstance. Therefore, we need to reacquaint the query suggestion task and search for the directions we should head towards.

To better investigate the context-aware query suggestion task itself, we conduct a meta-analysis on the session-level user reformulation behavior on a large-scale session data. The dataset totally contains more than 5,300,000 sessions extracted from a huge commercial search engine log[1]. In this paper, we propose three research questions as follows:

- **RQ1:** When will people submit a long search session?
- **RQ2:** How does the user reformulation pattern evolve within a session?
- **RQ3:** How do users reformulate their next query when inspired by the previous search round? Can we find any relationship between some interaction signals (such as clicks) and users' reformulation behavior?

These questions are fundamental but crucial for exploring the query suggestion task. The analysis results may contribute to the redefining of the problem and the redesigning of better query suggestion metrics. We then present some of our considerations of the query suggestion task itself to provide references for other researchers who are interested in relative domains.

2   Related Work

There are a number of existing work aiming to optimize the ranks of the intended query (or the next query) in the candidate query set. Some work mine the inter-query dependencies through the co-occurrences in the query log, the query flow graph or the bipartite graph [9,15]. Recently, Sordoni et al. [5] first employ RNN for sequential query prediction and generation. To handle the data sparsity problem in utilizing the "wisdom of crowds", some researchers begin to exploit manually extracted features or clickthrough data for better user intent modeling. Wu at el. [6] propose a feedback memory network to take the clicks and skips in previous search rounds as positive and negative feedbacks respectively and incorporate them into the session-level embeddings. Jiang et al. [7] employ node2vec [16] to train the node embeddings from a session flow graph and then feed them into a reformulation inference network for query suggestion.

Instead of just boosting the system performance, some other studies make some efforts on understanding user reformulation behaviors. Liu et al. [14] analyze the nature of the query recommendation process from the user' s perspective and use click-through rate and user click amount to evaluate the effectiveness of their proposed snippet click model. To gain precise and detailed insight into which terms the users show a particular interest in, Eickhoff et al. study query refinement using the eye-tracking technique [4]. Jiang et al. extract some heuristic features according to a user behavior analysis and apply the LambdaMart algorithm to learn user reformulation [3]. Except for analyzing user behavior, some Information Retrieval (IR) researchers focus on solving the query ambiguity problem. Shokouhi et al. not only utilize the context information within the

---

[1] To access the dataset, please contact chenjia0831@gmail.com.

session to provide unambiguous query suggestion but also propose a context-sensitive result fusion approach to improve the retrieval quality for ambiguous queries [10].

The difference between our work and the previous ones is: we make a detailed analysis of the session-level user reformulation behavior and the query suggestion task itself. We not only aim at exploring the reason why people submit long sessions, but also focus on the evolution of the user search pattern within the ongoing sessions. We further investigate to find the relationship between some signals and the user reformulation actions. Finally, we come up with some of our concerns for the query suggestion task and propose some potential directions for future work in this task.

3   Dataset

In this section, we will briefly introduce our dataset. We extract our session data from a log recorded by Sogou.com, which is a major Chinese commercial search engine. The log was sampled from April 1st to April 18th, 2015, containing abundant Web search data on the desktop. For each query, the URLs, vertical types and the click information (whether be clicked and the click timestamp) for all returned results and the user IDs are recorded. Similar to previous studies, we use the 30-min gap as the session boundary to split the queries submitted by the same users into search sessions. We then discard those sessions with only one query or more than 10 queries, because there is no context information to be utilized in single-query sessions while sessions that are too long may contain much noise. Because our dataset is Chinese-centric, we adopt an open-sourced tool called `jieba`[2] for word segmentation. We randomly sample 10% of all the sessions as our testing set and the rest as the training set. To ensure the consistency, we abandon the testing sessions whose last query does not appear in the training set. Then we randomly sample 10% of the training data as our validating set for further system parameter tuning. Finally, there are 5,045,625 training sessions (including 505,036 validating sessions) and 331,605 testing sessions, respectively.

Table 1. Basic statistics of sessions with different context lengths.

Data\Context length	Short(1)	Medium(2–3)	Long($\geq$4)	All
Training+Validating	3,261,183	1,393,824	390,618	5,045,625
Testing	223,467	85,324	22,814	331,605

Table 1 presents the statistics of sessions with different context lengths in our dataset. To explore the system performance across sessions with different lengths, we split the session data into three groups, i.e. short sessions with only

---

[2] https://pypi.org/project/jieba/.

one previous query, medium sessions with 2–3 query contexts, and long sessions with more than four previous search rounds. From Fig. 1(a), We can find that over 60% sessions are short sessions, which indicates that in the real-world Web search scenario people tend to submit only one query reformulation. We further explore the number of clicks within a session and present the statistical results in Fig. 1(b). Over 80% of all sessions have at least one click. Generally, compared to another search engine log AOL [1], our dataset owns more short sessions but contains obviously more clickthrough information.

4   Session-Level User Reformulation Behavior Analysis

In this section, we will make a detailed analysis of session-level user reformulation behavior on our training set (including the validating set). Here we leave the testing set as unknown.[3]

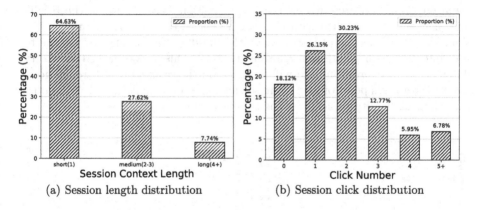

(a) Session length distribution   (b) Session click distribution

Fig. 1. Distributions for session lengths and clicks.

4.1   Analysis of Session-Level User Reformulation Pattern

It is crucial to investigate users' session-level behavior to find heuristics for designing better query suggestion algorithms or evaluation metrics. In this subsection, we will study the following two research questions:

- **RQ1:** When will people submit a long search session?
- **RQ2:** How does the user reformulation pattern evolve within a session?

To answer the above questions, we will make a stratified analysis of the users' session-level search patterns on our session data.

A search session is consist of a sequence of queries $S = \{q_0, q_1, ... q_{|K|}\}$. The query lengths may change a lot at different session positions because of

---

[3] Other researchers can use the testing set for system performance evaluation.

user intent shift. We present the trends of the query length and the user clicks across each search iteration in sessions with 2–10 queries in Fig. 2(a) and (b), respectively. As shown in Fig. 2(a), we find that generally the shorter a session is, the longer the queries within it are. This is different from the previous work [3], which reports longer sessions usually contain queries with more terms. We also observe that query lengths will always increase at the beginning, and then vibrate within a small range during the search processes. One possible explanation for this phenomenon is that although users may have complex information needs in longer sessions, they may not be able to express their needs clearly in the search query at the beginning and need to attempt multiple search rounds in a trial-and-error process to find an appropriate query expression. On the contrary, in short sessions, users may have higher-level cognition towards their information needs and thus can formulate their query with more terms and less ambiguity. We further explore the average click number in each session position. In Fig. 2(b), we can observe a sharp rise of click number in the last two search rounds within a session in all lengths. There is an average click of over 0.6 in the last search iteration. This indicates that at the end of sessions, users click on the results and may be more satisfied with the search task so they choose to end the session. The slight decline of the curve in the middle of a session may be due to user intent shifts or expression reformulations. At this period, users tend to try different query expressions and will not click on the results until there are good results. From this point of view, long sessions may be mainly directly caused by the intent ambiguity rather than the complex information needs.

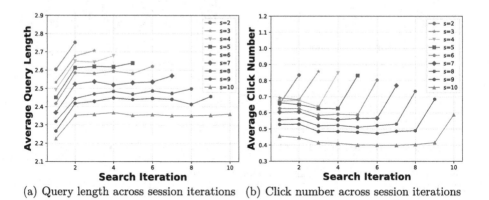

(a) Query length across session iterations   (b) Click number across session iterations

Fig. 2. Trends of query length and click number across session iterations

Query lengths and click numbers cannot provide details for user behaviors. Therefore, we compare the proportions of each reformulation type in short sessions and long sessions in our dataset, respectively. In the search process, users may learn from the search results and reformulate her next query. User reformulation behavior in our data can be normally divided into four main groups: *specification*, *generalization*, *repetition* and *others*. Specification includes those reformulations adding constraints to the original queries to narrow down the scope of search results. So the query lengths usually increase in this condition. On the other hand, users may also generalize the queries by loosening the search constraints and deleting some terms. Some other reformulation types include spelling change (or character change in Chinese), parallel shift, synonym, intent shift, and etc. Note that there are differences between the parallel shift and intent shift. In parallel shift, users may focus on various facets of the same object or problem. However, they may focus on two different objects when their search intents have shifted. In our session data, there are a proportion of query repetitions. We think that this is because the paging down operations by users are also recorded as new query submissions by the search engine. Some typical examples of each reformulation types in our data are presented in Table 2. Note that our session data is huge so we can only roughly label the reformulation type for every two continuous queries q_{t-1} and q_t according to the following definitions:

- **Specification:** $+\triangle q_t \neq \emptyset, -\triangle q_t = \emptyset$;
- **Generalization:** $+\triangle q_t = \emptyset, -\triangle q_t \neq \emptyset$;
- **Repetition:** $+\triangle q_t = \emptyset, -\triangle q_t = \emptyset$;
- **Others:** $+\triangle q_t \neq \emptyset, -\triangle q_t \neq \emptyset$.

where $+\triangle q_t = \{s|s \in S(q_t), s \notin S(q_{t-1})\}$, $-\triangle q_t = \{s|s \notin S(q_t), s \in S(q_{t-1})\}$, and $S(q)$ denotes the term set of a query q. Here we do not consider the semantic similarity, so the proportion of the "others" reformulation type we report can be higher than the ground truth value because a portion of specification or generalization cases might also be labeled as the "others" type.

Table 2. Typical examples of each reformulation types (translated from Chinese).

Reformulation		Examples
Specification		Minecraft → Minecraft skin websites
Generalization		*Transformers: Age of Extinction → Transformers*
Repeated Queries		Xiaomi→ taobao.com → taobao.com
Others	spelling change	Datong Securities(大同证券) → Datong Securities(大通证券)
	parallel shift	*Conan* the movie version → *Conan* the mandarin version
	synonym	*Running Man 2*(跑男 2) → *Running Man 2*(奔跑吧兄弟第二季)
	intent shift	Ultra Magnus(通天晓) → The Fallen(堕落金刚)

Table 3 presents the comparison between short and long sessions in terms of the proportion of each reformulation type. We notice that there is no significant difference in the repetition action. This shows that there might be equal chances that users may repeat their last query or click the page-down button in short and long sessions. However, there is a rise of about 50% in the specification action from the long session condition to short session condition (i.e. from 9.93% to 14.14%). This gap is distributed to the generalization and the "others" reformulation types. We can learn from Table 2 that in generalization and the "others" reformulation types, users are more likely to shift their intents or expand the search scope. They choose to reformulate their queries in this way maybe because they have scanned the results of the current query and believe that this query is not heading for the desired information. Not sufficiently acknowledging their information needs and submitting queries with ambiguity to the search engines may be the direct cause of why people submit a long search session.

Table 3. Probabilities of each reformulation type in short and long sessions

Session length	Generalization	Specification	Repetition	Others
Short(2)	0.0366	0.1414	0.3085	0.5136
Long(5+)	0.0480	0.0993	0.3042	0.5486

Having figured out the possible reason why users will submit a long session, we further explore how the user search pattern evolves within a session. The user search pattern is closely related with their reformulation behaviors, thus we calculate the proportions of each reformulation type across the session and plot the results in Fig. 3. Generally, we notice there are much more repetition and other reformulation cases than either the generalization or specification at all steps. Due to its small proportion, it is hard to find any markable trends for users' generalization behavior across the session process. However, we find a

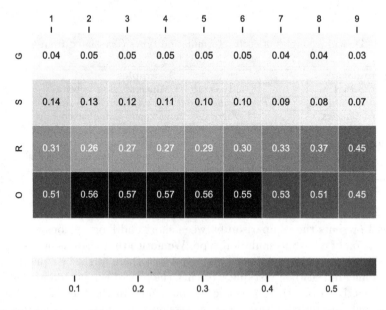

Fig. 3. The heatmap of the proportion of each reformulation pattern (G-generalization, S-specification, R-repetition, O-others) across reformulation steps within a search session. Here we take all sessions into consideration

stable decay (14% to only 7%) of the specification action from the first to the last reformulation step. This huge decline suggests that users are more and more clear about their search intents thus are less likely to add some constraints on their next queries to narrow down the search scope.

As for the "others" reformulation type, there is a sharp rise from the first to the second reformulation step, and then a slow decay from the fifth step to the eighth one, and finally a huge drop. This trend is exactly opposite to that of the repetition whose proportion first declines and then increases. The darker blocks in the fourth row of the heatmap indicate that people may shift their intents more frequently and submit more various queries in the middle of a session. In the last several search rounds, they tend to repeat their previous queries or examine more results. Finally, they end the search session because their information needs are mostly satisfied. From this analysis, we find that users' exploration process of searching for an appropriate query can be up to 7–8 search rounds. Reflect on the current query suggestion task that mainly aims at optimizing the rank of the predicted query, a more urgent goal may be helping users to reformulate their queries with less ambiguity and shortening the search process.

4.2 User Reformulation Behavior

It is of vital importance to study the mechanism of how users reformulate their queries within a session. In this subsection, we will investigate the following research question:

– **RQ3:** How do users reformulate their next query when inspired by the previous search round? Can we find any relationship between some interaction signals (such as clicks) and users' reformulation behavior

We first compare the dwell time across each reformulation step in Fig. 4(a). The results show that users spend more time browsing the results in shorter sessions. This finding is also consistent with our previous analysis that users tend to have a clear search intent in shorter sessions so they can receive better results and spend more time reading on them. In long sessions, the dwell time first declines and then increases, which implies users usually engage more at the beginning and the end of a session. There might be more attempts in the middle of a session.

In the last subsection, we have shown that the search engine users will change their reformulation patterns during the search process. Inspired by some contents in the previous search round, users will rewrite the following query to obtain more appropriate results. To make sense how users can be influenced by the previous search round and reformulate their next queries, we crawl the titles for each search result in our data and analyze the relationship between these titles and the newly-formed query. For over 92% queries, we have crawled the titles for at least five results. We then count up the number of the cases in which the terms added in the specification action or deleted in the generalization action also appear in the result titles of the previous query. All cases are divided into four groups according to whether the result has been clicked or not: *click*, *skip*, *non-click*, and *others*. Here we define the skips as those results that have not been clicked but ranked higher than the last clicked result. Other results without clicks are denoted as the non-clicks. Users may also be impacted by other contents such as the texts in the search snippets, the landing pages, and etc. We regard these conditions as others.

The statistics are shown in Table 4. Note that there are less long sessions than short sessions, so the numbers of cases always decay across the reformulation steps. An interesting finding is: both $+\triangle q_t$ and $-\triangle q_t$ are more likely to be influenced by the clicked results than the skipped results. To our surprise, the probability of a user being affected by the clicked results is around five times of that by the skipped ones if she deletes some words from her previous query. However, this margin drops to only three times in the case of the added terms in the specification condition. This finding indicates that clicks are not always the positive feedback signals for user information needs. Users may first check the results, realize the current query is not suitable for their search purposes, and then delete some terms from the current query according to the result titles. Another finding is that the users' reformulation behavior can also be largely impacted by those non-click titles. Especially, the non-click cases account for more than a half of the amount in the generalization condition. One possible reason may be: although the users do not click these results, they are likely to examine them and somehow judge them as not relevant. In addition, the "others" condition occupies a much larger proportion in term of $+\triangle q_t$ than $-\triangle q_t$. This gap suggests that the user specification behavior can be influenced more by other elements such as the snippets, the landing page contents, and etc. In contrast, they may not engage too much in the generalization case. They may just scan the result titles and then decide to delete some terms if they estimate that the current query is not appropriate or too specified.

Table 4. Statistics for the cases in which the terms in $+\triangle q_t$ and $-\triangle q_t$ also appear in the result titles of the previous query. Here we only consider the results whose titles we have successfully crawled.

Condition		Reformulation step								
		1	2	3	4	5	6	7	8	9
$+\triangle q_t$	clicks	11,890	4,223	1,655	756	401	185	76	40	23
	skips	3,494	1,479	596	255	130	59	29	20	9
	non-clicks	39,669	14,120	6,058	2,897	1,485	759	365	172	83
	others	109,670	39,834	17,764	8,706	4,552	2,439	1,296	659	271
$-\triangle q_t$	clicks	48,646	18,664	7,634	3,675	1,881	922	473	250	104
	skips	9,822	4,450	1,940	901	464	234	122	62	28
	non-clicks	98,200	36,939	16,131	7,923	4,120	2,172	1,076	592	233
	others	27,998	10,829	4,889	2,441	1,244	678	404	174	71

To further investigate the relationship between clicks and user reformulation behavior, we calculate the proportion of each kind of reformulation type given the previous query causes clicks or not. The results are shown in Fig. 4(b). We can learn that for the queries do not cause clicks, there is a higher probability (64.45%) that the user may copy some terms from these queries to reformulate her next query. However, the probability drops to only 52.92% if there is no click in the previous search round. This find is consistent with the results reported in previous work [3]. On one hand, users are more likely to reformulate specified or repeated queries if she clicks no result of the current query. One possible explanation is that users do not find any relevant results so they tend to click the page-down button or add some constraints on the current query to search for more relevant results. On the other hand, there is a higher probability of other reformulation behaviors when people click some results. In this condition, people may find relevant documents and feel satisfied to some extent. Therefore, they may tend to end up the current search subtask or even shift their intents to start another subtask.

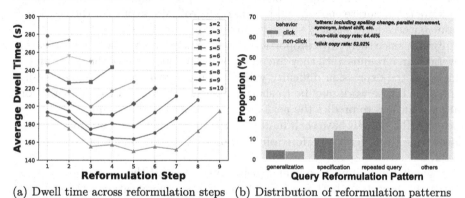

(a) Dwell time across reformulation steps   (b) Distribution of reformulation patterns

Fig. 4. Some statistics of users' session-level reformulation behaviors.

4.3 Conclusions

To sum up, the above analysis suggests that:

- It may be the intent ambiguity or expression difficulty that directly cause longer sessions rather than users' complex information needs.
- Users tend to specify their queries in the first reformulation step to narrow down the search scope, and then continue their search processes in a trial-and-error manner.
- Surprisingly, for both the added terms $+\triangle q_t$ and the deleted terms $-\triangle q_t$ in the reformulation actions, users are possibly impacted more by the clicked results than the skipped ones.
- Users can be influenced more by the result titles when they decide to delete some terms in the current query, while they may be more likely to refer to

other contents such as the result snippets or the texts in the landing pages for query specification.

- If a user clicks some results in this search round, then there is a higher probability she will copy some terms from the current query to reformulate her next query.
- Users will click more documents at the end of a session. They may find some relevant documents, feel satisfied with them, and then end their search processes.

From the above analysis, we find several assumptions in some previous work may not be so meticulous and should be further improved.

5   Discussions and Future Work

In this paper, we make a detailed investigation of users' session-level reformulation behavior. We find that some of the assumptions adopted by the previous work are not accurate enough and may hurt the robustness of their theory. Some main concerns for the query suggestion task are:

Firstly, since there are a proportion of long sessions, many users may endeavor several search rounds until they find an appropriate query. Since the query ambiguity and the expression difficulty will cause users struggled in a long session, a possible future work may be to shorten the search process by disambiguation rather than just to predict the next query. Also, the existing evaluation metrics such as MRR and SR have their limitations as they do not take the semantic similarities into consideration. More robust evaluation system should be constructed so far.

Secondly, according to our analysis results, titles of the clicked results can have great impacts on both users' specification and generalization actions. There may be problems if we just regard the click signals as the positive feedbacks and the skips as the negative feedbacks. More evidences should be collected for designing better query suggestion algorithms.

Last but not least, we have found that there are obvious marginal effects on the user clickthrough and reformulation behaviors. So the session boundary detection can also be an issue. Most existing work roughly adopt the 30 min as the threshold to split the query sequence into sessions and then continue their experiments on these sessions. However, when it comes to practice, it is hard to know when the user will end their search processes. Therefore, it is also crucial to predict the end of a session.

References

1. Brenes, D.J., Gayo-Avello, D.: Stratified analysis of AOL query log. Inf. Sci. **179**(12), 1844–1858 (2009)
2. He, Q., Jiang, D., Liao, Z. et al.: Web query recommendation via sequential query prediction. In: International Conference on Data Engineering, pp. 1443–1454 (2009)

3. Jiang, J.Y., Ke, Y.Y., Chien, P.Y., et al.: Learning user reformulation behavior for query auto-completion. In: Proceedings of the 37th International ACM SIGIR Conference on Research and Development in Information Retrieval, pp. 445–454. ACM (2014)

4. Eickhoff, C., Dungs, S., Tran, V., et al.: An eye-tracking study of query reformulation. In: International ACM SIGIR Conference on Research and Development in Information Retrieval, pp. 13–22 (2015)

5. Sordoni, A., Bengio, Y., Vahabi, H. et al.: A hierarchical recurrent encoder-decoder for generative context-aware query suggestion. In: Conference on Information and Knowledge Management, pp. 553–562 (2015)

6. Wu, B., Xiong, C., Sun, M. et al.: Query suggestion with feedback memory network. In: The Web Conference, pp. 1563–1571 (2018)

7. Jiang, J., Wang, W.: RIN: reformulation inference network for context-aware query suggestion. In: Conference on Information and Knowledge Management, pp. 197–206 (2018)

8. Liu, X., et al.: Hierarchical attention network for context-aware query suggestion. In: Tseng, Y.-H., et al. (eds.) AIRS 2018. LNCS, vol. 11292, pp. 173–186. Springer, Cham (2018). https://doi.org/10.1007/978-3-030-03520-4_17

9. Cao, H., Jiang, D., Pei, J. et al.: Context-aware query suggestion by mining click-through and session data. In: Knowledge Discovery and Data Mining, pp. 875–883 (2008)

10. Shokouhi, M., Sloan, M., Bennett, P.N., et al.: Query suggestion and data fusion in contextual disambiguation. In: The Web Conference, pp. 971–980 (2015)

11. Gao, B.J., Anastasiu, D.C., Jiang, X., et al.: Utilizing user-input contextual terms for query disambiguation. In: International Conference on Computational Linguistics, pp. 329–337 (2010)

12. Song, Y., Zhou, D., He, L. et al.: Post-ranking query suggestion by diversifying search results. In: International ACM SIGIR Conference on Research and Development in Information Retrieval, pp. 815–824 (2011)

13. Dang, V., Croft, B.: Query reformulation using anchor text. In: Web Search and Data Mining, pp. 41–50 (2010)

14. Liu, Y., Miao, J., Zhang, M., et al.: How do users describe their information need: query recommendation based on snippet click model. Expert. Syst. Appl. **38**(11), 13847–13856 (2011)

15. Huang, C.K., Chien, L.F., Oyang, Y.J.: Relevant term suggestion in interactive web search based on contextual information in query session logs. J. Am. Soc. Inf. Sci. Technol. **54**(7), 638–649 (2003)

16. Grover, A., Leskovec, J.: node2vec: scalable feature learning for networks. In: Proceedings of the 22nd ACM SIGKDD International Conference on Knowledge Discovery and Data Mining, pp. 855–864. ACM (2016)

LTRRS: A Learning to Rank Based Algorithm for Resource Selection in Distributed Information Retrieval

Tianfeng Wu, Xiaofeng Liu, and Shoubin Dong[✉]

Communication and Computer Network Key Laboratory of Guangdong,
School of Computer Science and Engineering,
South China University of Technology, Guangzhou, China
sbdong@scut.edu.cn

Abstract. Resource selection is a key task in distributed information retrieval. There are many factors that affect the performance of resource selection. Learning to rank methods can effectively combine features and are widely used for document ranking in web search. But few of them are explored for resource selection. In this paper, we propose a resource selection algorithm based on learning to rank called LTRRS. By analyzing the factors affecting the effectiveness of resource selection, we extract multi-scale features including term matching features, topical relevance features and central sample index (CSI) based features. By training LambdaMART learning to rank model, we directly optimize NDCG metric of resource ranking list in LTRRS. Experiments on the Sogou-QCL dataset show that LTRRS algorithm can significantly outperform the baseline methods in NDCG and precision metrics.

Keywords: Resource selection · Learning to rank ·
Distributed Information Retrieval

1 Introduction

With the rapid development of the Internet, a large amount of network information is available in the websites. Search engines play an important role in searching information and gaining knowledge in people's daily life. The goal of information retrieval is to return a ranking result list that satisfies a user's information needs according to the given query. As the sources of information continues to increase, people's search needs become more diverse and may not be satisfied with a single source of information.

Distributed Information Retrieval (DIR), or Federated Search is an important task to search from multiple distributed collections (resources) [1]. By forwarding the queries to appropriate content providers, the DIR system merges the results of different collections to get more relevant and diverse results. There are three key phases in DIR: resource description, resource selection and results merging. In resource description phase, the DIR system uses as much information as possible to describe the content of a resource. Resource selection aim to select some relevant resources for the query. Then in the results merging phase, the DIR system merges multiple retrieval results from selected resources and returns a single rank list to user.

© Springer Nature Switzerland AG 2019
Q. Zhang et al. (Eds.): CCIR 2019, LNCS 11772, pp. 52–63, 2019.
https://doi.org/10.1007/978-3-030-31624-2_5

Resource selection plays a key role in distributed information retrieval. By selecting a small number of relevant resources out of all resources to forward the queries, it would significantly improve the efficiency of the retrieval system. Considerable efforts in recent years have been made to resource selection, which can be divided into large-document methods, small-document methods and supervised methods. In large-document methods, each resource is treated as a big bag of words and is selected according to the similarity with the query. Small-document methods use sample ranking in CSI to estimate complete ranking of each resources and rank resources based on the sample ranking or scores. Supervised methods train a classifier or ranking function for resource selection.

Different resource selection algorithms consider different factors to rank resources, which are mainly limited to term matching similarity or scores of sample documents. Combining multiple factors can often improve the performance of resource selection. In addition, learning to rank algorithms have been widely used in web search to rank documents, few of them has been used for resource selection.

In this paper, we propose a learning to rank based resource selection algorithm named LTRRS. By using term matching features, CSI based features and topical relevance features, we train a LambdaMART model to combine these features and optimize resources ranking list NDCG metric to rank resources. Experimental results show that the proposed algorithm LTRRS significantly outperform the classical algorithms.

2 Related Works

Resource selection methods can broadly be categorized into three types: large-document methods, small-document methods and supervised methods. This section will discuss these three kinds of methods.

2.1 Large-Document Methods

Large-document methods take each resource as a big document containing a large bag of words and rank resource according to the similarity of this large document with query. The similarity calculation and document ranking methods in the traditional document ranking are adopted to rank resource, such as matching by term frequency, or the query likelihood method in the language model. The CORI algorithm [2] adopted the inference network in INQUERY, by combining the factors like document frequency, collection frequency of the query and collection size to calculate query likelihood probability. Xu and Croft et al. [3] use a document clustering method to establish a language model for each resource. And then, the similarity between the query and the resource can be measured by calculating the KL distance between the query language model and the resource language model.

In this kind of methods, the documents in the resource are not distinguished and only be treated as a whole to calculate the similarity with query. However, When the number of documents in the resource is getting much bigger, it will difficult to distinguish relevance resource only calculating the whole similarity between query and resource.

2.2   Small-Document Methods

Small-document methods use sample ranking to estimate the relevance of each resource. In this type of method, the DIR system firstly sample a small number of documents from all resources to form central sample documents. And then a centralized sample index (CSI) is built on the central sample documents. Finally, the score of the resource is calculated according to the scores or ranking of the documents in the CSI.

In ReDDE algorithm [4], the system retrieve from CSI to get document result list firstly, and then the rank of top n documents in the result list are used to calculate the score of each resource. The ReDDE.top algorithm [4] is the improvement from ReDDE algorithm, using the scores of documents in CSI result list instead of ranking information to calculate the relevance of each resource. Similarly, the CRCS algorithm [5] considers the ranking of the documents in CSI to calculate the scores.

2.3   Supervised Methods

Supervised methods use machine learning methods to train model for resource selection. There are mainly three kinds of supervised methods for it: query classification methods, resource classification methods and learning to rank methods.

In query classification methods, training data is used to train a classifier for query. Kang and Kim [6] combine query features and document features to classify the query.

Resource classification methods train model to assign each resource to select or not class. Arguello et al. [7] proposed the classification method for resource selection. In their work, three categories of features are used to train LR models, including the score features from the traditional resource selection algorithm, the topical category features of the query, and the click rate related features.

Learning to rank resource methods train learning to rank model and ranking functions for resource selection. Xu and Li [8] proposed features for collection selection and using SVM and RankingSVM to learn ranking functions. Dai and Kim et al. [9] train SVMrank model to rank resources in selective search, combining query-independent features, term-based features, and CSI-based features.

Furthermore, some resource selection methods [10, 11] aim to improve the efficiency of the resource selection. By using appropriate strategies such as load balancing methods, they pay more attention to the efficiency of the system.

3   Framework

3.1   Definitions

Given a query, and a set of resources $R = \{r_1, r_2, \ldots, r_n\}$, in which n represent the number of all resources. Let $v(q, r_i)$ denote features extracted from the ith resource r_i and query q pair. The goal of resource selection is to select top k resources from resources set R. While the learning to rank methods for resource selection are aimed at learning ranking function $F(v(q, r_i))$ to rank resources.

3.2 Architecture

Figure 1 shows the architecture of the proposed algorithm LTRRS. The whole archi-tecture can be divided into two stages: offline stage and online stage. The offline stage includes the offline calculation and preparation for online stage. While the online stage is ranking for resources in real time. Furthermore, the offline stage can be divided into four module including preprocess module, resource description module, query expansion and learning module. In this section, we describe the details of each part.

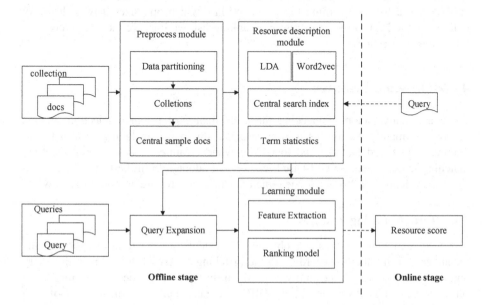

Fig. 1. The architecture of LTRRS

3.3 Preprocess Module

The preprocessing module is mainly responsible for data preparation. In an uncoop-erative environment, the resources may represent search engines, we need to get sample documents for each search engine. While in a cooperative environment, like large scale collection retrieval, we need to partition collections to get a number of resources.

3.4 Resource Description Module

Resource description module is responsible for using information from collection to describe each resource. In this module, we use four parts including LDA model part, word2vec part, CSI part and term statistics part. Latent Dirichlet Allocation (LDA) is a kind of topic model [12], and word2vec [13] is a word embedding technique. An LDA model is trained on central sample documents, getting the topic distribution vector of each resource centroid. The word2vec part uses the central sample documents to train word2vec model, so as to use in query expansion. CSI part uses the central sample documents to build index and retrieve results from it to get scores of each document, while the term statistics part calculates the lexical statistics of each resource offline.

Each part will extract features for training learning model to rank resources. Details of feature calculations are described in the Sect. 4.

3.5 Learning Module

In learning module, all features are combined to train ranking model for resource selection. In this work, we use LambdaMART [14] model to rank resources. LambdaMART is a listwise learning to rank algorithm, which optimizes listwise loss. By optimizing the NDCG metric of resource ranking list, we improve the effectiveness of the resource selection.

4 Multi-scale Features

There are many factors influencing the performance of resource selection. In this section, we mainly discuss the features using in this paper, including term matching features, CSI-based features and topical relevance features. Among them, the term matching features and the CSI-based features are adopted from the features proposed by Dai and Kim et al. [9], while the topic relevance features are proposed in this work.

4.1 Term Matching Features

The term matching features are obtained by calculating the term statistics of the resources and the query. According to the matching degree of the terms in the query and the resource, we get the similarity of them. In the resource description module in offline stage of LTRRS algorithm, the DIR system calculate the term statistics of each resource. After the precomputation, the DIR system can calculate the term matching features efficiently in online stage.

Query Likelihood Features: This kind of features calculate the likelihood of resource language models generating query. The terms use unigram and bigram sequences applying for document title and body, generating 4 features totally. The calculating equations are shown as Eq. (1)–(3).

$$logP(q|r_i) = \sum_{w \in q} log(\lambda P(w|r_i) + (1 - \lambda)P(w|G)) \tag{1}$$

$$P(w|r_i) = (\sum_{d_j \in r_i} \frac{TF(w, d_j)}{LEN(d_j)})/|r_i| \tag{2}$$

$$P(w|G) = \sum_{r_i \in R} \frac{P(w|r_i)}{|R|} \tag{3}$$

where $logP(q|r_i)$ is the log likelihood of the ith resource r_i generating the query, $P(w|r_i)$ is the probability of the ith resource r_i generating the term w in query q.

Meanwhile, $P(w|G)$ is the probability of all resources generating the term w, used to smooth $P(w|r_i)$ in case of zero probability problem. And λ is a smoothing parameter, set to 0.8 in this work. $TF(w, d_j)$ is the term frequency of w, $LEN(d_j)$ is the document length of d_j, $|r_i|$ is the resource size, $|R|$ is the number of resources.

Query Term Statistics Features: This type of features are created by calculating the statistics of query terms in resource, including maximum and minimum resource term frequency, TFIDF value of query terms. Similarly, Unigram and bigram sequences of terms are used in calculation for document title and body, generating 16 features totally. The details are as follows:

$$tf_{max}(q, r_i) = \max_{w \in q} tf(w, r_i) \tag{4}$$

$$tf_{min}(q, r_i) = \min_{w \in q} tf(w, r_i) \tag{5}$$

$$tfidf_{max}(q, r_i) = \max_{w \in q} tf(w, r_i) * idf(w, r_i) \tag{6}$$

$$tfidf_{min}(q, r_i) = \min_{w \in q} tf(w, r_i) * idf(w, r_i) \tag{7}$$

4.2   CSI-Based Features

CSI-based features are calculated by building the central sample index. In offline stage, the DIR system build central sample index from central sample documents in resource description module. While in online stage, the DIR system retrieves from the central sample index, and calculate the features in real time.

ReDDE Features: We create ReDDE features using ReDDE and ReDDE.top resource selection algorithm [4], the ReDDE and ReDDE.top scores are used as two features. Besides, we use the inverse rank of each resource in ReDDE.top scores as another feature, generating 3 features totally. The inverse rank calculation is defined as follows.

$$inverseRank = 1/(rank + k) \tag{8}$$

where $rank$ denotes the ranking value of each resource using ReDDE.top score, and k is a parameter setting to 10 in this work.

Centroid Distance Features Centroid distance Features capture the distance between each resource centroid and top k documents of retrieval results from CSI. The assumption of this type of features is that the closer the resource centroid is to the top-k document in retrieval results from CSI, the more relevant the resource is to the query. Therefore, we compute the KL divergence and cosine similarity between average vectors of top k documents and resource centroid vector. In Addition, we use the inverse of KL divergence as the feature in this work. We compute features using $k = \{10, 50, 100\}$, generating 6 features totally as follows:

$$kl\_CentDist(q, r_i) = 1/KL(mean(dt(docs_{topk})), cen_{r_i}) \tag{9}$$

$$cos\_CentDist(q, r_i) = cosine(mean(dt(docs_{topk})), cen_{r_i}) \tag{10}$$

where $dt(docs_{topk})$ denotes for topic distributions of top k document results retrieved from CSI, cen_{r_i} is the topic distribution of the ith resource r_i.

4.3   Topical Relevance Features

Topic model is widely used to get the abstract topic of the documents in a collection, Latent Dirichlet Allocation (LDA) is an example of topic model [12]. Topical relevance features are based on the topical similarity of the query and the resource documents. By training LDA model on sample documents, we apply k-means clustering method on topic distributions of sample documents to get the centroid of each resource. By calculating the similarity of the topic distribution of resource centroid and query, we get topical relevance features.

Considering that the query is usually too short to get topic information, query expansion using word2vec is used in this work to expand query. we train word2vec model on title of central sample documents, in which the dimension is set to 100 and single word and phrases are both used to learn a word2vec model. Then in online stage, for each term w in a query, we use the trained word2vec model to select top 20 most similar words to was expansion words of w. Similarly, we use unigram and bigram sequences in query terms to form w. All the expansion words of a query constitute the query expansion words.

After query expansion, the trained LDA model are used to infer query expansion words to get query topic distribution. By calculating the KL divergence and cosine similarity of the topic distribution of resource centroid and query, we get topical relevance features. Similarly, we use the inverse of KL divergence as the feature in this work. And the unigram and bigram sequences in query terms are used to calculate features separately, generating 4 features totally. We compute the inverse KL divergence and cosine similarity features as follows:

$$kl\_sim(q, r_i) = 1/KL(dt(qextend), cen_{r_i}) \tag{11}$$

$$cos\_sim(q, r_i) = cosine(dt(qexpand), cen_{r_i}) \tag{12}$$

where $qextend$ denotes the query expansion words for given query q, $dt(qextend)$ denotes for topic distribution of $qextend$, cen_{r_i} is the topic distribution of the ith resource r_i.

5   The Proposed Algorithm

The goal of resource selection is to select k relevant resources from resources. We use LambdaMART model as the learning to rank model in the proposed algorithm LTRRS. In LTRRS, we optimize NDCG@20 metric of resource ranking list in learning model, so as to learn to get the optimal resource ranking list. It is worth mentioning that other evaluation metrics such as Precision@k can also be used in the algorithm.

The Proposed algorithm LTRRS are summarized in Algorithm 1, which is divided into offline stage and online stage. In the training phase, we use central sample documents to build CSI, and use the retrieval results from CSI to compute CSI-based features. Meanwhile, we gather the term statistics from each resource, and compute term matching features based on term statistics. In addition, the term statistics information include unigram, bigram term frequency and document frequency on body and title of resource documents. While in topical relevance features calculation phase, a LDA model and word2vec model are trained on central sample documents, and then we compute topical similarity between query and resources to get topical relevance features. Finally, all features are combined to train a LambdaMART model and optimize resource ranking list evaluation metric NDCG@20. In online stage, we use the information and model calculated in offline stage to get resource score online.

Algorithm 1. The LTRRS algorithm

Offline stage: Ranking model training

Input: Query Q, Resources $R = \{R_1, R_2, ..., R_n\}$, Resource relevance score Rel

output: Ranking model m, Central index Inx, Resources term statistics $TermStatistic$, LDA model $ldamodel$, word2vec model $w2vmodel$

1:    $S \leftarrow$ Sample($R, |S|$) //Sample $|S|$ documents from Resources

2:    $Inx \leftarrow$ BuildCentralIndex(S) //build central sample index on sample docs

3:    $ldamodel \leftarrow$ train_LDA_model(S)

4:    $w2vmodel \leftarrow$ train_Word2vec_model(S)

5:    $TermStatistic \leftarrow$ Calculate_Term_Statistic(R)

6:    $Feat \leftarrow$ calculate features using methods in section 4.

7:    $m \leftarrow$ LambdaMART($Q, Feat, Rel$)

Online stage: Resource selection

Input: Query q

output: Resources ranking list $RList$

1:    $Feat \leftarrow$ calculate features using methods in section 4.

2:    $Rscores \leftarrow m.$infer($q, Feat$) // get resources scores

3:    $RList \leftarrow$ rankingByScore($Rscores$)

4:    **Return** $RList$

6   Experiments

6.1   Dataset

Sogou-QCL dataset [15] is used in this work, which is sampled from query logs of commercial search engine Sogou. Five relevance labels from click model are provided in each query document pair. Each document record contain title, body, html page, frequency and relevance labels information. Besides, a small dataset contains 2000 queries and about 50 thousand documents is also in Sogou-QCL dataset, which is annotated by crowdsourcing. We use this small dataset to evaluate the effectiveness of resource selection algorithm in this work. Models were trained by 5-fold cross-validation. For a given query, the relevance score of each resource are the sum of the documents relevance under corresponding resource.

We use the partitioning method in preprocess module to construct resource lists. First, we sample 2% documents randomly from 7736480 query-document pairs in Sogou-QCL Dataset. Then we train LDA model to get topic distribution of sample documents. After that, we use K-means clustering algorithm to cluster topic distribution of sample documents to get 100 clusters centroid. The 100 clusters centroid are the resources centroid. We partition all the documents into 100 resource according to the distance of each document with 100 clusters centroid. The statistics are show in Table 1.

Table 1. Statistics of resources

#Resources	#Documents	Largest resource	Smallest resource	Average docs number
100	5438462	241285	1191	54385

6.2   CSI Setup

The Indri search engine was used to index and retrieve from CSI. For a given query, top 200 documents retrieved from CSI are used to calculate the score of each resource. Language model with Dirichlet smoothing are used as the retrieval model, in which the smoothing parameter μ are set to the default value 2500. For each query, we use the sequential dependency model (SDM) to construct our query. In particular, the similarity between the query and the document in the experiment is computed by the weighted sum of the following three sequential dependent methods. The weights set to the unigram, bigram and unordered window bigram are 0.5, 0.25, 0.25, and the window size of the unordered window is set to 8.

6.3   Result Analysis

The Baseline methods in the experiment are the ReDDE algorithm [4], the ReDDE.top [4] algorithm, and the method using LDA [12] to calculate topical relevance in this work denoted as LDA. We use the Ranklib implementation of AdaRank and LambdaMART model in the LTRRS. We use the default parameters in AdaRank and LambdaMART model and the learning rate is set to 0.05. The evaluation metrics of the experiment are NDCG@k and P@k.

6.3.1 Performance Comparison

We compare LTRRS and the baselines in this section. As can be seen from Table 2, LTRRS outperforms the baselines significantly in all metrics. ReDDE and ReDDE.top have similar performance, while LDA method has a worse performance. The result shows that LTRRS have obvious advantage when we want to select top 5 to 20 resources out of all resources. We also compared two ranking model of AdaRank and LambdaMart, and LTRRS based on LambdaMart achieves better results.

Table 2. Comparision between LTRRS and baselines

Method	NDCG@10	NDCG@20	P@5	P@10
ReDDE	0.530	0.563	0.544	0.428
ReDDE.top	0.536	0.568	0.533	0.415
LDA	0.437	0.467	0.442	0.319
LTRRS(AdaRank)	0.6879	0.7079	0.6646	0.5047
LTRRS	**0.758**	**0.776**	**0.693**	**0.521**

6.3.2 Feature Analysis

Based on above results, we investigate different kinds of features on LTRRS in this section. The comparison of the contributions of three kinds of features is shown in Table 3. LTRRS_csi represents for the effectiveness of using CSI-based features while LTRRS_term denotes for using term matching features and LTRRS_topic using topical relevance features. LTRRS_all is the performance of using all the features in this work. As can be seen from Table 3, the performance of LTRRS_all using all features is better than the method using single type of features. The results indicate that three types of features have different contributions to the LTRRS algorithm by covering different aspects of information. By incorporating three kinds of features, LTRRS_all improves the performance compared to that using any single kind of features.

In the comparison of the three kinds of features, LTRRS_term has a best performance compared to other two types of features. LTRRS_csi method rank second and LTRRS_topic has the worst performance. The results suggest that term matching features have a biggest contribution to LTRRS algorithm. The method combining query likelihood method in language model and other term matching method still have great help for resource selection.

The three types of features have different computational costs. In the calculation of CSI-base features, the central search index should be built in offline stage, while in online stage, the DIR system need to retrieve results from CSI and calculate CSI-based features. As a result, it has a high computational cost in both online stage and offline stage. In the term matching feature calculation, the term statistics information is computed in offline stage, while in online stage, the DIR system just need to calculate the matching of query and each resource term statistics. So term matching feature calculation has a low computational cost in online stage but a high computational cost in offline stage. Similarly, in the topical relevance feature calculation, after the computation in offline stage, it would have a low computational cost in online stage.

Overall, term-matching features have a low computational cost in online stage and best performance. The result suggests that combining features from term statistics of each resource can effectively improve the performance of resource selection algorithm.

Table 3. Performance of LTRRS using different feature sets

Method	NDCG@10	NDCG@20	P@5	P@10
LTRRS_csi	0.552	0.586	0.530	0.409
LTRRS_term	0.719	0.737	0.687	0.516
LTRRS_topic	0.460	0.492	0.438	0.316
LTRRS_all	**0.758**	**0.776**	**0.693**	**0.521**

7   Conclusion

In this paper, we present a learning to rank based resource selection algorithm named LTRRS. There are many factors that affect the performance of resource selection method. Learning to rank resources method can effectively combine the characteristics from various aspects. By combining term matching features, topical relevance features and CSI-based features, a listwise learning to rank model LambdaMART is trained to optimize resources ranking list in LTRRS. Experiments on Sogou-QCL dataset show that LTRRS can effectively combine all features and outperform the classical resource selection algorithm.

Acknowledgement. The research of this paper was supported by Guangdong Natural Science Foundation (2015A030308017).

References

1. Callan, J.: Distributed information retrieval. In: Croft, W.B. (ed.) Advances in Information Retrieval: Recent Research from the Center for Intelligent Information Retrieval, pp. 127–150. Springer, Boston (2000). https://doi.org/10.1007/0-306-47019-5_5
2. Callan, J.P., Lu, Z., Croft, W.B.: Searching distributed collections with inference networks. In: Proceedings of the 18th Annual International ACM SIGIR Conference on Research and Development in Information Retrieval, pp. 21–28. ACM (1995)
3. Xu, J., Croft, W.B.: Cluster-based language models for distributed retrieval. In: Proceedings of the 22nd Annual International ACM SIGIR Conference on Research and Development in Information Retrieval, pp. 254–261. Citeseer (1999)
4. Si, L., Callan, J.: Relevant document distribution estimation method for resource selection. In: Proceedings of the 26th Annual International ACM SIGIR Conference on Research and Development in Information Retrieval, pp. 298–305. ACM, New York (2003)
5. Shokouhi, M.: Central-rank-based collection selection in uncooperative distributed information retrieval. In: Amati, G., Carpineto, C., Romano, G. (eds.) ECIR 2007. LNCS, vol. 4425, pp. 160–172. Springer, Heidelberg (2007). https://doi.org/10.1007/978-3-540-71496-5_17

6. Kang, I.-H., Kim, G.: Query type classification for web document retrieval. In: Proceedings of the 26th Annual International ACM SIGIR Conference on Research and Development in Information Retrieval, pp. 64–71. ACM, New York (2003)

7. Arguello, J., Callan, J., Diaz, F.: Classification-based resource selection. In: Proceedings of the 18th ACM Conference on Information and Knowledge Management, pp. 1277–1286. ACM, New York (2009)

8. Xu, J., Li, X.: Learning to rank collections. In: Proceedings of the 30th Annual International ACM SIGIR Conference on Research and Development in Information Retrieval - SIGIR 2007, Amsterdam, The Netherlands p. 765. ACM Press (2007)

9. Dai, Z., Kim, Y., Callan, J.: Learning to rank resources. In: Proceedings of the 40th International ACM SIGIR Conference on Research and Development in Information Retrieval - SIGIR 2017, Shinjuku, Tokyo, Japan, pp. 837–840. ACM Press (2017)

10. Kim, Y., Callan, J., Culpepper, J.S., Moffat, A.: Load-balancing in distributed selective search. In: Proceedings of the 39th International ACM SIGIR conference on Research and Development in Information Retrieval, pp. 905–908. ACM (2016)

11. Kulkarni, A., Callan, J.: Selective search: Efficient and effective search of large textual collections (TOIS). ACM Trans. Inf. Syst. 33, 17 (2015)

12. Blei, D.M., Ng, A.Y., Jordan, M.I.: Latent Dirichlet allocation. J. Mach. Learn. Res. 3, 993–1022 (2003)

13. Mikolov, T., Sutskever, I., Chen, K., Corrado, G.S., Dean, J.: Distributed representations of words and phrases and their compositionality. In: Burges, C.J.C., Bottou, L., Welling, M., Ghahramani, Z., Weinberger, K.Q. (eds.) Advances in Neural Information Processing Systems 26, pp. 3111–3119. Curran Associates, Inc. (2013)

14. Wu, Q., Burges, C.J., Svore, K.M., Gao, J.: Adapting boosting for information retrieval measures. Inf. Retr. 13, 254–270 (2010)

15. Zheng, Y., Fan, Z., Liu, Y., Luo, C., Zhang, M., Ma, S.: Sogou-QCL: a new dataset with click relevance label. In: The 41st International ACM SIGIR Conference on Research and Development in Information Retrieval, pp. 1117–1120. ACM (2018)

Knowledge and Entities

Simplified Representation Learning Model Based on Parameter-Sharing for Knowledge Graph Completion

Yashen Wang[1(✉)], Huanhuan Zhang[1], Yifeng Li[1], and Haiyong Xie[1,2]

[1] China Academy of Electronics and Information Technology of CETC,
Beijing, China
yashen_wang@126.com, huanhuanz_bit@139.com, yliu@csdslab.net,
haiyong.xie@ieee.org
[2] University of Science and Technology of China, Hefei, Anhui, China

Abstract. Knowledge graphs (KG) contain knowledge about the world and provide a structured representation of this knowledge. Current knowledge graphs contain only a small subset of what is true in the world. Knowledge Graph Completion (KGC) task aims to findin missing or errant relationships with the goal of improving the general quality of KGs. Recent years have witnessed great advance of represent learning (RL) based KGC models, which represent entities and relations as elements of a continuous vector space. However, with the deepening of the research, the scale of parameters and the complexity of KGC models become larger and larger, resulting in a serious imbalance between accuracy and computational complexity. Finally, not only the efficiency is not satisfactory, but also the training cost becomes high, which seriously restricts the flexibility and scalability of the KGC model. Therefore, this paper investigates how to enhance the simplicity of KGC model and achieve a reasonable balance between accuracy and complexity. Extensive experiments show that the proposed framework improves the performance of the current represent learning models for KGC task.

Keywords: Knowledge Graph Completion · Simplified model · Parameter-sharing · Representation learning

1 Introduction

Knowledge graphs such as Freebase, YAGO, and WordNet are among the most widely used resources in the Natural Language Processing (NLP) applications [8,12,18,34,39,42]. Typically, a knowledge graph consists of a set of triples (h, r, t) where h, r, t stand for head entity, relation and tail entity respectively. KGs are widely used for many practical tasks, however, their completeness are not guaranteed. Although large-scale KGs have contained billions of triples [1,14,27], the extracted knowledge is still a small part of the real-world knowledge and probably contains errors and contradictions. For example, 71% of

© Springer Nature Switzerland AG 2019
Q. Zhang et al. (Eds.): CCIR 2019, LNCS 11772, pp. 67–78, 2019.
https://doi.org/10.1007/978-3-030-31624-2_6

people in Freebase have no known place of birth, and 75% have no known nationality. Therefore, the task of Knowledge Graph Completion (KGC) emerges at a historic moment for completing the missing elements in the current knowledge graph [6,17,23].

Recent years have witnessed great advance of represent learning (RL) based Knowledge Graph Completion models, which represent entities and relations as elements of a continuous vector space. Although these most RL-based models have significantly improved the knowledge graph embedding representations and increased the Knowledge Graph Completion accuracy, there is still room for improvement. This is because, at the same time, the existing Knowledge Graph Completion models improve the accuracy of calculation, and its spatial scale and computing complexity are also increasing, resulting in increased computing overhead, poor scalability, and high training costs. Therefore, many current KGC models could not be applied to large-scale knowledge graphs or online task. Moreover, many recent RL-based KGC models rely heavily on the pre-trained embedding representation of knowledge graph from traditional representation learning models as input [13,44]. Apparently, in this instance, if we get rid of this pre-trained embedding representation, the performance of the model will be greatly reduced.

To overcome the challenging faced with current KGC models, this paper investigates how to explore solutions towards these problems mentioned above, and proposes a novel simplified model for KGC task, from the following aspects. Firstly, take triple $(?, r, t)$ for predicting the head entity h as an example. We project the candidate head entity $h_?$ into a target vector, which represents the existing entity (i.e., t) and the existing relation (i.e., r) in the given triple $(?, r, t)$. Secondly, The projection matrices occurred in previous RL-based KGC models [17,36,40], are superseded by a novel and simple combination operator in this paper. Thirdly, the traditional pairwise-based loss function, which is widely-used in current RL-based KGC models, is superseded by listwise-based loss function in this paper, and we verify the feasibility of listwise-based loss function and explore to simultaneously optimize the loss function of the entire list of candidate entities (or candidate relations).

Finally, the extensive experiments show that our simplified model improves the performance of the current represent learning models for knowledge graph completion task, without the need for complex feature engineering.

2   Notation and Definition

This paper represents vectors with lowercase letters and matrices with uppercase letters. Let $\mathbf{x} \in R^k$ be vectors of length k, i.e., the embedding dimensionality is k. V indicates the vocabulary, and accordingly $|V|$ indicates the number of all the words in the vocabulary. Let E and R represent the set of entities and relations respectively. A triple is represented as (h, r, t), where $h \in E$ is the head entity, $r \in R$ is the relation, and $t \in E$ is the tail entity of the triple. A knowledge graph (KG) is denoted as G. Given a knowledge graph G, it contains

$|E|$ entities and $|R|$ types of relations. The set of triples $T = \{(h, r, t)\}$ could be obtained by the representation learning models. An embedding is a function from an entity or a relation to one vector, more vectors or matrices of numbers. A representation learning model generally defines two aspects: (i) the embedding functions for entities and relations; and (ii) a function taking the embeddings for h, r and t as input and generating a prediction of whether (h, r, t) is "true" in a world or not. The values of the embeddings are learned using the triples in a KG G. Matrix is denoted as $\mathbf{M}$ here, wherein diagonal matrix is denoted as $\mathbf{D}$. RL-based KGC models usually generate entity embeddings, which contribute to entity vector matrix $\mathbf{M}_E$. In the same vein, $\mathbf{M}_R$ denotes the relation vector matrix in the current RL-based models.

3   Related Work

During the past two decades, several knowledge graphs (KGs) containing (perhaps probabilistic) facts about the world have been constructed. These KGs have applications in several fields including search, question answering, natural language processing, recommendation systems, etc [12,18,35,39,42]. Due to the enormous number of facts that could be asserted about our world and the difficulty in accessing and storing all these facts, KGs are incomplete. However, it is possible to predict new relations or entities in a KG based on the existing ones. Knowledge Graph Completion (KGC) and several other related problems aiming at reasoning with entities and relationships are studied under the umbrella of statistical relational learning.

To complete or predict the missing relation element of triples, such as $(h, ?, t)$, Representation Learning (RL) is widely deployed. RL embeds entities and relations into a vector space, and has produced many successful translation models including TransE [3], TransH [36], TransR [17], TransG [40], etc. These models aim to generate precise vectors of entities and relations following the principle $\mathbf{h} + \mathbf{r} \approx \mathbf{t}$, which means t is translated from h by r. Besides, these methods usually learn continuous, low-dimensional vector representations (i.e., embeddings) for entities and relationships by minimizing a margin-based pairwise ranking loss.

Motivated by the linear translation phenomenon observed in well trained word embeddings [20], TransE [3] represents the head entity h, the relation r and the tail entity t with vectors $\mathbf{h}, \mathbf{r}, \mathbf{t} \in R^k$ respectively, which were trained so that $\mathbf{h} + \mathbf{r} \approx \mathbf{t}$. They define the energy function as

$$f_r(h, t) = \|\mathbf{h} + \mathbf{r} - \mathbf{t}\|_l \tag{1}$$

where $l = 1$ or $l = 2$, which means either the l_1 or the l_2 norm of the vector $\mathbf{h} + \mathbf{r} - \mathbf{t}$ will be used depending on the performance on the validation set. We follow previous work to minimize the following hinge loss function:

$$\ell = \sum_{(h,r,t) \sim \Delta, (h',r',t') \sim \Delta'} [\gamma + f_r(h, t) - f_r(h', t')]_+ \tag{2}$$

Wherein Δ is the training set consisting of correct triples (i.e., fact), Δ' is the distribution of corrupted triples (i.e., negative samples)[1], and $[\cdot]_+ = max(\cdot, 0)$. $f_r(h, t)$ is the energy function of each model and γ is the margin.

Furthermore, many translation-based methods are introduced, including TransH [36], TransD [10], TransR [17]. Moreover, [40] proposed a manifold-based embedding principle to deal with the overstrict geometric form of translation-based assumption. [33] employed complex value embeddings to understand the structural information. RESCAL [25] maps each relation r into a matrix $\mathbf{M}_r \in \mathbb{R}^{k \times k}$, and utilize the following energy function:

$$f_r(h, t) = \mathbf{h}^\top \mathbf{M}_r \mathbf{t} \tag{3}$$

The loss function is defined as follows:

$$\ell = \sum_{r \in R} \sum_{h \in E} \sum_{t \in E} [\chi(h, r, t) - f_r(h, t)]^2 \tag{4}$$

Wherein, $\chi(h, r, t) = 1$ if (h, r, t) is a fact.

We could conclude that, recent years have witnessed great advance of represent learning (RL) based KGC models [19,21], which represent entities and relations as elements of a continuous vector space. However, with the deepening of the research, the scale of parameters and the complexity of KGC models become larger and larger, resulting in a serious imbalance between accuracy and computational complexity. Finally, not only the efficiency is not satisfactory, but also the training cost becomes high, which seriously restricts the flexibility and scalability of the KGC model. To address this challenge, this paper investigates how to reduce the scale of parameters and the complexity of KGC models, and finally enhance the simplicity of KGC model and achieve a reasonable balance between accuracy and complexity.

4   Simplified Representation Learning Model Based on Parameter-Sharing for Knowledge Graph Completion

Knowledge Graph Completion (KGC) tasks usually could be divided into Entity Prediction task and Relationship Prediction task. Take predicting head entity h in the triple $(?, r, t)$ as an example. Firstly, the prediction task is transformed into a *ranking* problem, wherein the candidate entity $h_?$ with the highest ranking-score is regarded as the correct answer, i.e., a "fact". Secondly, we optimize the entire list of candidate entities. In the aforementioned triple, relation r and tail entity t are known. Hence, combination matrix, in form of diagonal matrix, is constructed by combing the relation vector $\mathbf{r}$ and tail entity vector $\mathbf{t}$. Then, all the candidate entities could be projected into the same ranking-score vector, denoted as target vector here. The dimensionality of the target vector is equal to the number of candidate entities, and therefore each dimensionality of this

---

[1] (h', r', t') usually denotes the "corrupted" triple which does not exist in Δ.

vector corresponds to each candidate's ranking-score. The great advantage of this proposed strategy is that, the ranking-score in each dimensionality could explicitly represent the similarity among candidate entity $h_?$ and known elements (i.e., relation r and tail entity t in the given triple $(?, r, t)$), and all the candidate entities in the entire candidate entity list could be optimized simultaneously.

To sum up, the proposed model provides novel model for achieving dual improvement compared with the traditional RL-based KGC models, which reduces the scale of trained parameters and meanwhile improves the performance of the model for KGC task, and breaks away from the dependence on complex feature engineering.

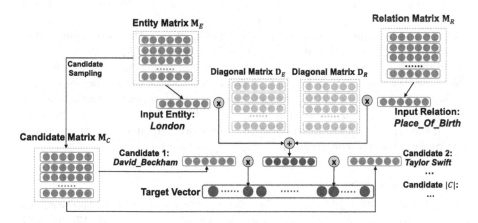

Fig. 1. The sketch of the proposed parameter-sharing neural network architecture based on listwise-base ranking (Take entity prediction task as example). (Color figure online)

4.1 Overview

Concretely, the proposed simplified model is essentially a parameter-sharing neural network. Because the parameters are reused and shared, the scale of parameters is greatly reduced. Figure 1 overviews the processing-flow of the proposed model in the form of an example. Given the triple $(?, Place\_Of\_Birth, London)$ to predicting by the missing head entity $h_?$, the proposed model aims at calculating the ranking-score of each candidate head entity (e.g., $David\_Beckham$ and $Taylor\_Swift$ shown in Fig. 1), wherein the entity vector of the candidate entity $David\_Beckham$ or $Taylor\_Swift$ is derived from the entity matrix $\mathbf{M}_E$.

In the previous RL-based KGC models [6,23], specific matrix-formed combination operators are introduced. Conversely, we utilize diagonal matrix here, which is sparse and could reduce computational overhead. Therefore, the combination operator is defined as follows[2]:

$$\mathbf{r} \circ \mathbf{t} = \mathbf{M}_R \mathbf{r} + \mathbf{M}_E \mathbf{t} + \mathbf{b}_{\text{comb}} \qquad (5)$$

---

[2] Take the prediction of head entity h of triple $(?, r, t)$ as example.

Wherein, $\mathbf{M}_E \in R^{|V| \times |V|}$ and $\mathbf{M}_R \in R^{|V| \times |V|}$ are the diagonal matrices representing the entity matrix and the relationship matrix, respectively (shown as the orange matrices in Fig. 1) $|V|$ denotes the number of all the words in the vocabulary V (as discussed in Sect. 2). Besides, $\mathbf{b}_{comb}$ is the combination bias vector as a trained parameter.

With efforts above, the projection function for candidate entity i, could be written as follows:

$$h_i(\mathbf{r}, \mathbf{t}) = \frac{\exp(\mathbf{M}_C^i \tanh(\mathbf{r} \circ \mathbf{t}) + b_{proj})}{\sum_j \exp(\mathbf{M}_C^j \tanh(\mathbf{r} \circ \mathbf{t}) + b_{proj})} \tag{6}$$

Wherein, $\mathbf{M}_C \in R^{|C| \times |V|}$ is the candidate-entity matrix, wherein $|C|$ denotes the scale of the entire candidate entity list as shown in Fig. 1. b_{proj} is the projection bias as a parameter to be trained. Hence, $\mathbf{M}_C^i$ denote the embedding vector of the i-th candidate entity in candidate entity matrix $\mathbf{M}_C$. Apparently, the output of the project function $h(\mathbf{r}, \mathbf{t})$ is the target vector mentioned above (shown as the red vector in Fig. 1), and $h_i(\mathbf{r}, \mathbf{t})$ denotes to the value of i-th dimensionality in this target vector indicating the ranking-score of the corresponding candidate entity derived from $\mathbf{M}_C$. Note that, as shown in Fig. 1, $\mathbf{M}_C$ is derived from $\mathbf{M}_E$, due to the strategy of parameter-sharing. Therefore, $\mathbf{M}_C$ doesn't introduce any new parameters into the model, although $|C|$ may be large.

4.2 Optimization

The pairwise [7,30] ranking-based loss function is widely-used in the previous RL-based KGC models, such as TransE [3], TransH [36], TransR [17], TransG [40], HolE [24], etc. However, candidates are measured and ranked independently. In this paper, we investigate how to simultaneously optimize the loss function of the entire list of candidate entities (or candidate relations). Based on the architecture constructed in this paper (shown in Fig. 1), we explore the loss functions based on *listwise* ranking [38].

Especially, in the design of sorting based on listwise, we leverage the Softmax regression [11] strategy, which has good application effect in multi-label classification problem and etc. [29,32,43], for loss function based on listwise ranking in the proposed simplified model. Because this strategy could synergistically consider all the predicted rankling-scores at the same time [28], it is very suitable for multi-label classification problem, while our task could also be viewed as a multi-label classification problem. Therefore, we classify candidate entities simultaneously based on the aforementioned Softmax regression strategy, which comes down to a listwise methodology. Hence, the loss function in the proposed simplified model, could be defined as follows:

$$\ell = -\sum_{i=1}^{|\mathbf{y}|} \frac{\varphi(y_i = 1)}{\sum_j \varphi(y_j = 1)} \log(h_i(\mathbf{r}, \mathbf{t})) \tag{7}$$

Wherein, $\mathbf{y} \in R^{|C|}$ is binary vector, and candidate i represent a positive sample if $y_i = 1$. $\varphi(y_i = 1)$ is an indication function, where $\varphi(y_i = 1)$ if $y_i = 1$.

Table 1. Statistics of different datasets.

Dataset	WN11	WN18	FB13	FB15K
#Train	112,581	141,442	316,232	483,142
#Valid	2,609	5,000	5,908	50,000
#Test	10,544	5,000	23,733	59,071
$|E|$	38,696	40,943	75,043	14,951
$|R|$	11	18	13	1,345

Recall that we need to sample a negative triple (h', r, t') to compute hinge loss [15,26], given a positive triple $(h, r, t) \in \Delta$. The distribution of negative triple is denoted by Δ'. Previous work [3,17,22] generally constructs a set of corrupted triples by replacing the head entity or tail entity with a random entity uniformly sampled from the KG. With efforts above, we define the For a triple (h, r, t) in the training set Δ, we sample its negative triple $(h', r', t') \notin \Delta$ by replacing one element with another entity or relation. When predicting different elements of a triple, we replace the corresponding elements to obtain the negative triples, wherein the negative triple set could be denoted as $\Delta'_{(h,r,t)}$.

5   Experiments

In this section, we first describe the settings in our experiments, and then we conduct experiments of link prediction and triple classification tasks and compare our method with base models and the state-of-the-art baselines.

5.1   Experiment Settings

In this paper, we evaluate our model on four benchmark datasets: WN11, WN18, FB13 and FB15k [3,31,36]. The statistics of the datasets is shown in Table 1, wherein $|E|$ denotes the number of entities and $|V|$ denotes the number of relation types. We compare our model (denoted as **Ours**) with **TransE** [3], **HolE** [23],**PTransE** [16], **SME** [2], **TransH** [36], **RESCAL** [25], **SE** [4], **TransR** [17], **DKRL** [41] (listed in ascending order by parameter scale), and evaluate on two classical tasks: link prediction and triple classification. For the proposed simplified model, we set learning rate as 0.01, mini-batch size as 250, and dropout probability as 0.5, for both tasks, which releases the best results. More importantly, in link prediction task, embedding dimensionality $k = 200$, and in triple classification task, embedding dimensionality $k = 100$. We report the average results of 20 repeats here.

Besides, the statistical t-test [5,9] is employed here: To decide whether the improvement by algorithm A over algorithm B is significant, the t-test calculates a value p based on the performance of A and B. The smaller p is, the more significant the improvement is. If the p is small enough ($p < 0.05$), we conclude that the improvement is statistically significant. Moreover, all the models are implemented with Theano, and optimized simultaneously using Stochastic Gradient Descent (SGD).

5.2   Link Prediction

Link prediction aims to predict missing head or tail entity of a triple, which is a widely employed evaluation task for knowledge graph completion models [4,37]. Concretely, given a head entity h (or tail entity t) and a relation r, the system will return a rank list of candidate entities for tail entity (or head entity). Following [3,17], we conduct the link prediction task on WN18 and FB15k datasets. Based on the entity ranking list, we employ two evaluation metrics from [3]: (i) mean rank of correct entities (MR); and (ii) proportion of correct entities in top-10 rank entities (HIT@10). A good link predictor should achieve low MR and high Hit@10. We tuned model parameters using validate datasets. To create a test set, we replaced the relationship of each test triple with all relationships in the KG, and rank these replacement relationships in descending order. We follow [3] to report the *filter* results, i.e., removing all other correct candidates r' in ranking. The overall results are presented in Table 2, wherein $|E|$ denotes the number of entities, $|R|$ denotes the number of relation types, k denotes the number of embedding dimensionality, $|h|$ denotes the hidden layer size, and $|V|$ denotes the number of words in the vocabulary V. Besides, $\#Para$ describes the parameter scale of each model and all the comparative models in Table 2 are listed in ascending order by parameter scale.

Table 2. Evaluation results of link prediction task (all the comparative models are listed in ascending order by parameter scale). The superscript † and ‡ respectively denote statistically significant improvements over **HolE** and **DKRL** ($p < 0.05$).

Models	#Para	WN18		FB15K	
		MR	HIT@10	MR	HIT@10
TransE [3]	$O(k(|E| + |R|))$	251	89.2	125	47.1
HolE [23]	$O(k(|E| + |R|))$	**211**‡	92.5‡	67‡	73.9‡
PTransE [16]	$O(k(|E| + |R|))$	227	85.4	**54**	83.6
Ours	$O(k(|E| + |R| + 1))$	217‡	**93.7**†‡	59†‡	**87.2**†‡
SME [2]	$O(k(|E| + |R| + k))$	533	74.1	154	40.8
TransH [36]	$O(k(|E| + k|R|))$	303	86.7	87	64.4
RESCAL [25]	$O(k(|E| + k|R|))$	579	90.4	683	44.1
SE [4]	$O(k(|E| + 2k|R|))$	584	79.1	162	39.8
TransR [17]	$O(k(|E| + (1 + k)|R|))$	219	91.7	77	68.7
DKRL [41]	$O(k(|E| + |R| + |V| + 2|h|))$	224	89.1	113	57.6

From Table 2, we can see that the proposed **Ours** surpasses all baseline models in most cases on all metrics. This result verifies that the parameter-sharing strategy is beneficial for RL-based knowledge graph completion models. Moreover, we also generate a variant of **Ours**, which maintains the pairwise-ranking strategy, and compare this variant with the proposed **Ours** to verify the effect of the listwise-ranking strategy. From the experimental results, we find that proposed model performs better than its pairwise-ranking variant in most cases. Moreover, Observed from the 2th column in Table 2, the extensive experiments show that our simplified model improves the performance of the current represent learning models for knowledge graph completion task, without the need for complex feature engineering.

5.3 Triple Classification

This section evaluates different models on the triple classification task. Triple classification aims to judge whether a given triple (h, r, t) is true fact or not, and it is usually modeled as a binary classification task [3,31,37]. Following [31] we evaluate different systems on WN11 and FB13 datasets.

Given a triple (h, r, t) and all its accurate relation mentions and entity descriptions of this triple, In our experiments, a triple will be classified as a true fact if the score obtained by function $f_r(h, t)$ is below the relation-specific threshold δ_r, otherwise it will be classified as a false fact. The δ_r is optimized by maximizing classification accuracy on validation dataset, and different values of δ_r will be set for different relations. We use the same settings as link prediction task, all parameters are optimized on the validation datasets to obtain the best accuracies. We compare our model with all baseline models, and we report the best results in Table 3.

Table 3. Evaluation results of triple classification task (all the comparative models are listed in ascending order by parameter scale). The superscript † and ‡ respectively denote statistically significant improvements over **HolE** and **DKRL** ($p < 0.05$).

Models	#Para	WN11	FB13	AVG.
TransE [3]	$O(k(|E| + |R|))$	75.9	81.5	78.7
HolE [23]	$O(k(|E| + |R|))$	86.1‡	81.9	84.0‡
PTransE [16]	$O(k(|E| + |R|))$	76.4	82.7	79.6
Ours	$O(k(|E| + |R| + 1))$	**87.5**†‡	82.4	**85.0**†‡
SME [2]	$O(k(|E| + |R| + k))$	65.9	58.1	62.0
TransH [36]	$O(k(|E| + k|R|))$	78.8	83.3	81.1
RESCAL [25]	$O(k(|E| + k|R|))$	83.4	82.8	83.1
SE [4]	$O(k(|E| + 2k|R|))$	74.2	80.6	77.4
TransR [17]	$O(k(|E| + (1 + k)|R|))$	85.9	82.5	84.2
DKRL [41]	$O(k(|E| + |R| + |V| + 2|h|))$	79.3	**84.2**†	81.8

Similar to last experiment, form Table 3, the results demonstrate that, our method has achieved the best performances on the triple classification task, which verifies that it is critical to utilize listwise-ranking strategy to determine whether a triple should be added into knowledge graph or not. We can see that, the proposed **Ours** is ranked at 4th position according to parameter scale, which is far from the parameter scale of **DKRL**, however **Ours** improves the average accuracy of more complex **DKRL** by 3.91% and achieve the similar results as **TransR** and **HolE**.

6   Conclusions

In summary, we propose a novel Knowledge Graph Completion framework for knowledge graph. The candidate entity is mapped into a target vector representing the existing entity and the existing relationship in the given triple. Besides, each dimensionality in this target vector could be used to measure the similarity between the candidate element and the known elements (relations or entities) in the given triple. Empirically, we show the proposed simplified model can improve the performance of the current RL-based KGC models on several benchmark datasets.

Acknowledgements. The authors are very grateful to the editors and reviewers for their helpful comments. This work is funded by: (i) the China Postdoctoral Science Foundation (No. 2018M641436); (ii) the Joint Advanced Research Foundation of China Electronics Technology Group Corporation (CETC) (No. 6141B08010102); (iii) 2018 Culture and tourism think tank project (No. 18ZK01); (iv) the New Generation of Artificial Intelligence Special Action Project (18116001); and (v) the Joint Advanced Research Foundation of China Electronics Technology Group Corporation (CETC) (No. 6141B0801010a).

References

1. Bollacker, K., Evans, C., Paritosh, P., Sturge, T., Taylor, J.: Freebase: a collaboratively created graph database for structuring human knowledge. In: SIGMOD Conference, pp. 1247–1250 (2008)
2. Bordes, A., Glorot, X., Weston, J., Bengio, Y.: Joint learning of words and meaning representations for open-text semantic parsing. In: AISTATS (2012)
3. Bordes, A., Usunier, N., Garcia-Duran, A., Weston, J., Yakhnenko, O.: Translating embeddings for modeling multi-relational data. In: Advances in Neural Information Processing Systems, pp. 2787–2795 (2013)
4. Bordes, A., Weston, J., Collobert, R., Bengio, Y.: Learning structured embeddings of knowledge bases. In: AAAI Conference on Artificial Intelligence, AAAI 2011, San Francisco, California, USA, August 2011
5. Ding, A.A., Chen, C., Eisenbarth, T.: Simpler, faster, and more robust t-test based leakage detection. In: Standaert, F.-X., Oswald, E. (eds.) COSADE 2016. LNCS, vol. 9689, pp. 163–183. Springer, Cham (2016). https://doi.org/10.1007/978-3-319-43283-0_10

6. Dong, X., et al.: Knowledge vault: a web-scale approach to probabilistic knowledge fusion. In: ACM SIGKDD International Conference on Knowledge Discovery and Data Mining, pp. 601–610 (2014)
7. Hastie, T., Tibshirani, R.: Classification by pairwise coupling. In: Conference on Advances in Neural Information Processing Systems (1998)
8. Huang, H., Wang, Y., Feng, C., Liu, Z., Zhou, Q.: Leveraging conceptualization for short-text embedding. IEEE Trans. Knowl. Data Eng. $30(7)$, 1282–1295 (2018)
9. Jankowski, K.R.B., Flannelly, K.J., Flannelly, L.T.: The t-test: an influential inferential tool in chaplaincy and other healthcare research. J. Health Care Chaplain. $24(1)$, 30 (2018)
10. Ji, G., He, S., Xu, L., Liu, K., Zhao, J.: Knowledge graph embedding via dynamic mapping matrix. In: ACL (2015)
11. Jiang, M., et al.: Text classification based on deep belief network and softmax regression. Neural Comput. Appl. 7, 1–10 (2016)
12. Kazemi, S.M., Poole, D.: Simple embedding for link prediction in knowledge graphs. In: NeurIPS (2018)
13. Li, J., Li, Y., Zhai, F.: Initial fine alignment based on self-contained measurement in erection manoeuvre. IET Sci. Meas. Technol. $12(3)$, 375–381 (2018)
14. Liang, Y., Xu, F., Zhang, S.H., Lai, Y.K., Mu, T.: Knowledge graph construction with structure and parameter learning for indoor scene design. Comput. Vis. Media $4(2)$, 1–15 (2018)
15. Lin, C., Fang, B., Shang, Z., Tang, Y.: Negative samples reduction in cross-company software defects prediction. Inf. Softw. Technol. $62(1)$, 67–77 (2015)
16. Lin, Y., Liu, Z., Luan, H.B., Sun, M., Rao, S., Liu, S.: Modeling relation paths for representation learning of knowledge bases. In: EMNLP (2015)
17. Lin, Y., Liu, Z., Zhu, X., Zhu, X., Zhu, X.: Learning entity and relation embeddings for knowledge graph completion. In: Twenty-Ninth AAAI Conference on Artificial Intelligence, pp. 2181–2187 (2015)
18. Ma, S., Ding, J., Jia, W., Wang, K., Guo, M.: TransT: type-based multiple embedding representations for knowledge graph completion. In: Joint European Conference on Machine Learning and Knowledge Discovery in Databases, pp. 717–733 (2017)
19. Meilicke, C., Fink, M., Wang, Y., Ruffinelli, D., Gemulla, R., Stuckenschmidt, H.: Fine-grained evaluation of rule- and embedding-based systems for knowledge graph completion. In: Vrandečić, D., et al. (eds.) ISWC 2018. LNCS, vol. 11136, pp. 3–20. Springer, Cham (2018). https://doi.org/10.1007/978-3-030-00671-6_1
20. Mikolov, T., Sutskever, I., Chen, K., Corrado, G., Dean, J.: Distributed representations of words and phrases and their compositionality. In: Advances in Neural Information Processing Systems 26, pp. 3111–3119 (2013)
21. Nguyen, D.Q., Vu, T., Nguyen, T.D., Nguyen, D.Q., Phung, D.: A capsule network-based embedding model for knowledge graph completion and search personalization (2018)
22. Nguyen, D.Q., Sirts, K., Qu, L., Johnson, M.: STransE: a novel embedding model of entities and relationships in knowledge bases. In: HLT-NAACL (2016)
23. Nickel, M., Rosasco, L., Poggio, T.: Holographic embeddings of knowledge graphs. In: Thirtieth AAAI Conference on Artificial Intelligence, pp. 1955–1961 (2016)
24. Nickel, M., Rosasco, L., Poggio, T.A.: Holographic embeddings of knowledge graphs. In: AAAI (2016)
25. Nickel, M., Tresp, V., Kriegel, H.P.: A three-way model for collective learning on multi-relational data. In: International Conference on International Conference on Machine Learning (2011)

26. Qian, C., Yu, Y., Tang, K., Jin, Y., Yao, X., Zhou, Z.H.: On the effectiveness of sampling for evolutionary optimization in noisy environments. Evol. Comput. **26**(2), 237–267 (2018)
27. Quan, W., Mao, Z., Wang, B., Li, G.: Knowledge graph embedding: a survey of approaches and applications. IEEE Trans. Knowl. Data Eng. **29**(12), 2724–2743 (2017)
28. Read, J., Pfahringer, B., Holmes, G.: Multi-label classification using ensembles of pruned sets. In: Eighth IEEE International Conference on Data Mining (2008)
29. Read, J., Pfahringer, B., Holmes, G., Frank, E.: Classifier chains for multi-label classification. Mach. Learn. **85**(3), 333–359 (2011)
30. Slatkin, M., Hudson, R.R.: Pairwise comparisons of mitochondrial dna sequences in stable and exponentially growing populations. Genetics **129**(2), 555–562 (1991)
31. Socher, R., Chen, D., Manning, C.D., Ng, A.Y.: Reasoning with neural tensor networks for knowledge base completion. In: International Conference on Neural Information Processing Systems, pp. 926–934 (2013)
32. Sun, Y., Wen, G.: Ensemble softmax regression model for speech emotion recognition. Multimedia Tools & Appl. **76**, 8305–8328 (2016)
33. Trouillon, T., Welbl, J., Riedel, S., Gaussier, É., Bouchard, G.: Complex embeddings for simple link prediction (2016)
34. Wang, Y., Huang, H., Feng, C.: Query expansion based on a feedback concept model for microblog retrieval. In: International Conference on World Wide Web, pp. 559–568 (2017)
35. Wang, Y., Huang, H., Feng, C., Zhou, Q., Gu, J., Gao, X.: CSE: conceptual sentence embeddings based on attention model. In: 54th Annual Meeting of the Association for Computational Linguistics, pp. 505–515 (2016)
36. Wang, Z., Zhang, J., Feng, J., Chen, Z.: Knowledge graph embedding by translating on hyperplanes. In: Twenty-Eighth AAAI Conference on Artificial Intelligence, pp. 1112–1119 (2014)
37. Wang, Z., Li, J.: Text-enhanced representation learning for knowledge graph. In: International Joint Conference on Artificial Intelligence (2016)
38. Xia, F., Liu, T.Y., Wang, J., Zhang, W., Hang, L.: Listwise approach to learning to rank: theory and algorithm. In: International Conference on Machine Learning (2008)
39. Xiao, H., Huang, M., Meng, L., Zhu, X.: SSP: semantic space projection for knowledge graph embedding with text descriptions. In: AAAI (2017)
40. Xiao, H., Huang, M., Zhu, X.: TransG: a generative model for knowledge graph embedding. In: Meeting of the Association for Computational Linguistics, pp. 2316–2325 (2016)
41. Xie, R., Liu, Z., Jia, J.J., Luan, H., Sun, M.: Representation learning of knowledge graphs with entity descriptions. In: AAAI (2016)
42. Yi, T., Luu, A.T., Hui, S.C.: Non-parametric estimation of multiple embeddings for link prediction on dynamic knowledge graphs. In: Thirty First Conference on Artificial Intelligence (2017)
43. Yuan, Z., et al.: Softmax regression design for stochastic computing based deep convolutional neural networks. In: On Great Lakes Symposium on VLSI (2017)
44. Zeman, O., Tennekes, H.: A self-contained model for the pressure terms in the turbulent stress equations of the neutral atmospheric boundary layer. J. Atmos. Sci. **32**(9), 1808–1813 (2010)

Document-Level Named Entity Recognition by Incorporating Global and Neighbor Features

Anwen Hu, Zhicheng Dou[✉], and Ji-rong Wen

Beijing Key Laboratory of Big Data Management and Analysis Methods,
Renmin University of China, Beijing 100872, China
{anwenhu,dou,jrwen}@ruc.edu.cn

Abstract. State-of-the-art named entity recognition models mostly process sentences within a document separately. Sentence-level named entity recognition is easy to cause tagging inconsistency problems for long text documents. In this paper, we first propose to use the neural network to encode global consistency and neighbor relevance among occurrences of a particular token within a document. We first encode sentences within a document independently by a sentence-level BiLSTM layer, then we design a document-level module to encode the relation between occurrences of a particular token. In our document-level module, we use CNN to encode global consistency features and apply BiLSTM to model neighbor relevance features. We further apply a gate to effectively fuse these two non-local features and use a CRF layer to decode labels. We evaluate our model on the CoNLL-2003 dataset. Experimental results show that our model outperforms existing methods.

Keywords: Document-level · Named entity · Global · Neighbor

1 Introduction

Named entity recognition (NER) is usually a basic step in many natural language processing (NLP) tasks, such as calculating reputation for entities [19] and relation extraction [16]. Due to the success of recurrent neural network (RNN) and its variants in modeling sequential data, many RNN-based neural network models [3,6,8,12,15] were proposed for NER. Most of these models are designed for sentence-level named entity recognition: they treat sentences in a document independently during training or predicting. This is easy to cause that an identical entity in two separated sentences might be classified as different entity types, which is called tagging inconsistency problem. For the example given in Fig. 1, a sentence-level model named BiLSTM-CNN-CRF [15] successfully recognized the first "Wenchang" as a 'LOCATION' (a city in China). However, it misclassified the second one appearing in the second sentence, from 'LOCATION' to 'PERSON' due to its ambiguous local context.

© Springer Nature Switzerland AG 2019
Q. Zhang et al. (Eds.): CCIR 2019, LNCS 11772, pp. 79–91, 2019.
https://doi.org/10.1007/978-3-030-31624-2_7

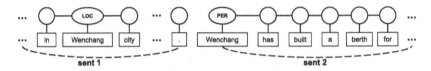

Fig. 1. An example of the label consistency problem within a document in the CoNLL-2003 English dataset.

Document-level NER has the potential to solve the tag inconsistency problem in sentence-level NER. For the example in Fig. 1, the first sentence explicitly tells Wenchang is a city. Using the context of "Wenchang" in the first sentence could help recognize the entity type of the same token in the second sentence. Many manually designed non-local features [2,5,9,10] were proposed to utilize context information in entire documents. To reduce reliance on feature engineering, some studies [14,20,22,24] proposed using neural networks to model the relation across sentences. For example, a global self-attention mechanism [24] was introduced to find useful contextual information across sentences based on semantic relevance.

In this paper, we propose a novel neural network leveraging global consistency and neighbor relevance for document-level NER. Our model uses BiLSTM to encode sentences within a document independently. Then, we apply a document-level module to model the relation between occurrences of a particular token across sentences. According to the statistic on CoNLL-2003 English dataset [21], we find more than 80% sequences of occurrences of a particular token refer to an identical entity. Thus, we use a CNN layer to learn global consistency features among all occurrences of the current token. Besides, when our humans are confused about a concept during reading, we will look for clearer contents in the document from near to far. To imitate this human's habit, we use a BiLSTM layer in the document-level module to learn neighbor relevance features from adjacent occurrences. The global consistency feature encodes how the token appears in the entire document. The neighbor relevance feature encodes the context of nearby occurrences. To decide how much information of these two features should be introduced respectively, we fuse these two features by a gated fusion module. At last, we use a CRF layer to decode labels for each sentence.

We evaluate our model on the CoNLL-2003 dataset. Experimental results show that adding either document-level feature can significantly improve the F1 score, and our gated fusion model obtains the best recognition quality.

The main contributions of this paper are:

- We propose a novel method for document-level named entity recognition. We use a sentence-level BiLSTM layer to encode sentences dependently and then use a document-level module to generate document-level features.
- We introduce two kinds of automatically learned document-level features: a global consistency feature extracted by CNN and a neighbor relevance feature encoded by BiLSTM. These features are fused by a gating mechanism.
- Experimental results confirm that our proposed method outperforms the state-of-the-art sentence-level and document-level NER models.

2   Related Work

2.1   Sentence-Level NER

Many statistics-based models, like HMM [13] and CRF [11], were effectively employed in sentence-level NER. With the development of the neural network, many RNN-based methods with CRF as the decoding layer [8,12] achieved better performance than statistic models. Besides, character-level information encoded by CNN [3] or BiLSTM [12] was proven to be significant for NER quality. BiLSTM-CNNS-CRF model [15] was truly end-to-end, which didn't require feature engineering, task-specific resources or data-processing. We propose to add a document-level module to the architecture of BiLSTM-CNNS-CRF to introduce non-local information within the entire document.

2.2   Document-Level NER

To make use of non-local information, many manually designed non-local features [2,5,10,18] were utilized for statistic-based methods and exhibited promising results. Some studies aimed to design global features to make occurrences of a particular token within a document labeled consistently, such as Init-Caps of Other Occurrences (ICOC) [2] and Entity-majority feature [10]. Similarly, in this paper, we use a CNN based global vector to introduce a consistent document-level representation for all occurrences of a particular token within a document. Besides, the context aggregation feature [18] was proposed for the case that identical tokens may not have identical label assignments. For example, "Australia" can be labeled as 'LOC', and "The bank of Australia" should be labeled as 'ORG'. In this work, BiLSTM based neighbor vector is different for each occurrence, and we incorporate local context representations and non-local representations. Both points avoid all occurrences of a particular token are labeled as the same entity type.

With the development of the neural network, there were also some neural network based methods that didn't rely on manually designed features. ID-CNN [20] iteratively applied 'block' (a stack of dilated convolutions [23]) with the same parameters several times to encode document-level features. Att-BiLSTM-CRF [14] used an attention mechanism to find useful context information within a document for the chemical named entity. Both these two work encoded the whole long sequence concatenated by sentences within a document. NER reasoner [22] was designed as a multi-layer architecture, where each layer could utilize context information of entities predicted by the last layer with a candidate pool. Global-ATT [24] is the most relevant work to ours. They used BiLSTM to encode sentences within a document independently and used a self-attention mechanism to find useful context information from all occurrences of a particular token. The main difference between Global-ATT [24] and our model is how to generate reliable non-local features. Unlike using the self-attention mechanism to focus on semantically similar occurrences, our model generates non-local features by incorporate global consistency features and neighbor relevance features.

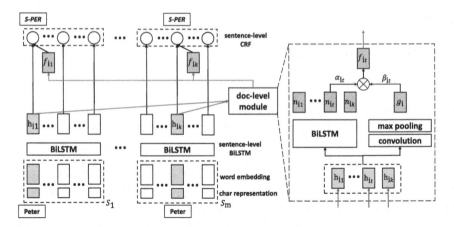

Fig. 2. The architecture of our model. $\mathbf{S} = (S_1, ..., S_{m-1}, S_m)$ is a list of sentences within a document. $\mathbf{h_i} = (h_{i1}, h_{i2}, ..., h_{ik})$ is a list of sentence-level BiLSTM outputs for occurrences of token 'Peter'. $\mathbf{n_i} = (n_{i1}, n_{i2}, ..., n_{ik})$ is a list of neighbor representations. g_i is a global representation. $\mathbf{f_i} = (f_{i1}, f_{i2}, ..., f_{ik})$ is a list of fused representations.

3   Our Document-Level NER Model: GNG

We propose a novel neural network architecture that fuses **G**lobal consistency features and **N**eighbor relevance features with a **G**ate mechanism, namely GNG. We design a document-level module to take into account context information from all occurrences of a particular token within a document. The architecture of our proposed model is shown in Fig. 2. We first encode sentences within a document independently in the sentence-level BiLSTM layer. Then for each token, we collect local contextual representations of its occurrences as the input of the document-level module. The document-level module returns a fused document-level feature vector for each occurrence. We concatenate sentence-level contextual representation and fused document-level feature vectors to new hidden states. At last, we apply a sentence-level CRF layer to decode the label sequences. We will introduce the details of each component in the remaining part of this section.

3.1   Sentence-Level Bi-directional LSTM

The Long Short-Term Memory Network (LSTM) [7] is a variant of the recurrent neural network (RNN) designed to learn long-term dependencies. LSTM is composed of a memory cell and three gates to control how much information to forget and to pass on to the next time step. However, LSTM only takes information from the past and ignore future information. Bidirectional LSTMs combine two LSTMs in two directions, one in the forward direction and the other in the backward direction. For each sentence, our sentence-level BiLSTM is fed a sequence of token representations which are concatenated by word embeddings

Table 1. Statistics of entity type consistency on the CoNLL-2003 dataset. **Consistent** and **Inconsistent** refer to counts and percentages of consistent tag sequences and inconsistent tag sequences.

Dataset	Consistent	Inconsistent
Train	19,460 (87.2%)	2,868 (12.8%)
Development	4,804 (86.4%)	753 (14.6%)
Test	4,734 (88.2%)	636 (12.8%)

and CNN based char representations [15]. At each time, BiLSTM concatenates two hidden states $\overrightarrow{h_t}$ and $\overleftarrow{h_t}$ to the output:

$$h_t = [\overrightarrow{h_t}, \overleftarrow{h_t}] \tag{1}$$

h_t aggregates context information of each token within a sentence, so we call h_t as local context feature/representation.

3.2 Document-Level Module

After the sentence-level BiLSTM layer, we apply a document-level module to aggregate local context features from all occurrences of a particular token within a document. For each token x_i, we collect its occurrences as $\mathbf{u_i} = (u_{i1}, u_{i2}, ..., u_{ik})$, where k is the count of occurrences for token x_i within a document. Then, according to the positions of these occurrences, we obtain a list of local context representations for $\mathbf{u_i}$:

$$\mathbf{h_i} = (h_{i1}, h_{i2}, ..., h_{ik}) \tag{2}$$

where $h_{it}(1 \leq t \leq k)$ is obtained by Eq. (1). h_{it} means the local context feature vector of the tth occurrence of token x_i. $\mathbf{h_i}$ is the input of the document-level module for token x_i.

Our document-level module can be divided into two parts. We use a CNN layer to extract a global consistency feature for all occurrences. And for each occurrence, we use a BiLSTM layer to capture another neighbor relevance feature from its adjacent occurrences. These two non-local features can be used alone or fused to a new feature.

CNN in Doc-Level Module. In most cases, different occurrences of a particular token in a document are labeled as the same entity type. The consistency statistic on the CoNLL-2003 shown in Table 1 supports this intuition. Table 1 shows the counts and percentages of consistent tag sequences and inconsistent tag sequences within a document. Consistent tag sequence means all occurrences of a particular token within a document are labeled as the same tag. For example, (B-PER, B-PER, B-PER) for token "Peter" is consistent, (B-PER, E-PER,

B-PER) or (B-PER, B-ORG, B-PER) for token "Peter" is inconsistent. Obviously, consistent tag sequences are much more than inconsistent tag sequences. So, in most cases, when the local context of a token is not sufficient for models to classify its entity type, information from other occurrences can provide some help. Based on this idea, we first introduce a global consistency feature for all occurrences of a particular token within a document. After getting sentence-level Bi-directional LSTM outputs $\mathbf{h_i}$, we apply a CNN with the max-pooling layer to extract the global consistency representation g_i. Its calculation is defined as:

$$g_i = \mathrm{CNN}(\mathbf{h_i})$$

where $\mathbf{h_i}$ is obtained by Eq. (2). CNN() refers to the convolution and the max-pooling layer in the document-level module. g_i is shared by all occurrences of a particular token within a document.

BiLSTM in Doc-Level Module. In cases where not all occurrences of a particular token are labeled as the same entity type, it's inappropriate to introduce an identical global feature for all occurrences of a particular token. While reading an article, if we humans have doubts about a certain concept in a sentence, we will first look for neighbor occurrences of the concept to get more context information across sentences. Based on this human habit, we introduce a neighbor relevance feature for each occurrence. Note "neighbor" means neighbor occurrences rather than neighbor context or neighbor sentences. Besides, news editors always organize articles in chronological order. So we think descriptions of an entity in an article can be seen as a time sequence. For example, there is an article about the Bank of Japan governor "Matsushita" in the CoNLL-2003 dataset. It is first mentioned that Matsushita's view on the yen was quoted in Japan's leading economic daily. Then it states the effects of his comments. Next, it says that Matsushita further expressed his point of view in the following interview. Therefore, to encode the sequence composed of local context representations with timing characteristics like this, we apply another BiLSTM layer to learn neighbor relevance representation $n_{it}(1 \leq t \leq k)$ for each occurrence.

$$\mathbf{n_i} = \mathrm{BiLSTM}(\mathbf{h_i}),$$
$$\mathbf{n_i} = (n_{i1}, n_{i2}, ..., n_{ik})$$

where $\mathbf{h_i}$ is obtained by Eq. (2). n_{it} means neighbor relevance representation for the tth occurrence of token x_i.

Gated Fusion. The influence of the global consistency representation and the neighbor relevance representation may be different in different cases, so we propose a gated fusion to fuse these two features. For each occurrence of a particular token, we get its global feature and neighbor feature. Then based on its local context feature, we compute the weights of the two non-local features and get a new fused feature. The two weights are calculated as follows:

$$\alpha_{it} = \sigma(W_\alpha(\tanh(W_{\hat{g}}g_i + b_{\hat{g}}) \oplus h_{it})),$$
$$\beta_{it} = \sigma(W_\beta(\tanh(W_{\hat{n}}n_{it} + b_{\hat{n}}) \oplus h_{it})),$$

where h_{it} is obtained by Eq. (1). g_i is global consistency representation for token x_i, n_{it} is neighbor relevance representation for the tth occurrence of token x_i. $W_{\hat{g}}$, $W_{\hat{n}}$, W_α, W_β are weight matrices. $b_{\hat{g}}$, $b_{\hat{n}}$ are bias vectors. $\oplus$ is the concatenating operation, σ is the sigmoid function. α_{it} and β_{it} is the weight vector for global representation and neighbor representation, respectively. The gated fusion is defined as:

$$f_{it} = \alpha_{it}g_i + \beta_{it}n_{it}$$

where f_{it} is the fused document-level feature for the tth occurrence of token x_i.

3.3   CRF Layer

To consider the correlations between labels in neighborhoods, we apply the sentence-level Condition Random Fields (CRF) layer [11] to decode the best label sequence for each sentence independently.

For a sentence $\mathbf{x} = (w_1, w_2, ..., w_l)$ (l is the number of tokens), we concatenate its local context representations and document-level representations and get new hidden states $\mathbf{h_x} = (\hat{h}_1, \hat{h}_2, ..., \hat{h}_l)$. Then, we reduce the dimension of vectors in $\mathbf{h_x}$ to the number of distinct tags e with two fully connected layers. We convert new low dimensional hidden states to a score matrix $\mathbf{P} \in \mathbb{R}^{l \times e}$. P_{ij} refers to the score of the jth tag for the ith token in the sentence. For any possible predicted sequence $\mathbf{y} = (y_1, y_2, .., y_l)$, its probability is defined as:

$$p(\mathbf{y}|\mathbf{x}; W^t) = \frac{\exp \psi(\mathbf{x}, \mathbf{y})}{\sum_{\tilde{\mathbf{y}} \in \mathcal{Y}_\mathbf{x}} \exp \psi(\mathbf{x}, \tilde{\mathbf{y}})}$$

where $\psi(\mathbf{x}, \mathbf{y}) = \sum_{i=1}^{l} P_{i,y_i} + \sum_{i=0}^{l} W^t_{y_i,y_{i+1}}$, and W^t is a learned transition matrix, $W^t_{y_i,y_{i+1}}$ represents the transition score from the tag y_i to the tag y_{i+1}. $\mathcal{Y}_\mathbf{x}$ is a set of all possible tag sequences. During training, we maximize the log-probability of the ground-truth tag sequence $\hat{\mathbf{y}}$. The loss function is defined as:

$$loss = -\log(p(\hat{\mathbf{y}}|\mathbf{x}; W^t)),$$

Decoding is searching for the tag sequence which obtains the maximum score:

$$\mathbf{y}^\star = \arg\max_{\tilde{\mathbf{y}} \in \mathcal{Y}_\mathbf{x}} \psi(\mathbf{x}, \tilde{\mathbf{y}})$$

4   Experiments

4.1   Dataset

We perform experiments on the CoNLL-2003 English dataset [21], which is taken from the Reuters Corpus comprised of news stories between August 1996 and August 1997. CoNLL-2003 English dataset contains four different types of named entities: persons (PER), organizations (ORG), locations (LOC), and miscellaneous names (MISC). The statistics of the dataset are shown in Table 2. We use the BIOES tagging scheme, which has been proven better than standard BIO2 by previous studies [12, 18].

Table 2. Statistics of the CoNLL-2003 dataset. **#token, #sentence** and **#document** refer to counts of tokens, sentences and documents respectively.

Dataset	#token	#sentence	#document
Train	20,3621	14,987	946
Test	46,435	3,684	231
Development	51,362	3,466	216

4.2   Baselines

To verify the effectiveness of GNG, we compare our model with several state-of-the-art NER models. These models can be divided into two groups: sentence-level models and document-level models.

Sentence-Level Models

- **LSTM-CRF** [12], which uses a BiLSTM layer to extract character-level representation and uses another BiLSTM layer to encode sentences.
- **BiLSTM-CNN-CRF** [15], which uses CNN to extract morphological information from characters of words, and a BiLSTM layer to encode sentences.
- **BiLSTM-CNN** [3], which extracts character features with a CNN layer and encodes sentences with a BiLSTM layer. Besides, it uses lexicons as a form of external knowledge.
- **Parallel-RNNs** [6], which is a parallel LSTM model for NER.

Document-Level Models

- **Two-stage CRF** [10], which designs three features corresponding to a function of aggregate statistics of the output of the first CRF at the document level, namely Token-majority features, Entity-majority features and Superentity-majority features.

- **Ratinov09** [18], which uses three non-local features (context aggregation, two-stage prediction aggregation, extended prediction history) and external knowledge to improve the performance of perceptron based NER system.
- **Att-BiLSTM-CRF** [14], which concatenates sentences within a document to a sequence, and uses an attention layer to extract global information.
- **ID-CNN** [20], which uses Iterated Dilated Convolutional Neural Network to handle a very long sequence concatenated by sentences of a document.
- **Global-ATT** [24], which applies a self-attention mechanism on occurrences of a particular token within a document to generate global representation.
- **NER reasoner** [22], which is a multi-layer architecture, where each layer makes use of named entities recognized by the last layer.

Other Baselines. To analyze the contribution of each component in our document-level module, we also experiment with using each document-level feature alone or concatenating two document-level features directly.

- **GNG-DOC**: Previous sentence-level methods randomly shuffled sentences in the dataset during training. GNG needs complete document information, so we shuffle documents randomly during training. To compare the impact of training strategies, we train our basic sentence-level model GNG-DOC like GNG. The architecture of GNG-DOC is the same as BiLSTM-CNN-CRF.
- **GNG-LSTMN**: This model only uses global consistency representations extracted by the CNN layer in the document-level module.
- **GNG-CNNG**: This model only uses neighbor relevance representations encoded by the BiLSTM layer in the document-level module.
- **GNG-GATE**: This model concatenates global consistency representations and neighbor relevance representations, other than using a fusion gate.

4.3 Parameter Setting

We perform experiments with conventional Glove 100-dimensional embedding [17] or word embeddings produced by pre-trained language models named bert-base [4] and flair [1]. The optimizer is stochastic gradient descent (SGD) with batch size 2 and momentum 0. 9. Word length in character-level CNN is set to 64, sentence length in sentence-level BiLSTM is set to 130, both of which are slightly bigger than the maximum in the CoNLL-2003 dataset, and we apply zero-operation as necessary. We find entity tokens which appear more than 20 times within a document in the CoNLL-2003 are very rare. Thus, the maximum length of a list consisting of occurrences of a particular token is set to 20. If the number of occurrences of a particular token within a document is bigger than 20, its document-level information will be ignored.

4.4 Results and Discussion

In this paper, we use standard F1-score (F1) as the evaluation metrics. We conduct each experiment 4 times and report its mean. Experimental results are shown in Tables 3 and 4. We find:

(1) **GNG outperform existing sentence-level models and document-level models.** GNG-DOC achieves comparable performance with LSTM-CRF. It shows that for the sentence-level model, there is no obvious difference between shuffling all sentences and shuffling documents like GNG during training. So, the improvement of GNG in F1 has nothing to do with our training strategies. Our document-level module can indeed significantly improve the NER quality based on the sentence-level model.

(2) **All components in document-level modules are important.** Both GNG-CNNG and GNG-LSTMN underperform GNG, which indicates both global consistency features and neighbor relevance features are essential in our document-level module. Besides, GNG-GATE underperforms our GNG, which shows our fusion gate can fuse these two non-local features more effectively.

Table 3. F1 scores of different approaches on the test set of CoNLL-2003. ‡ marks the neural model. ∗ marks model which uses external resources. Our models use the glove as default word embedding. **F1** refers to F1-score.

Model	F1
LSTM-CRF‡	90.94
BiLSTM-CNN-CRF‡	91.21
BiLSTM-CNN‡∗	91.62
Parallel-RNNs‡	91.48
Two-stage CRF	87.24
Ratinov09∗	90.57
Att-BiLSTM-CRF‡	90.49
ID-CNN‡	90.65
Global-ATT‡	91.43
NER reasoner‡	91.44
GNG-DOC‡	90.92
GNG-LSTMN‡	91.76
GNG-CNNG‡	92.05
GNG-GATE‡	91.78
GNG‡	**92.12**

Table 4. F1 scores of GNG-DOC and GNG on CoNLL-2003 with different word embeddings. **bert-base** [4] and **flair** [1] are word embeddings produced by pre-trained language models.

Model	glove	bert-base	flair
GNG-DOC	90.92	90.76	92.64
GNG	**92.12**	**91.45**	**92.96**

(3) As shown in Table 4, with either **bert-base** [4] or **flair** [1] as initialized word embedding, GNG outperforms GNG-DOC. Our document-level module learns features across sentences, which are overlooked in these state-of-the-art sentence-level language models. Thus our document-level feature can further improve NER quality at the base of word embeddings produced by these pre-trained language models.

5 Conclusion

In this paper, we propose a novel neural network named GNG that incorporates global consistency feature and neighbor relevance feature for document-level named entity recognition. GNG encodes sentences within a document independently, and utilizes a document-level module to model relations between occurrences of a particular token. In the document-level module, there is a CNN layer to learn global consistency and a BiLSTM layer to encode neighbor relevance. A gate mechanism is further used to fuse these two non-local representations. GNG achieves the state-of-the-art result on the CoNLL-2003 English dataset.

Acknowledgments. This work was supported by National Natural Science Foundation of China No. 61872370, National Key R&D Program of China No. 2018YFC0830703, and the Fundamental Research Funds for the Central Universities, and the Research Funds of Renmin University of China No. 2112018391.

References

1. Akbik, A., Blythe, D., Vollgraf, R.: Contextual string embeddings for sequence labeling. In: Proceedings of the 27th International Conference on Computational Linguistics, pp. 1638–1649 (2018)
2. Chieu, H.L., Ng, H.T.: Named entity recognition with a maximum entropy approach. In: Proceedings of the Seventh Conference on Natural Language Learning, CoNLL 2003, Held in cooperation with HLT-NAACL 2003, Edmonton, Canada, 31 May–1 June 2003, pp. 160–163 (2003)
3. Chiu, J.P.C., Nichols, E.: Named entity recognition with bidirectional lstm-cnns. TACL **4**, 357–370 (2016)
4. Devlin, J., Chang, M.W., Lee, K., Toutanova, K.: Bert: Pre-training of deep bidirectional transformers for language understanding. arXiv preprint arXiv:1810.04805 (2018)
5. Finkel, J.R., Grenager, T., Manning, C.D.: Incorporating non-local information into information extraction systems by Gibbs sampling. In: Proceedings of the 43rd Annual Meeting of the Association for Computational Linguistics, pp. 363–370 (2005)
6. Gregoric, A.Z., Bachrach, Y., Coope, S.: Named entity recognition with parallel recurrent neural networks. In: Proceedings of the 56th Annual Meeting of the Association for Computational Linguistics (Volume 2: Short Papers), vol. 2, pp. 69–74 (2018)
7. Hochreiter, S., Schmidhuber, J.: Long short-term memory. Neural Comput. **9**(8), 1735–1780 (1997). https://doi.org/10.1162/neco.1997.9.8.1735

8. Huang, Z., Xu, W., Yu, K.: Bidirectional LSTM-CRF models for sequence tagging. CoRR abs/1508.01991 (2015)
9. Kazama, J., Torisawa, K.: A new perceptron algorithm for sequence labeling with non-local features. In: Proceedings of the 2007 Joint Conference on Empirical Methods in Natural Language Processing and Computational Natural Language Learning, EMNLP-CoNLL 2007, pp. 315–324 (2007)
10. Krishnan, V., Manning, C.D.: An effective two-stage model for exploiting non-local dependencies in named entity recognition. In: Proceedings of the 21st International Conference on Computational Linguistics and 44th Annual Meeting of the Association for Computational Linguistics, ACL 2006, Sydney, Australia, 17–21 July 2006 (2006)
11. Lafferty, J., McCallum, A., Pereira, F.C.: Conditional random fields: probabilistic models for segmenting and labeling sequence data (2001)
12. Lample, G., Ballesteros, M., Subramanian, S., Kawakami, K., Dyer, C.: Neural architectures for named entity recognition. In: The 2016 Conference of the North American Chapter of the Association for Computational Linguistics: Human Language Technologies, NAACL HLT 2016, pp. 260–270 (2016)
13. Leek, T.R.: Information extraction using hidden Markov models. Master's thesis, University of California, San Diego (1997)
14. Luo, L., Yang, Z., Yang, P., Zhang, Y., Wang, L., Lin, H., Wang, J.: An attention-based BiLSTM-CRF approach to document-level chemical named entity recognition. Bioinformatics 34, 1381–1388 (2017)
15. Ma, X., Hovy, E.H.: End-to-end sequence labeling via bi-directional LSTM-CNNs-CRF. In: Proceedings of the 54th Annual Meeting of the Association for Computational Linguistics, Volume 1: Long Papers, ACL 2016, Berlin, Germany, 7–12 August 2016 (2016)
16. Mintz, M., Bills, S., Snow, R., Jurafsky, D.: Distant supervision for relation extraction without labeled data. In: ACL/IJCNLP, pp. 1003–1011. The Association for Computer Linguistics (2009)
17. Pennington, J., Socher, R., Manning, C.: Glove: global vectors for word representation. In: Conference on Empirical Methods in Natural Language Processing, pp. 1532–1543 (2014)
18. Ratinov, L., Roth, D.: Design challenges and misconceptions in named entity recognition. In: Proceedings of the Thirteenth Conference on Computational Natural Language Learning, CoNLL 2009, Boulder, Colorado, USA, 4–5 June 2009, pp. 147–155 (2009)
19. Seghouani, N.B., Bugiotti, F., Hewasinghage, M., Isaj, S., Quercini, G.: A frequent named entities-based approach for interpreting reputation in Twitter. Data Sci. Eng. 3(2), 86–100 (2018)
20. Strubell, E., Verga, P., Belanger, D., McCallum, A.: Fast and accurate entity recognition with iterated dilated convolutions. In: Proceedings of the 2017 Conference on Empirical Methods in Natural Language Processing, EMNLP 2017, Copenhagen, Denmark, 9–11 September 2017, pp. 2670–2680 (2017)
21. Tjong Kim Sang, E.F., De Meulder, F.: Introduction to the CoNLL-2003 shared task: language-independent named entity recognition. In: Proceedings of the Seventh Conference on Natural Language Learning at HLT-NAACL 2003-Volume 4, pp. 142–147. Association for Computational Linguistics (2003)

22. Yin, X., Zheng, D., Lu, Z., Liu, R.: Neural entity reasoner for global consistency in ner. arXiv preprint arXiv:1810.00347 (2018)
23. Yu, F., Koltun, V.: Multi-scale context aggregation by dilated convolutions. In: ICLR (2016)
24. Zhang, B., Whitehead, S., Huang, L., Ji, H.: Global attention for name tagging. In: Proceedings of the 22nd Conference on Computational Natural Language Learning, pp. 86–96 (2018)

NLP for IR

Ensemble System for Identification of Cited Text Spans: Based on Two Steps of Feature Selection

Jin Xu, Chengzhi Zhang$^{(\boxtimes)}$, and Shutian Ma

Department of Information Management,
Nanjing University of Science and Technology, Nanjing 210094, China
zhangcz@njust.edu.cn

Abstract. CL-SciSumm Shared Task proposed a novel approach which is to generate scientific summary based on cited text spans (CTS) in target paper. This mechanism requires identifying CTS from reference paper according to citation sentence (citance) firstly. Therefore, CTS identification has then arisen the attention of many scholars since identified sentences will finally be aggregated for summary generation. Prior studies viewed this task as a text classification problem and feature selection is one key step for modeling the linkage between CTS and citance. Since most studies have paved the work by building features arbitrarily and applying them directly to model training. There is a lack of investigation to evaluate the effectiveness of features. Performance variation caused by different classifiers are barely taken into consideration as well. To further improve the performance of CTS identification, this paper builds an ensemble system based on two steps of feature selection. In the first step, we construct a set of features and do correlation analysis to select those which are higher-correlated with CTS. The second step is responsible for assigning several basic classifiers (SVM, Decision Tree and Logistic Regression) with their best performing feature sets. Experimental results demonstrate that our proposed systems can surpass the previous best performing one.

Keywords: Cited text spans · Feature selection · Negative sampling · Text classification · Ensemble system

1 Introduction

The increasing amount of scientific papers has made it difficult for users to catch up with the development in each field of study. In order to overcome this problem, scientific summarization, which provides people a general understanding of papers, has attracted many researchers and developed quickly in the last decade. Especially, citation sentence (citance) is widely used to generate the summary of target paper since it contains the key information about the reference, such as the research problem it addressed, approaches it proposed, good results it obtained, and even its drawbacks and limitations (Abu-Jbara and Radev 2011; Elkiss et al. 2008; Nanba and Okumura 1999). However, citance also contains information from citing paper. Since authors will hold different opinions due to their different writing backgrounds and citing intentions,

© Springer Nature Switzerland AG 2019
Q. Zhang et al. (Eds.): CCIR 2019, LNCS 11772, pp. 95–107, 2019.
https://doi.org/10.1007/978-3-030-31624-2_8

citation-based summarization is unable to express the idea of original text accurately (Teufel et al. 2006).

In recent years, many shared tasks, such as 2014 TAC Biomedical Summarization Track[1] and Computational Linguistics Scientific Document Summarization Shared Task (CL-SciSumm)[2] proposed a new scientific summarization framework. Different from above-mentioned method, this framework generates scientific summary based on cited text spans (CTS). Given one citance and its reference, CTS refers to the set of sentences located in reference that best reflect the citance. After identifying CTS from reference, these sentences are then grouped according to the predefined facet and integrated into summary. Compared with the citation-based summarization, CTS-based one is derived from original content in reference. It can not only reflect paper impact, but also reveal the information of reference comprehensively. Therefore, it would be very essential to identify CTS accurately to generate a better summary.

Currently, researchers have mainly regarded CTS identification as a text classification task, which is to find the most similar sentences from reference for the given citance (Jaidka et al. 2018). In this respect, feature selection plays an important role in building the linkage between CTS and citance. However, there exist two main limitations in the usage of features according to current studies. Firstly, most researchers generally build feature sets based on their prior experience without taking feature effectiveness into account. Secondly, features are fed directly into classifiers during model training while the discrepancies of feature performance in different classifiers are rarely considered. Therefore, this paper aims at building ensemble system for CTS identification by two steps of feature selection. The first step is in charge of selecting significantly correlated features with CTS via correlation analysis. In the second step, based on the different performances of features in different classifiers, we assign our basic classifiers with their best performing feature sets. Furthermore, we conduct negative sampling to overcome the class imbalance data problem. Finally, we apply voting strategy to integrating the decisions made by basic classifiers and obtain the final results.

2 Related Work

2.1 Feature Selection in CTS Identification

In order to model the patterns between CTS and citance, there mainly exist four types of features: location (position)-based features, sentence importance-based features, similarity-based features and rule-based features etc. Location-based features reveal the locational information of candidate CTS in reference paper. Sentence importance-based features consider the importance of candidate CTS as a factor affecting whether they are being cited or not. Similarity-based features refer to measuring similarity between citance and candidate CTS from different aspects. Rule-based features are responsible for modeling the linkage between sentences based on manual rules.

---

[1] https://tac.nist.gov/2014/BiomedSumm/index.html.

[2] http://wing.comp.nus.edu.sg/~cl-scisumm2019.

For example, Ma et al. classified their features into three categories: position-based features, similarity-based features and rule-based features (Ma et al. 2017). By using these features, they proposed a weighted voting system to integrate results obtained from all the four classifiers. Davoodi, Madan and Gu treated the identification of CTS as a binary classification problem and also grouped their features into three categories: similarity-based features, positional features and frequency-based features. In CIST@CLSciSumm-17, Li et al. extracted lexical features from sentences and calculate a set of similarities like IDF similarity, Jaccard similarity and context similarity. In order to match the citance with correct CTS, they tried Convolutional Neural Network to establish citation linkage (Li et al. 2017). In 2018, they built a rich feature set based on their preceding work in 2017. The word-level similarity features contain Word Mover's Distance (also known as optimal transport) (Kusner et al. 2015), IDF similarity, Jaccard similarity, Word vector similarity and WordNet similarity, while the sentence-level similarity features contain LDA similarity (Li et al. 2018).

2.2 Solutions to Class Imbalance Data Problem

In classification problems, class imbalance problem will cause huge influence on the performance of model training because classification algorithms tend to lay emphasis on the majority while disregard the minority (He and Garcia 2009).

There exist two types of approaches: dataset-based and algorithm-based adoptions. Dataset-based adoptions aim at obtaining balanced data distribution through some mechanisms, including over sampling methods and negative sampling methods. Over sampling methods first randomly select part of minority and copy them. Then, the new generated samples are added to training samplings set. In particular, Chawla et al. proposed one of classic algorithms, synthetic Minority Over-sampling TEchnique (SMOTE) (Chawla et al. 2002). Negative sampling randomly removes part of majority from original dataset, which reduces the size of the majority in samples to alleviate the quantitative gap between classes. For example, Cover proposed Nearest Neighbor (NN) rule (Cover 1968) to extract a part of majority samples according to the number of minority. Specifically, for each minority sample, only its nearest neighbor is pitched on as training data (Cover and Hart 1967). For algorithm-based adoptions, they realize probability density estimation for the targets (minority samples) via statistical distribution and judge the new points (majority samples) to be training samples according to the predetermined threshold. For example, Gunetti and Picardi utilized Gaussian distribution for target sample density estimation (Gunetti and Picardi 2005). Hong et al. applied kernel spatial density estimation to class-imbalance data classification (Hong et al. 2007).

3 Methodology

In this paper, we transform our work into binary classification problem which is to classify every single sentence in reference into CTS or non-CTS. As is shown in Fig. 1, first of all, we build a set of features and select those with higher correlation and significance in correlation analysis. Then, we solve the problem of class imbalance through negative sampling. In this way, classifier-feature selection is employed to assign the suitable features set to each classifier. When identifying CTS in test data, classifiers are trained individually and integrated to get final results via the voting.

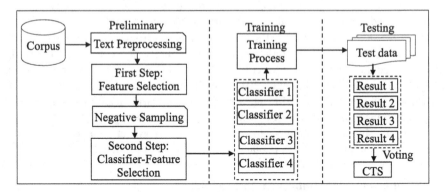

Fig. 1. Framework of CTS identification

3.1 Feature Selection: Correlation Analysis of Features

We perform correlation analysis on each feature to explore whether it is correlated with CTS. In this way, we aim at revealing which features are more effective in distinguishing CTS and non-CTS. Based on the prior study (Ma et al. 2017, 2018), we built three types of features in Table 1 and test their correlation coefficient with CTS.

Table 1. Features in this paper

	Feature	Feature description
Position-based feature	Sentence length(sl)	The number of words in candidate CTS
	Sid(sid)	The serial number of candidate CTS in full text
	Ssid($ssid$)	The serial number of candidate CTS in paragraph it belongs to
	Sentence position ($senp$)	The ratio of Sid and the number of sentences in full text
	Section position ($secp$)	The position of paragraph candidate CTS is located, divided by the number of paragraphs in full text
	Inner position($innp$)	The ratio of CTS's Ssid and the number of sentences in the paragraph it belongs to
Similarity-based feature	Longest common subsequence($lseq$)	See citance and candidate CTS as two sets of sequences with words as basic unit, find the longest subsequence (not necessarily consecutive in original sequences) common to two
	Longest common substring($lstr$)	See citance and candidate CTS as two sets of strings with words as basic units, find the longest string(s) that is a substring(s) (required to occupy consecutive positions within the original strings) of two

(continued)

Table 1. (*continued*)

Feature	Feature description
Dice similarity(*dice*)	Segment citance and candidate CTS into sets of words (s_1, s_2). It is calculated by: $2*$ intersection(s_1, s_2)/ (length(s_1) + length(s_2))
Jaccard similarity (*jacc*)	Segment sentences into set of words, calculate the division of the intersection and union between two sets
Doc2Vec similarity (*d2v*)	Represent sentences as low-dimensional and dense vectors via Doc2Vec algorithm, calculate cosine value between two vectors
Levenshtein distance[a] (*leven*)	Calculate the average of Levenshtein distance (the minimum number of single character edits required to change one to the other) for all the words between two sentences
LDA similarity(*lda*)	Represent probability distribution of sentences according to their topics, calculate cosine value between two sentence vectors
WordNet similarity (*wn*)	Based on WordNet ontology, calculate the average of the similarity between words from two sentences
Bigram_overlap(*bo*)	Segment sentences into sets of bigram, calculate the number of overlap between two sets
Word_overlap(*wo*)	Segment sentence into sets of words, calculate the number of overlap between two sets
Word2Vec similarity (*w2v*)	Represent words as low-dimensional and dense distributed representation by Word2Vec, calculate the average of the similarity between words from two sentences via cosine value
Importance-based feature	TextSentenceRank (*tsr*)	The weight of candidate CTS modeled by TextRank algorithm

[a]https://pypi.org/project/python-Levenshtein/

Here, we calculate Pearson Correlation Coefficient (Pearson 1895) between each feature and annotated label as our metric. Pearson Correlation Coefficient $(\rho_{X,Y})$ is used to measure the linear correlation between variables and ranges from -1 to 1. Its definition is presented in formula (1). Given a pair of variables, feature $(X = \{x_1, x_2, \ldots, x_n\})$ and labels $(Y = \{y_1, y_2, \ldots, y_n\})$, $\rho_{X,Y}$ is the covariance of the two variables divided by the product of their standard deviations (Yeager 2019). In particular, $\bar{x}_i$ and $\bar{y}_i$ refer to the average of X and Y, and n means the number of samples.

$$\rho_{X,Y} = \frac{cov(X, Y)}{\sigma_X \sigma_Y} = \frac{\sum_{i=1}^{n}(x_i - \bar{x}_i)(y_i - \bar{y}_i)}{\sqrt{\sum_{i=1}^{n}(x_i - \bar{x}_i)^2}\sqrt{\sum_{i=1}^{n}(y_i - \bar{y}_i)^2}} \tag{1}$$

Table 2. Pearson correlation coefficients of different features

sl	sid	ssid	lseq	lstr	senp	secp	innp	tsr
0.129**	−0.126**	−0.104**	**0.385****	**0.305****	−0.126**	−0.102**	−0.067**	0.092**
dice	jacc	d2v	leven	lda	wn	bo	wo	w2v
0.343**	**0.355****	0.050**	−0.071**	0.127**	0.066**	**0.327****	**0.374****	0.184**

**Correlation is significant at the 0.01 level (2-tailed).
*Correlation is significant at the 0.05 level (2-tailed).

From Table 2, we can find that none of these features are significantly correlated with CTS ($p > 0.5$). There are only six features with comparatively higher correlation ($p > 0.3$). The highest is from longest common subsequence (*lsubseq*) while the lowest is from Doc2Vec similarity (*d2v*). Therefore, we reserve these six features as our experimental feature set. Compared with the current approaches of feature selection based on subjective experiences in CTS identification, the correlation analysis is useful to reveal the effectiveness of different features and help us improve the identification performance further.

3.2 Data Negative Sampling: The Imbalance of Dataset

In training process, serious class-imbalance problem turns up. For one citance, only few are labelled "CTS" since most of candidate sentences are non-CTS, leading to huge quantitative discrepancy between classes.

We randomly extract a part of samples in majority class to reduce its size. The number of extracted samples is dependent on the amount of minority class multiplied by a random integer (T). In order to choose suitable T, we let it range from 1 to 20, with 1 as the interval, aiming at formulating a sampling parameter (T) for each classifier. On the training data, we put the six features (*lseq*, *lstr*, *dice*, *jacc*, *bo*, *wo*) into four classifiers and use 10-fold cross validation to observe the performances with the gradual increase of T. The results are shown in the Fig. 2.

As we can see from the figure, with the gradual increase of T, the performances of CTS identification show a decline tendency. Even though classifiers show perfect results in training data via 10-cross validation with smaller T, they are likely to overfit and behave badly in test data. It will lead to information loss of training data if we exclude too many negative samples. Thus, it is important to make a trade-off between the model fitting and information intactness. From the Fig. 2, we can find that all the F_1-score curves undergo a sharp decline first, then go down slightly for a period and finally decline fast again. We must ensure that F_1-score cannot be too small when determining parameter T. In the meanwhile, we consider the parameter from the point where F_1-score undergo slight descent. The slowing down of F_1-score falling in certain period means that the added negative samples contain useful information and contribute to model learning. Based on this, we choose the spot where F_1-score descends slightly and appears relatively higher as the sampling parameter for each classifier. Parameter T of every classifier is displayed in Table 3.

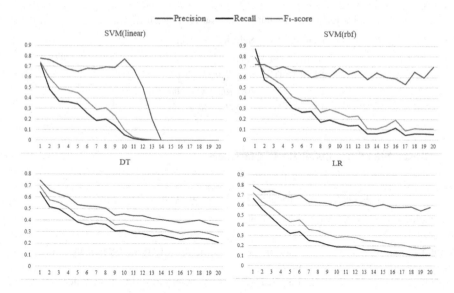

Fig. 2. Evaluation when T is increasing under different classifiers

Table 3. Negative sampling schemes for basic classifiers

Classifier	SVM (linear)	SVM (rbf)	DT	LR
T	5	7	7	6

3.3 Classifier-Feature Selection

Due to the discrepant performance of each feature on different classifiers, it will not be the best choice to train basic classifiers with all significantly correlated features. It is more rational to assign them with their best-performing feature sets respectively. Therefore, to find the efficient classifier-feature combination, we test features separately on training data via 10-fold cross validation.

From Table 4, *lseq*, *dice*, *jacc* and *wo* behave badly in SVM (linear). In other classifiers, there are also one or two features which obtain poor results. Consequently, we drop the bad-performing features (F_1-score < 0.1, red in the table). Each classifier is assigned with its best features set (See Table 5).

Table 4. Evaluation of all features under different classifiers via 10-fold cross validation

	SVM (linear)			SVM (rbf)			DT			LR		
	Precision	Recall	F_1-score	Precision	Recall	F_1-score	Precision	Recall	F_1-score	Precision	Recall	F_1-score
lseq	0.0000	0.0000	0.0000	0.7318	0.1539	0.2533	0.4071	0.0252	0.0470	0.6225	0.3029	0.4054
lstr	0.7544	0.1065	0.1856	0.7191	0.1064	0.1845	0.6726	0.1694	0.2441	0.7737	0.1065	0.1852
dice	0.0000	0.0000	0.0000	0.7933	0.0271	0.0520	0.5974	0.1898	0.2859	0.6608	0.1918	0.2949
jacc	0.0000	0.0000	0.0000	0.7917	0.0271	0.0522	0.6344	0.2159	0.3208	0.2729	0.0319	0.0558
bo	0.5624	0.3147	0.3872	0.5777	0.3611	0.4442	0.7557	0.1394	0.2341	0.7864	0.1422	0.2390
wo	0.0000	0.0000	0.0000	0.6214	0.2061	0.3079	0.6575	0.2100	0.3178	0.4011	0.0504	0.0890

Table 5. Final features selection for four classifiers

Classifier	Selected features
SVM (linear)	*lstr, bo*
SVM (rbf)	*lseq, lstr, bo, wo*
DT	*lstr, dice, jacc, bo, wo*
LR	*lseq, lstr, dice, bo*

3.4   Ensemble of Results of Basic Classifiers

Table 6. Four ensemble systems with different threshold

Ensemble system	Threshold	Description
System 1	1	Labelled "CTS" when at least one classifier decide sentence to be
System 2	2	Labelled "CTS" when at least two classifiers decide sentence to be
System 3	3	Labelled "CTS" when at least three classifiers decide sentence to be
System 4	4	Labelled "CTS" when at least four classifiers decide sentence to be

To get better performances, we integrate the decisions from basic classifiers as final results through voting. Firstly, we use threshold to define how we integrate four results from basic classifiers into one. Then we alter thresholds (1 to 4) here to distinguish different ensemble systems (system 1 to system 4, See Table 6). For example, threshold in system 1 is 1, so the candidate sentence will be identified as CTS when at least one classifier labels it to be.

4   Experiments and Results Analysis

4.1   Dataset and Preprocessing

Our experimental dataset is from the corpus released by CL-SciSumm Shared Task 2017[3]. The dataset contains 30 topics of training data and 10 topics of test data. In every topic there is one annotation file. Figure 3 shows one example in it. Every record refers to one citation relationship between two papers. It has the following items: Citance Number, Reference Article, Citing Article, Citation Offset, Citation Text, Reference Offset, and Reference Text. There exist two attributes affiliated to Citation Text and Reference Text—Sid and Ssid (Table 1). Apart from the annotation file, full text of one reference paper and its over 10 citing papers are given.

---

[3] https://github.com/WING-NUS/scisumm-corpus.

Citance Number: 2 | Reference Article: C02-1025.txt | Citing Article: C10-2167.txt | Citation Marker Offset: ['65'] | Citation Marker: Chieu et al., 2002 | Citation Offset: ['65'] | Citation Text: <S sid ="65" ssid = "25">In statistical methods, the most popular models are Hidden Markov Models (HMM) (Rabiner, 1989), Maximum Entropy Models (ME) (Chieu et al., 2002) and Conditional Random Fields (CRF) (Lafferty et al., 2001).</S> | Reference Offset: ['4'] | Reference Text: <S sid ="4" ssid = "4">In this paper, we show that the maximum entropy framework is able to make use of global information directly, and achieves performance that is comparable to the best previous machine learning-based NERs on MUC6 and MUC7 test data.</S> | Discourse Facet: Results_Citation | Annotator: Aakansha Gehlot |

Fig. 3. An example of annotation file

Before model training, we need to preprocess the text to reduce the noise. We drop the stop words in the light of stop word dictionary[4] and transform all the words into stem form by using Porter Stemmer[5]. After that, in text representing process, we adopt Word2Vec[6] and Doc2Vec[7] model in Gensim, python package of LDA[8] and TextRank[9] model and WordNet[10] ontology to represent documents. Our basic classifiers were implemented through Scikit-learn[11] python package.

4.2   Results Analysis

The current best performance is derived from the NUDT team in CL-SciSumm 2018 (Jaidka et al. 2018). In their experiment, they utilized a random forest model with multiple features. In addition, multiple random forest model with BM25 and VSM model are firstly combined. They then applied a voting strategy based on threshold to select the most related CTS. Finally, NUDT also explored the language model with word embeddings and integrated it into voting system to improve the performance (Wang et al. 2018). Their experimental results are displayed in Table 7.

Table 7. Performances of different running sets in NUDT team

Number of random forest models	Best threshold	Precision	Recall	F_1-score
50	34	0.118	0.179	0.1426
30	20	0.120	0.179	0.1436
25	17	0.122	0.179	**0.1453**
20	14	0.121	0.179	0.1451
15	9	0.1209	0.179	0.1444

---

[4] https://blog.csdn.net/shijiebei2009/article/details/39696523/.

[5] http://tartarus.org/~martin/PorterStemmer/.

[6] https://radimrehurek.com/gensim/models/word2vec.html.

[7] https://radimrehurek.com/gensim/models/doc2vec.html.

[8] https://pypi.org/project/lda/.

[9] https://pypi.org/project/pytextrank/.

[10] https://wordnet.princeton.edu/download.

[11] http://scikit-learn.org/.

Here, we present the results of experimental schemes before and after classifier-feature selection in Tables 8 and 9.

Table 8. Evaluations in different experimental schemes without classifier-feature selection

	SVM (linear)	SVM (rbf)	DT	LR	System 1	System 2	System 3	System 4
Precision	0.1200	0.0915	0.0835	0.0938	0.0756	0.1024	0.1295	0.1037
Recall	0.1977	0.2101	0.3376	0.2406	0.3142	0.2757	0.1831	0.2183
F_1-score	0.1409	0.1232	0.1351	0.1308	0.1213	0.1451	0.1463	0.1347

Table 9. Evaluations in different experimental schemes after classifier-feature selection

	SVM (linear)	SVM (rbf)	DT	LR	System 1	System 2	System 3	System 4
Precision	0.1266	0.1132	0.1035	0.1160	0.0811	0.1331	0.1427	0.1369
Recall	0.1989	0.2618	0.3398	0.2975	0.3598	0.3480	0.2856	0.2061
F_1-score	0.1420	0.1523	0.1451	0.1613	0.1322	0.1783	0.1734	0.1591

From Table 8, we can find that before classifier-feature selection, the highest F_1-score (0.1463) comes from system 3, which is neck and neck with 0.1453. Overall, the performances are decent even though no remarkable improvement has been achieved both in basic classifiers and in ensemble systems. This proves the effectiveness of feature selection via correlation analysis.

From Table 9, we can find that classifier-feature selection has a positive impact on the CTS identification, both in basic classifiers and voting systems. Especially, in system 2, the F_1-score has increased by about 3% compared with 0.1453.

The two tables also illustrate that there exist discrepancies among basic classifiers, even they have been proved best in our previous study and equipped with optimal feature sets and sampled training data respectively. This prove the rationality of our approach of integrating all results to obtain better performance. In Table 9, two of the ensemble systems prove to be better than basic classifiers in F_1-score. Especially, system 2 obtains 0.1783 while System 1 has the lowest F_1-score (0.1322) among these schemes. Its higher recall and extremely low precision may account for this. The constraint in system 1 is relatively loose, which permit more sentences to be identified as CTS. Consequently, it obtains higher recall at the cost of judging non-CTS as CTS wrong. In contrast, since system 4 appears to be too rigorous, its recall is too disappointing although it has decent precision.

In general, no matter in basic classifiers or in ensemble systems, our approaches have brought great improvements after classifier-feature selection. That achievements also result from the first step feature selection based on correlation analysis (See Table 8). The results support our methods' effectiveness in both two steps of feature selection.

5   Discussion

5.1   Correlation Analysis-Based Feature Selection

Among all the eighteen features, only six of them are relatively higher-correlated with whether one sentence is CTS or not. And interestingly, these features are about literal similarities, rather than semantic ones. Our suspicion is that the CTS identification work is more like finding connections between short texts. The literal or surface information may play a more important role in building connections. In addition, scientific terminology is of particular significance and rarely changed or adapted in citing process. It is a helpful indication when calculating similarity between sentences pair. In contrast, owing to the limited training corpus, it seems difficult to discover the relation between short sentences with semantic information like LDA, Doc2Vec.

5.2   Classifier-Feature Selection

By comparison of Tables 8 and 9, we can find that the second step of feature selection can improve the identification of CTS. Furthermore, according to Table 9, we can observe that classifiers appear different performances when fed with different feature sets. In particular, SVM (linear) is the pickiest classifier. It behaves well when combined with features like longest common string and bigram overlap. In contrast, DT proves relatively compatible with most features. Furthermore, jaccard similarity seems to be not so suitable for these basic classifiers, except DT.

5.3   Ensemble of Results of Basic Classifiers

We integrate the decisions of basic classifiers as final results via voting approaches. The final results reveal that ensemble systems can outweigh basic classifiers. And more importantly, besides voting systems, basic classifiers can also produce good results, better than 0.1453. We argue that this is mainly from the two steps of feature selection. As mentioned previously, all the six features are correlated with CTS and each basic classifier is equipped with best-performing feature set, which are the main cause of the improvements in our study. Another one reason is that the data size is not big enough for classifiers to learn hidden patterns in CTS identification. With the gradual enlarging of data volume, results on test data may not be so good. Anyway, the improvements in our experiments manifest the effectiveness of our proposed voting strategies by integrating different basic predictions.

6   Conclusion and Future Work

In this article, our goal is to improve the performance of CTS identification. We employ two steps of feature selection to choose effective features sets to obtain higher-correlated features and to assign each basic classifier with suitable feature set. Then, the decisions made by basic classifiers are integrated as final results via voting strategies.

Our results demonstrate that two steps of feature selection and voting strategies have potential effects in improving the performance in this task.

This work has few limitations. In this paper, we only extract a portion of negative samples randomly and have no idea whether they are representative or not. It is possible that the chosen samples only contain meaningless information. Besides, we treat all the word equally when calculating similarity. Some words include important information in scientific papers, and they should be emphasized. Similarly, it is irrational to treat all the classifiers equally. They are supposed to be given different weights based on some indicators. In the future, we aim to achieve these goals. (1) Adopting a new sampling method that can extract representative data. (2) Conducting syntactic parsing based on part of speech to calculate the similarity between sentences.

Acknowledgements. This work is supported by Major Projects of National Social Science Fund (No. 17ZDA291).

References

Abu-Jbara, A., Radev, D.: Coherent citation-based summarization of scientific papers. In: Proceedings of the 49th Annual Meeting of the Association for Computational Linguistics: Human Language Technologies-Volume 1, pp. 500–509. Association for Computational Linguistics (2011)

Chawla, N.V., Bowyer, K.W., Hall, L.O., Kegelmeyer, W.P.: SMOTE: synthetic minority over-sampling technique. J. Artif. Intell. Res. **16**, 321–357 (2002). https://doi.org/10.1613/jair.953

Cover, T., Hart, P.: Nearest neighbor pattern classification. IEEE Trans. Inf. Theory **13**(1), 21–27 (1967). https://doi.org/10.1109/TIT.1967.1053964

Cover, T.: Estimation by the nearest neighbor rule. IEEE Trans. Inf. Theory **14**(1), 50–55 (1968)

Elkiss, A., Shen, S., Fader, A., Erkan, G., States, D., Radev, D.: Blind men and elephants: what do citation summaries tell us about a research article? J. Am. Soc. Inf. Sci. Technol. **59**(1), 51–62 (2008). https://doi.org/10.1002/asi.20707

Gunetti, D., Picardi, C.: Keystroke analysis of free text. ACM Trans. Inf. Syst. Secur. **8**(3), 312–347 (2005)

He, H., Garcia, E.A.: Learning from imbalanced data. IEEE Trans. Knowl. Data Eng. **21**(9), 1263–1284 (2009)

Hong, X., Chen, S., Harris, C.J.: A kernel-based two-class classifier for imbalanced data sets. IEEE Trans. Neural Netw. **18**(1), 28–41 (2007). https://doi.org/10.1109/TNN.2006.882812

Jaidka, K., Yasunaga, M., Chandrasekaran, M.K., Radev, D., Kan, M.-Y.: The CL-SciSumm shared task 2018: results and key insights. In: CEUR Workshop Proceedings, Ann Arbor, MI, United States, vol. 2132, pp. 74–83 (2018)

Kusner, M., Sun, Y., Kolkin, N., Weinberger, K.: From word embeddings to document distances. In: International Conference on Machine Learning, pp. 957–966 (2015)

Li, L., Chi, J., Chen, M., Huang, Z., Zhu, Y., Fu, X.: CIST@CLSciSumm-18: methods for computational linguistics scientific citation linkage, facet classification and summarization. In: CEUR Workshop Proceedings, Ann Arbor, MI, United States, vol. 2132, pp. 84–95 (2018)

Li, L., Zhang, Y., Mao, L., Chi, J., Chen, M., Huang, Z.: CIST@ CLSciSumm-17: multiple features based citation linkage, classification and summarization. In: Proceedings of the 2nd Joint Workshop on Bibliometric-Enhanced Information Retrieval and Natural Language Processing for Digital Libraries (BIRNDL2017), Tokyo, Japan, August 2017

Ma, S., Xu, J., Wang, J., Zhang, C.: NJUST @ CLSciSumm-17. In: CEUR Workshop Proceedings, Tokyo, Japan, vol. 2002, pp. 16–25 (2017)

Ma, S., Xu, J., Zhang, C.: Automatic identification of cited text spans: a multi-classifier approach over imbalanced dataset. Scientometrics **116**(2), 1303–1330 (2018). https://doi.org/10.1007/s11192-018-2754-2

Nanba, H., Okumura, M.: Towards multi-paper summarization using reference information. IJCAI **99**, 926–931 (1999)

Pearson, K.: Notes on regression and inheritance in the case of two parents. Proc. R. Soc. Lond. **58**, 240–242 (1895)

Teufel, S., Siddharthan, A., Tidhar, D.: Automatic classification of citation function. In: Proceedings of the 2006 Conference on Empirical Methods in Natural Language Processing, pp. 103–110 (2006). http://www.aclweb.org/anthology/W/W06/W06-1613

Wang, P., Li, S., Wang, T., Zhou, H., Tang, J.: NUDT @ CLSciSumm-18. In: CEUR Workshop Proceedings, Ann Arbor, MI, United States, vol. 2132, pp. 102–113 (2018)

Yeager, K.: LibGuides: SPSS tutorials: pearson correlation. https://libguides.library.kent.edu/SPSS/PearsonCorr. Accessed 5 May 2019

Joint Learning for Aspect Category Detection and Sentiment Analysis in Chinese Reviews

Zihang Zeng[1], Junteng Ma[1], Minping Chen[1], and Xia Li[1,2(✉)]

[1] School of Information Science and Technology,
Guangdong University of Foreign Studies, Guangzhou, China
`raymondtseng0912@126.com`, `juntengma@126.com`,
`minpingchen@126.com`, `shelly_lx@126.com`
[2] Eastern Language Processing Center, Guangzhou, China

Abstract. Aspect based sentiment analysis (ABSA) is a valuable task, aiming to predict the sentiment polarities of the given aspects (terms or categories) in review texts. Aspect-category sentiment analysis is a sub-task of ABSA, which mainly focus on aspect category detection and aspect category polarity identifying. Most of the previous methods employ a pipeline strategy, regarding aspect category detection and category sentiment analysis as two separate tasks, which could not meet the needs of practical application. To address this limitation, we propose an end-to-end neural network model based on joint learning, which can detect aspect category and identify aspect category polarity simultaneously. We conduct several comparable experiments on a Chinese review dataset and the experimental results show that our proposed model is simpler and more effective than the baseline models.

Keywords: Fine-grained sentiment analysis · Joint learning ·
Aspect-category sentiment analysis

1 Introduction

Sentiment analysis [1, 2] provides valuable information for both providers and consumers, aiming to determine the sentiment polarities of user's reviews. Aspect based sentiment analysis (ABSA) is a fundamental task in sentiment analysis, which consists of two challenge sub-tasks, namely aspect-term sentiment analysis (ATSA) and aspect-category sentiment analysis (ACSA). ATSA is a challenge task that mainly focuses on the aspect terms, which appear in the texts. Two well-known sub-tasks in ATSA are aspect term extraction and aspect term polarity analysis. The task of aspect term extraction aims to identify the aspect terms present in the review sentence while the task of aspect term polarity analysis aims to determine whether the polarity of each aspect term is positive, negative or neutral by giving a set of aspect terms within a review sentence. On the other hand, ACSA is another challenge task in ABSA that considers more about the aspect categories which need to be predefined. Two popular sub-tasks are defined in ACSA. One is aspect category detection which aims to identify the aspect categories discussed in a given sentence from a set of predefined categories while the other is aspect category polarity analysis which aims to determine the

Q. Zhang et al. (Eds.): CCIR 2019, LNCS 11772, pp. 108–120, 2019.
https://doi.org/10.1007/978-3-030-31624-2_9

polarities (positive, negative or neutral) of every aspect category in the review sentence with a set of given aspect categories. An illustration of an example for the two tasks (ABSA and ACSA) is shown in Fig. 1.

This car is cost efficient, and the brakes are very sensitive, but the interior is not wide enough.

Aspect-term sentiment analysis(**ATSA**)	Aspect-category sentiment analysis (**ACSA**)
(aspect-term,sentiment)	(aspect-category, sentiment)
(cost, positive)	*(price, positive)*
(the brakes, positive)	*(safety, positive)*
(the interior, negative)	*(interior, negative)*

Fig. 1. Example illustrator of ATSA and ACSA. For a review "This car is cost efficient, and the brakes are very sensitive, but the interior is not wide enough". ATSA task is to detect the aspects and their sentiments, for example, (cost, positive) means that cost is one of the aspect of the review and its sentiment is positive. ACSA task, on the other hand, is to detect the categories of the review and their sentiments, for example, (price, positive) means that the review is belong to "price" category and its sentiment is positive.

Although the work of ATSA and ACSA have been very popular in sentiment analysis [3–6] in recent years, in this paper, we mainly focus on the task of ACSA. Aspect category detection and aspect category polarity analysis have been included in the subtask of SemEval evaluation from 2014 to 2016 [7–9], nevertheless, most of the previous work only focus one of the two tasks, which limits its practical applications. As we know, the aspect categories of a user review are unknown in practical application, which means that the determination of aspect category polarity should be done after finishing the process of aspect category detection, namely the pipeline based methods. However, the errors of the model will be transferred from upstream task to downstream task when using the pipeline strategy, leading to the wrong determination. To fill this gap, an end-to-end framework based on multi-label classification for joint learning aspect category detection and aspect category polarity analysis is proposed in this paper, which can be seen as a framework of multi-task learning. We use the multi-task based learning method to detect each category and its polarity, where the detection of each category is regarded as a sub-task. To make the joint learning for aspect category detection and aspect category polarity analysis, all sub-tasks share the same sentence encoder with independent classifier. From this strategy, we can jointly identify the sentence's categories and polarities simultaneously.

The main contributions of this work are as follows:

(1) We propose a joint learning model which has a share encoding layer and an independent layer to solve the ACSA task. The share encoding layer is used to learn the shared sentence representation for the recognition of different aspect categories and the independent layer is used to modify the shared sentence representation for different aspect categories. To the best of our knowledge, this is the first work using joint learning framework for the detection of aspect category and aspect category polarity simultaneously.

(2) We conduct several comparable experiments on a Chinese reviews dataset and we will show that our model outperforms the baseline models which using complex structure and large scale of parameter sizes, showing the simplicity and effectiveness of our model.

2   Related Work

According to the methods used in the task of aspect-category sentiment analysis (ACSA), previous work can be divided into feature-based methods [10–13] and neural-network-based methods [3, 14–17]. The formers usually use handcrafted features such as n-gram features and dictionary features, then a series of one-vs-all classifiers are trained for each aspect category.

Compared with feature-based methods, neural-network-based methods can avoid a lot of heavy feature extraction work and achieve better results. Wang et al. [14] use the LSTM model with attention mechanism for aspect category polarity, they achieve state-of-the-art on the SemEval 2014 dataset. He et al. [15] propose a deep neural network model with attention mechanism for aspect category detection. They use a model similar to auto-encoder to realize unsupervised aspect category detection, which can discover more meaningful and coherent aspects and achieve good performance. Khalil et al. [16] integrate a CNN model using pre-trained word vectors and SVM model based on bag-of-word features for aspect category detection. For aspect category polarity, in order to capture emotional information, they use external data and CNN model to fine-tune the word vectors, and use them as input to train three CNN models which fuse the aspect category features. The final aspect category polarity results are obtained by voting on three models. Xue et al. [3] propose a simple but effective network based on CNN and gate mechanism. Its core idea is to use ReLU and TanH gate mechanisms to select sentiment features and aspect category features respectively on the basis of CNN. Then, the results of the two gate mechanisms are performed element-wise product and max pooling to get the final representation. Tay et al. [17] propose to integrate the information of aspect category into the neural network by modeling the relationship between words and aspect categories. Unlike many models which simply use concatenation to model the similarity between words and aspect categories, the authors use circular convolution and circular correlation to calculate the similarity between words and aspect categories.

The above previous studies either focus on aspect category detection or aspect category polarity analysis, to the best of our knowledge, no study is found to jointly implements the two tasks. Another similar task is aspect-term sentiment analysis (ATSA) which contains two sub-tasks: aspect term extraction and aspect term polarity analysis. Most of the previous work also only focus on one of the sub-tasks, the work of Li et al. [18] is one of the exception. The authors proposed a unified sequence labeling model to complete ATSA task in an end-to-end fashion. However, the ACSA task can not be solved though sequence labeling, as the aspect categories may not appear in the sentences and the sentence (review) may belong to several categories.

To this end, we propose an end-to-end framework based on multi-label classification for joint learning aspect category detection and aspect category polarity analysis. We use the multitask-based learning method to detect each category and its polarity, where the detection of each category is regarded as a sub-task. We will show that our model performs well compared with the baseline models, and to the best of our knowledge, this is the first work using joint learning framework for the detection of aspect category and aspect category polarity simultaneously.

3   Our Model

3.1   Architecture of Our Model

In order to implement the task of aspect category detection and aspect category sentiment analysis in an end-to-end fashion, a joint learning framework is proposed in this paper to detect aspect categories of the review and its sentiment simultaneously. Firstly, CNN [19, 20] is used to learn the character-level representation of each word, which is concatenated with word embedding, producing a new vector as word-level representation of the model. After that the vector is input into a highway network, finally, another CNN is used to learn sentence representation on the basis of word-level representation. By combining average pooling with max pooling, the final sentence representation is obtained and input into different classifiers for joint learning. The whole architecture of our proposed model is shown in Fig. 2. The sentence encoding part, i.e., the part surrounded by dotted lines, are parameter-sharing layers, while each classifier is parameter-exclusive. The share encoding layer is used to learn the shared sentence representation for the recognition of different aspect categories and the independent layer is used for modify the shared sentence representation for different aspect categories.

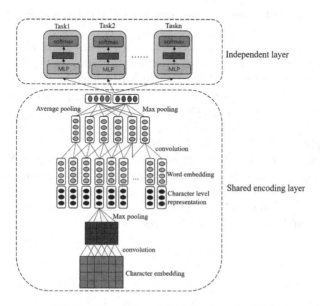

Fig. 2. The whole architecture of our model.

3.2   Character-Level Representation and Word-Level Representation

Given a review sentence S = {w_1, w_2, ..., w_n}, where n is the number of words in the sentence. First of all, each word must be expressed as a dense vector. It is found that more than 24% of the words in the dataset are out-of-vocabulary (OOV). Some of these words are emotional words, which are important for the task. One way to deal with these out-of-vocabulary words is to assign them random vectors. However, this method will result in many rich semantic information of these OOV words cannot be captured. Therefore, we use CNN to learn the character-level representation to address this problem. The details of getting character-level and word-level representation are shown in Fig. 3.

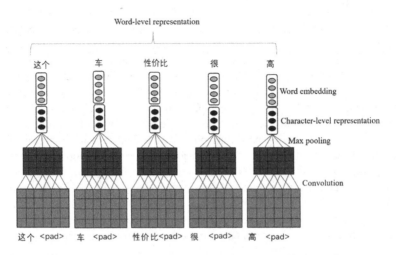

Fig. 3. Character-level and word-level representation encoding

Specifically, each word w_i is divided into character sequences and a preliminary vector is given to each character through random initialization, getting w_i = {c_1, c_2, ..., c_m}, where m is the longest word length, which is defined as 10 in this paper. For example, an work example sentence S={这个, 车, 性价比, 很, 高}, the word "这个" is divided into character sequences {"这", "个"}, the word {"性", "价", "比"} is divided into character sequences. If the length of the sequences is no longer than 10, then the sequences is padded with zero vector, as shown in Fig. 3.

Then the character vector matrix of each word is convoluted by CNN. The convolution layer slides in the input sequence using several convolution kernels with a fixed window size. The operation of convolution is shown in Eq. (1),where k is the window size of convolution and f is a non-linear activation function. In this paper, tanh is employed, W and b are weights and bias respectively.

$$z_i = f(W \cdot c_i : c_{i+k} + b) \tag{1}$$

On top of the convolution layer, a max pooling layer is adopted, and the feature dimension can be reduced. Finally, the character-level representation of each word can be obtained after pooling. The character vectors of each word will be updated during training, and eventually the semantic vectors of each word can be learned. As shown in Fig. 3, the pre-trained word vectors of each word and their character-level representation are concatenated to get the final word-level representation.

3.3 Highway Network and Sentence-Level Representation

Inspired by the gate mechanism in LSTM, Srivastava et al. [21] proposed highway network, which aims to solve the problem that the gradient of deep neural network disappears with the depth increasing, making the network difficult to train. As what it is called, highway network allows information to pass through all layers of deep neural network without hindrance, which effectively alleviates the gradient problem. Because the experimental dataset in this paper is relatively small, in order to facilitate the training of the network, after concatenating word embedding and character-level representation, obtaining a new matrix, we input it into a highway network structure, which is shown in Eqs. (2–4). Where W_1 and W_2 are weights, b_1 and b_2 are biases, and * denotes the element-wise product.

$$x_{dense} = \tanh(W_1 x + b_1) \tag{2}$$

$$x_{gate} = sigmoid(W_2 x + b_2) \tag{3}$$

$$x_{highway} = x_{dense} * x_{gate} + (1 - x_{gate}) * x \tag{4}$$

On top of the highway block, we use another CNN to learn sentence representation. CNN can learn the n-gram features of the input text. For the task of this paper, different segments of each review, namely n-grams, usually discuss different aspect categories, and the sentiment words are often close to discussed aspect categories, thus CNN is more suitable for the task of this paper. After CNN layer, the max pooling and average pooling are performed at the same time and the results of the two pooling are concatenated together to get the final sentence-level representation S.

3.4 Joint Learning

After obtaining the sentence representation, in order to recognize the aspect categories and the corresponding sentiment in an end-to-end manner, the sentence-level representation is input into different classifiers for classification. Each classifier represents a aspect category and has different classes, indicating its sentiment. In each classifier, in order to obtain the features related to the aspect category, the sentence representation is input into a fully-connected layer, then another fully-connected layer with softmax activation function is used to predict the final class, as shown in Eqs. (5–6). Where S is the shared sentence representation and S^* is the new representation after the fully-connected layer, $W_i^s, W_i^{S^*}$ and $b_i^s, b_i^{S^*}$ are the parameters, $q_i(x)$ is the predicted probability distribution of sample x in the ith task.

$$S^* = \left(W_i^s S + b_i^s\right) \tag{5}$$

$$q_i(x) = softmax\left(W_i^{S^*} S^* + b_i^{S^*}\right) \tag{6}$$

In this paper, we use parameter hard-sharing mechanism for joint learning. Parameter hard-sharing mechanism is one of the most common methods in multi-task learning. It means that all tasks in the network share the same parameters for encoding the text and only retain their respective output layers. Hard-sharing mechanism can reduce the risk of over-fitting which is suit for our model with not very large dataset for trainning. For each task, cross-entropy loss is used, as shown in Eq. (7):

$$\text{Loss}_i = -\sum\nolimits_{j=1}^{N} p_i(x)\log(q_i(x)) \tag{7}$$

Where Loss_i denotes the loss function of the ith task, $p_i(x)$ is the ground truth of sample x in the ith task, and $q_i(x)$ is the predicted probability distribution of sample x in the ith task. As the reviews on different aspect categories distribute differently in the dataset and the number of them varies greatly, we argue that the weights of different tasks in the model training should be different. So we use the weighted sum of the losses of different tasks as the final loss. At the beginning, the weights of each task are all 1.0, and they will be updated in the process of training. The final loss function is shown in Eq. (8), where n is the number of the sub-tasks.

$$\text{Loss} = \sum\nolimits_{i=1}^{n} a_i Loss_i \tag{8}$$

4   Experiment Results and Analysis

4.1   Dataset

We use the data from the 2018 CCF Big Data and Computational Intelligence Competition (BDCI 2018)[1] as our experiment dataset. Because the organizer only released the labels of the training set, we divide the original training set into a new training set, development set and test set. The specific information of our dataset is shown in Table 1. This dataset contains reviews about automobile. There are 10 predefined aspect categories in the dataset: *power, price, interior, configuration, safety, appearance, control, fuel consumption, space* and *comfort*. And there are three sentiment categories for each aspect category which are *positive, neutral* and *negative*. The task of this paper is to identify the aspect categories and their sentiments discussed in each review. A review may cover multiple aspect categories (Table 1).

---

[1] https://www.datafountain.cn/competitions/310/details.

Table 1. The statistics information of our dataset in the experiment.

	Training set	Development set	Test set
The number of samples	6290	1000	1000

4.2 Experiment Setup

In terms of preprocessing, we use Jieba[2] to tokenize the sentences, and replace all numbers in sentences with string "num". This paper uses the open source 300-dimensional Chinese word embedding trained on Wikipedia corpus as pre-trained word representation[3] and it is fine-tuned during training. For CNN of learning character-level representation, the window size is set to 2 and the number of convolution kernels is 20. For CNN learning sentence representation, we set its window size to 1 and the number of convolution kernels to 100. The hidden size of fully-connected layer is 100.

In order to reduce the risk of over-fitting, several dropout layers are added in the network, the rate of which is 0.2. Besides, L2 regularization is added to the loss function, and the ratio is 0.001. The initial learning rate is 0.0003 and the batch size is 32. The model has been trained for 50 epochs. The model which has best performance on development set during 50 epochs is tested on the test set. The hyper-parameters of the model are shown in Table 2.

Table 2. The hyper-parameters of the model in this paper.

Hyperparameter	Value
Char CNN window	2
Char CNN filters	20
Sentence CNN window	1
Sentence CNN filters	100
Dropout	0.2
Fully connected layer hidden	100
L2	0.001
Learning rate	0.0003
Batch size	32
Epoch	50

4.3 Evaluation Index

Following the official competition BDCI 2018, we use $F1$ score as our evaluation index. The calculation of $F1$ score is as follows: for a review, if it is correctly identified a aspect category and its corresponding sentiment, the number of Tp will plus 1, and if one of them is misidentified, the number of Fp will plus 1. If a review is identified with

---

[2] https://github.com/fxsjy/jieba.

[3] https://fasttext.cc/docs/en/pretrained-vectors.html.

less "aspect category + sentiment" than the actual number it has, the missing amount is added to *Fn*. If a review is identified as having more "aspect category + sentiment" than it actually contains, the amount exceeded is added to *Fp*.

After obtaining the values of *Tp*, *Fp* and *Fn*, the accuracy *P*, recall *R* and the final F1 score can be calculated, as shown in Eqs. (9).

$$P = \frac{T_p}{T_p + F_p}, R = \frac{T_p}{T_p + F_n}, F1 = \frac{2PR}{P + R} \tag{9}$$

4.4   Baseline Models

In our experiment, several models are used as our baselines to compare with our model which is named Char-CNN-CNN. We use SVM-based method and different neural network encoding structure based models as the baselines, they are: TFIDF-SVM, Char-CNN-LSTM, Char-CNN-SRU, Char-LSTM-LSTM, Char-CNN-Transformer, CNN-W/O-Char and Embed-Char-Avg+Max model. These baseline models are as follows:

TFIDF-SVM. In this model, one SVM classifier is trained for each aspect category using TFIDF features to represent the sentences.

Char-CNN-LSTM. The difference between Char-CNN-CNN and this model is that the former uses CNN to learn sentence representation while the latter uses LSTM to learn sentence representation.

Char-CNN-SRU. SRU (Simple Recurrent Unit) is a recurrent unit proposed in document [22] that can calculate parallel as fast as CNN. The difference between Char-CNN-SRU model and Char-CNN-LSTM is that their sentence encoders are SRU and LSTM respectively.

Char-LSTM-LSTM. This method uses LSTM to learn character level representation, and other settings are the same as Char-CNN-LSTM model.

Char-CNN-Transformer. This method uses Transformer [23] to encode sentences on the basis of word embedding and character level representation. Other settings are the same as Char-CNN-CNN.

CNN-W/O-Char. This method directly uses CNN to encode sentences without character level representation learning.

Embed-Char-Avg+Max. The method first learns the character level representation of each word through CNN, which is concatenated with the word embedding. Then, average pooling and max pooling are directly performed respectively, and the two result vectors are concatenated to get the final sentence representation.

4.5   Experimental Results and Analysis

4.5.1   Experimental Results of Different Models on the Dataset

The experimental results of different models on the development set and test set are shown in Table 3. As shown in Table 3, we can see that our model achieves higher F1 score than all the other models on both development set and test set. Our model outperforms TFIDF-SVM by 6.08% and 7.09% on development set and test set respectively. As we can see, all the neural-network-based methods outperform TFIDF-SVM method which indicates that the representation of sentence encoding with neural network can learn some of high and non-linear features of the sentence compared with TFIDF features encoding. For example, Embed-Char-Avg+Max is the simplest model among the neural-network-based models, but it also significantly outperforms the TFIDF-SVM method.

Table 3. Experimental results of different models on development set and test set.

Model	Development set	Test set
TFIDF-SVM	0.5880	0.5733
Embed-Char-Avg+Max	0.6193	0.6109
Char-CNN-LSTM	0.6374	0.6381
Char-CNN-SRU	0.6400	0.6272
Char-LSTM-LSTM	0.6437	0.6363
Char- CNN-Transformer	0.6439	0.6378
CNN-W/O-Char	0.6312	0.6298
Char-CNN-CNN(Ours)	**0.6488**	**0.6442**

Compared with Char-CNN-LSTM and Char-CNN-SRU, our model Char-CNN-CNN improves the F1 score by 0.61% and 1.7% on test set respectively. One of the reasons may be that LSTM and SRU mainly capture the whole semantic information of sentences, while CNN pays more attention to local features. For joint learning, the information that each sub-task should pay attention to is different. For example, in sentence "This car has good configuration and is cheap!", when identify the aspect category of "configuration", we should focus on the fragment of "good configuration", while when identify the aspect category of "price", we should pay attention to the fragment of "is cheap". Therefore, CNN which can learn the n-gram features in a sentence is more effective than LSTM and SRU for this task.

4.5.2   Validity of Character Level Representation

In order to verify the validity of character level representation for this task, we take CNN-W/O-Char method which does not learn character level representation as a comparative experiment. The results show that Char-CNN-CNN method which learns character level representation outperforms CNN-W/O-Char method by 1.72% on development set and 1.76% on test set, indicating that the character level representation is helpful when the number of OOV words is relative large.

In addition, we also tries to use LSTM to learn character level representation, i.e. Char-LSTM-LSTM model. However, it does not outperform Char-CNN-CNN method. One of the reasons may be that the number of parameters of LSTM is more than that of CNN, and the experimental dataset used in this paper is rather small, which makes it easier to become over-fitting.

4.5.3   Word Embedding Impact Analysis

In order to compare the quality of different pre-trained Chinese word embedding, we compare the performance of three kinds of Chinese pre-trained word embedding using Char-CNN-CNN method. The proportion of OOV words of three kinds of word embeddings and the experimental results are shown in Table 4.

Table 4. Experimental results of three kinds word embedding.

	OOV proportion	Development set	Test set
Word_embedding_Facebook	24.1%	**0.6488**	**0.6442**
Word_embedding_Baidu [24] [a]	28.8%	0.6333	0.6328
Word_embedding_Merge [24][a]	27.0%	0.6346	0.6343

[a]https://github.com/Embedding/Chinese-Word-Vectors

As we can see from Table 4, the F1 score of Char-CNN-CNN method using Facebook Chinese word embedding is 1.42% and 0.99% higher than using Word_embedding_Merge on development set and test set respectively, and 1.55% and 1.14% higher than using Word_embedding_Baidu on development set and test set respectively. As the basic input of deep learning model, the quality of word embedding affects the performance of downstream NLP tasks. The smaller the proportion of OOV words, the better the performance can be achieved, as shown in Table 4.

5   Conclusion

To implement aspect category detection and aspect category polarity two tasks in an end-to-end manner, an end-to-end neural network framework based on joint learning is proposed in this paper. Firstly, we use CNN structure to learn character-level representation and concatenate the character-level representation of each word with the pre-trained word embedding as final word-level representation. Then a highway network is used to modify the input embedding in order to make them better suit for the training of the network. Finally, another CNN structure is used to learn sentence representation on the basis of word-level representation, and the average pooling and max pooling are perform together to get the final sentence representation, which is input into the different classifiers representing different aspect categories. Several comparative experimental results show that the proposed model is simple and effective, and can be applied to simultaneous analysis and prediction for the task of aspect-category sentiment analysis.

In our future work, we believe that there are some relationship between the aspect categories and the emotional words. The relationship between them can be captured by using the features of syntax tree and lexical, which can be fused with the neural network to further improve the performance of the model.

Acknowledgments. This work is supported by National Nature Science Foundation of China (61976062) and the Science and Technology Program of Guangzhou, China (201904010303).

References

1. Pang, B., Lee, L.: Opinion mining and sentiment analysis. Found. Trends® Inf. Retrieval **2** (1–2), 1–135 (2008)
2. Liu, B.: Sentiment analysis and opinion mining. Synth. Lect. Hum. Lang. Technol. **5**(1), 1–167 (2012)
3. Xue, W, Li, T.: Aspect based sentiment analysis with gated convolutional networks. In: Proceedings of ACL, pp. 2514–2523 (2018)
4. Wang, B., Lu, W.: Learning latent opinions for aspect-level sentiment classification. In: Proceedings of AAAI, pp. 5537–5544 (2018)
5. Fan, F., Feng, Y., Zhao, D.: Multi-grained attention network for aspect-level sentiment classification. In: Proceedings of EMNLPg, pp. 3433–3442 (2018)
6. Ma, Y., Peng, H., Cambria, E.: Targeted aspect-based sentiment analysis via embedding commonsense knowledge into an attentive LSTM. In: Proceedings of AAAI, pp. 5876–5883 (2018)
7. Pontiki, M., Galanis, D., Papageorgiou, H., Manandhar, S., Androutsopoulos, I., Manandhar, S.: Semeval-2014 task 5: aspect based sentiment analysis. In: Proceedings of SemEval-2014, pp. 19–30 (2014)
8. Pontiki, M., Galanis, D., Papageorgiou, H., Manandhar, S., Androutsopoulos, I.: Semeval-2015 task 12: aspect based sentiment analysis. Proc. SemEval **2015**, 486–495 (2015)
9. Pontiki M, Galanis D, Papageorgiou H, et al.: Semeval-2016 task 5: aspect based sentiment analysis. In: Proceedings SemEval-2016, pp, 19–30 (2016)
10. Lakkaraju, H, Bhattacharyya, C, Bhattacharya, I, Merugu, S.: Exploiting coherence for the simultaneous discovery of latent facets and associated sentiments. In: Proceedings of SDM, pp. 498–509 (2011)
11. Zhuang, L., Jing, F., Zhu, X.Y.: Movie review mining and summarization. In: Proceedings of CIKM, pp. 43–50 (2006)
12. Kiritchenko, S., Zhu, X., Cherry, C., Mohammad, S.: NRC-Canada-2014: detecting aspects and sentiment in customer reviews. Proc. SemEval **2014**, 437–442 (2014)
13. Xenos, D., Theodorakakos, P., Pavlopoulos, J., Malakasiotis, P., Androutsopoulos, I.: Auebabsa at semeval-2016 task 5: ensembles of classifiers and embeddings for aspect based sentiment analysis. In: Proceedings of SemEval-2016. pp. 312–317 (2016)
14. Wang, Y., Huang, M., Zhao, L.: Attention-based LSTM for aspect-level sentiment classification. In: Proceedings of EMNLP, pp. 606–615 (2016)
15. He, R., Lee, W.S., Ng, H.T., Dahlmeier, D.: An unsupervised neural attention model for aspect extraction. In: Proceedings of ACL, pp. 388–397 (2017)
16. Khalil, T., El-Beltagy, S.R.: Niletmrg at semeval-2016 task 5: deep convolutional neural networks for aspect category and sentiment extraction. In: Proceedings of SEMEVAL-2016, pp. 271–276 (2016)

17. Tay, Y., Tuan, L.A., Hui, S.C.: Learning to attend via word-aspect associative fusion for aspect-based sentiment analysis. In: Proceedings of AAAI, pp. 5956–5963 (2018)
18. MLA Li, X., Lam, W.: A unified model for opinion target extraction and target sentiment prediction. In: Proceedings of AAAI, pp. 6714–6721 (2018)
19. Kim, Y.: Convolutional neural networks for sentence classification. CoRR, abs/1408.5882 (2014). https://arxiv.org/abs/1408.5882
20. Kalchbrenner, N., Grefenstette, E., Blunsom, P.: A convolutional neural network for modelling sentences. In: Proceedings of ACL, pp. 655–665 (2014)
21. Srivastava, R.K., Greff, K., Schmidhuber, J.: Training very deep networks. In: Proceedings of NIPS, pp. 2377–2385 (2015)
22. Lei, T., Zhang, Y., Wang, S.I., Dai, H., Artz, Y.: Simple recurrent units for highly parallelizable recurrence. In: Proceedings of EMNLP, pp. 4470–4481 (2018)
23. Vaswani, A., et al.: Attention is all you need. In: Proceedings of NIPS, pp. 5998–6008 (2017)
24. Li, S., Zhao, Z., Hu, R., Li, W., Liu, T., Du, X.: Analogical reasoning on chinese morphological and semantic relations. In: Proceedings of ACL, pp. 138–143 (2018)

Selecting Paragraphs to Answer Questions for Multi-passage Machine Reading Comprehension

Dengwen Lin, Jintao Tang[✉], Kunyuan Pang, Shasha Li, and Ting Wang

College of Computer, National University of Defense Technology,
Changsha 410072, China
{lindengwen17,tangjintao,pangkunyuan,lishasha,tingwang}@nudt.edu.cn

Abstract. This paper addresses the problem of question answering style multi-passage Machine Reading Comprehension (MRC) and suggests that paragraph-level segments are suitable to answer questions in real Web query scenario. We propose to combine a learning to rank framework with an attention-based neural network to select the best-matching paragraph for a specific question. To estimate the quality of a paragraph with respect to a given query, its largest ROUGE-L score compared against the annotated answers is used as the ranking indicator. Experimental results on a real-world dataset demonstrate that the proposed method obtains a significant improvement compared to the state-of-the-art baselines.

Keywords: Learning to rank ·
Machine reading comprehension · Question answering

1 Introduction

Machine reading comprehension (MRC) requires a computer to answer questions after reading and understanding text [2]. In recent years, MRC has evolved from the task defined by SQuAD [16] whose answer is extracted from a single passage to a more complex question answering (QA) task such as MS MARCO [14] and DuReader [7] in which questions are sampled from user logs of search engine and answers should be retrieved from several web documents. However, the majority of studies in multi-passage MRC mostly follow the extraction-based method used to address single-passage MRC problem [18,21,24], which usually formulates MRC task as predicting the start and end positions of the answer span in a single passage. This method is suitable for SQuAD whose answers are usually entities and relatively short, 3.1 words on average [21]. But in real Web query scenario, there are diverse questions and most of them cannot be

This work was supported in part by the National Key Research and Development Program of China (2018YFB1004502) and in part by the National Natural Science Foundation of China (61532001).

answered by simple entities [25]. For example, DuReader classifies questions into three types including Entity, Description and YesNo. Therein, Description questions concern reasons, approaches, attributes of objects and so on and YesNo questions need to provide not only affirmative or negative opinions but also supportive evidences for these opinions. Therefore, longer answers are usually expected for multi-passage MRC and statistics in [7] show that the average length of answers in DuReader is 69.6 words, which is about 22 times longer than those in SQuAD. Longer answers are harder to predict [21] and the wrong prediction of start or end positions will result in loss of information and confuse users even if the prediction is located accurately. In addition, most previous works apply the extractive method in multi-passage MRC by concatenating all selected paragraphs [7,21] without considering that the quality of paragraphs is uneven and most of them make no contribution to the answer. There are even some contradictory paragraphs may mislead the model [24].

In community QA, researchers have pinpointed this problem and proposed some methods to select a suitable document [26] or several sentences [25] as the answer for a given question. However, for MRC, the whole document is too long and noisy for users to find the accurate answer while sentences are too short to contain enough information. Considering that a paragraph is a self-contained unit and contains isolate information, we propose a paragraph selecting model which combines a learning to rank framework with an attention-based neural network to select the best-matching paragraph from all paired paragraphs for a given question. At first, we adopt Bi-directional Long Short-Term Memory (BiLSTM) and Bi-Directional Attention Flow (BiDAF) mechanism [18] to model the semantic relation between the question and each paragraph. Then we use attention pooling mechanism to translate each paragraph into a fixed length vector and adopt two fully connected layers to grade each paragraph. In order to evaluate the quality of a paragraph, we adopt the largest ROUGE-L score compared against the annotated answers as its real score. After that, we use a listwise approach [1] to predict the ranking list on paragraphs. Finally, the top-1 paragraph is selected as the answer.

The main contributions of this paper can be summarized as follows: (1) We apply a listwise approach to learning to rank to solve multi-passage MRC task without manually defined features. (2) To the best of our knowledge, our paragraph selecting framework is the first approach that adopts ROUGE-L as the ranking indicator of paragraph quality which can measure the match degree of each paragraph to the annotated answers and is widely used for evaluating the quality of language generation. (3) The experimental results on a real-world dataset show that our paragraph selecting framework outperforms several strong baselines.

2 Related Work

2.1 Datasets

Openly available benchmark datasets play an important role in the progress of QA research. These datasets allow the community to rapidly develop new methods and get comparable performance to verify whether a method is effective. In terms of the task definition, QA datasets can be classified into three main categories including cloze-style, multiple-choice and question answering-based MRC [7]. Therein, Cloze-style datasets like CNN/Daily Mail [8] and the Children's Book Test (CBT) [9] define the QA task as predicting the missing word in a given context while multiple-choice datasets like RACE [12] and MCTest [17] provide each question with four candidate answers and require the model to select the single correct answer. For question answering-based MRC, there are single-passage MRC and multi-passage MRC according to whether questions are provided with multiple evidence passages. One of the most representative single-passage MRC datasets is SQuAD while MS MARCO and DuReader are multi-passage MRC datasets. The questions of these two datasets are sampled from search engine's query logs. Different from SQuAD whose answers are factoid, short snippets, MS MARCO and DuReader have more diverse types of questions and pay more attention on non-factoid questions which have longer and more complicated answers. WikiPassageQA introduced in [4] is similar to MS MARCO and DuReader in terms of non-factoid and multi-passage but it is defined to address the task of answer passage retrieval.

2.2 Neural Network Models for Machine Reading Comprehension

With the release of large-scale benchmark datasets, neural networks have gained promising results on MRC task. Hermann et al. [8] first incorporated attention mechanism into MRC models and proposed two models called Attentive and Impatient Readers respectively. Wang and Jiang [21] combined match-LSTM with Pointer Network [20] to predict the boundary of the answer. Inspired by [21], Wang et al. [23] proposed a gated self-matching network, which added an additional gate to an attention-based RNN model and introduced a self-matching mechanism. Seo et al. [18] proposed a co-attention mechanism called BiDAF to match the question and passage mutually. Besides, reinforcement learning was also applied in MRC filed, for example, the Reinforced Mnemonic Reader proposed in [10].

Most above models were trained and evaluated on single passage MRC datasets and can be applied in the multi-passage MRC task usually by concatenating all passages. But there are more and more studies start to construct specific architectures for multi-passage MRC and open domain QA. For example, Chen et al. [3] extended SQuAD to an open domain QA dataset and proposed a method which combined an Information Retrieval (IR) component and a Reading Comprehension (RC) model. Because the paragraphs retrieved from a large-scale corpus accompanied with noise, Lin et al. [13] proposed to employ a paragraph selector to filter out noisy paragraphs and a paragraph reader to extract the correct answer. For some datasets like MS MARCO, there are retrieved passages in the datasets and Tan et al. [19] proposed an extraction-then-synthesis framework which first extracted evidence snippets from existing passages and then synthesized the final prediction. Unlike dividing the pipeline into two stages, Wang et al. [22] jointly trained a deep learning-based Ranker along with an answer-extraction Reader model. Wang et al. [24] developed a framework consisting of answer boundary prediction, answer content modeling and answer verification. The three modules were trained together as multi-task learning. Das et al. [5] introduced a new framework in which the retriever and the reader iteratively interacted with each other. Most above models mainly focus on factoid questions. The key differences between our work and their works are that we mainly aim at non-factoid questions which have more complicated and longer answers and our goal is to select the best-matching paragraphs. Moreover, we combine a listwise approach to learning to rank with an attention-based model without manually defined features to solve multi-passage MRC task.

3   The Proposed Approach

In this section, we first formulate the task of selecting paragraphs for multi-passage MRC and then introduce the proposed paragraph selecting framework in detail.

3.1   Task Definition

The paragraph selecting task discussed in this paper is formulated as follows. Given a question $\mathbf{Q} = \{w_1^Q, w_2^Q, \ldots, w_N^Q\}$ with N words and a set of candidate paragraphs $\mathbf{P} = \{\mathbf{P}_1, \mathbf{P}_2, \ldots, \mathbf{P}_k\}$, in which each candidate paragraph $\mathbf{P}_i = \{w_1^{P_i}, w_2^{P_i}, \ldots, w_M^{P_i}\}$ has the same length M after padding or truncating, output the score distribution over candidate paragraphs. Finally, we will rank all paragraphs in descending order of the predicted scores and select the top-1 paragraph to answer the question directly.

3.2   Question and Paragraph Modeling

The overall structure of our paragraph selecting framework is illustrated in Fig. 1. Unlike previous works, an input instance of our model is a question and a set of candidate paragraphs. For each instance, we first translate each word into its d-dimensional pre-trained word embedding. And then we apply BiLSTM on top of the embeddings to encode the question and each paragraph separately.

$$\mathbf{u}_t^Q = \text{BiLSTM}(\mathbf{u}_{t-1}^Q, \mathbf{e}_t^Q) \tag{1}$$

$$\mathbf{u}_t^{P_i} = \text{BiLSTM}(\mathbf{u}_{t-1}^{P_i}, \mathbf{e}_t^{P_i}) \tag{2}$$

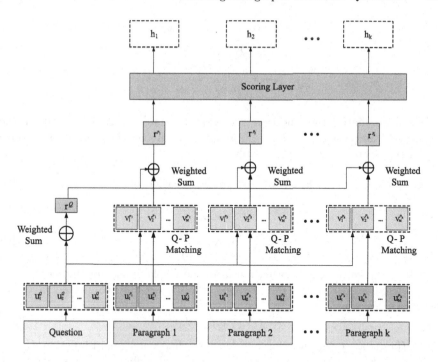

Fig. 1. Overview of our paragraph selecting framework

where $\mathbf{e}_t^Q$ and $\mathbf{e}_t^{P_i}$ are word embeddings. $\mathbf{u}_t^Q$ and $\mathbf{u}_t^{P_i}$ are the contextual embeddings which capture the interaction among words in the question and the i-th paragraph respectively.

After encoding layer, we use BiDAF [18] mechanism to match the question with each paragraph in word-level so that we can link and fuse information from both the context and the question words. Firstly, we compute the similarity matrix $\mathbf{S} \in \mathbf{R}^{N \times M}$. The similarity between the t-th word in the question and the j-th word in the i-th paragraph is computed as:

$$\mathbf{S}_{tj}^{P_i} = \mathbf{u}_t^Q \cdot \mathbf{u}_j^{P_i} \tag{3}$$

Then, we compute the paragraph-to-question and question-to-paragraph attentions following [18] to obtain a question-aware paragraph representation $\{\mathbf{g}_t^{P_i}\}$ for each paragraph $\mathbf{P}_i$. After that, we use another BiLSTM to produce a new representation $\{\mathbf{v}_t^{P_i}\}$ for each paragraph in order to aggregate matching information from the whole paragraph conditioned on the given query.

$$\mathbf{v}_t^{P_i} = \mathrm{BiLSTM}(\mathbf{v}_{t-1}^{P_i}, \mathbf{g}_t^{P_i}) \tag{4}$$

Next, we translate the word-level representation into paragraph-level representation [19] for each paragraph. We first use the attention pooling mechanism to translate a question into a fix-length vector based on a parameter $\mathbf{v}_r^Q$.

$$\mathbf{s}_t^Q = \mathbf{v}^T \tanh(\mathbf{w}_u^Q \mathbf{u}_t^Q + \mathbf{w}_v^Q \mathbf{v}_r^Q) \tag{5}$$

$$\mathbf{a}_t = \exp(\mathbf{s}_t^Q) / \sum\nolimits_{j=1}^{N} \exp(\mathbf{s}_j^Q) \tag{6}$$

$$\mathbf{r}^Q = \sum\nolimits_{t=1}^{N} \mathbf{a}_t \mathbf{u}_t^Q \tag{7}$$

Then we match the question representation $\mathbf{r}^Q$ with each word in the question-aware paragraph vector obtained from the previous layer to produce a fixed size vector for each paragraph.

$$\mathbf{s}_t^{P_i} = \mathbf{v}^T \tanh(\mathbf{w}_v^P \mathbf{v}_t^{P_i} + \mathbf{w}_r^Q \mathbf{r}^Q) \tag{8}$$

$$\mathbf{a}_t^{P_i} = \exp(\mathbf{s}_t^{P_i}) / \sum\nolimits_{j=1}^{M} \exp(\mathbf{s}_j^{P_i}) \tag{9}$$

$$\mathbf{r}^{P_i} = \sum\nolimits_{t=1}^{M} \mathbf{a}_t^{P_i} \mathbf{v}_t^{P_i} \tag{10}$$

After aggregating the information from the whole paragraph and converting it to a fixed length vector $\mathbf{r}^{P_i}$, we feed it into two fully connected layers to compute a score as:

$$h_i = f(\mathbf{v}_g^T(\tanh(\mathbf{W}_g \mathbf{r}^{P_i}))) \tag{11}$$

where $f(x)$ is a scoring function and here we choose a sigmoid function $f(x) = 1/(1+e^{-x})$. Finally, the model can output a score distribution over all candidate paragraphs for a specific question.

3.3   Objective Function

Our goal is to select the best-matching paragraph for a given question. To evaluate the match degree of a paragraph for a specific question, we calculate the largest ROUGE-L score of a paragraph compared against the annotated answers because ROUGE-L can measure the proximity of each paragraph to the answers and is widely used for evaluating the quality of language generation. Besides, lists of paragraphs are used as input instances in our task and we want to rank all paragraphs according to their ROUGE-L scores and then select the top one, therefore, we apply the listwise lose function introduced in [1] which represents the distance between the real ranking list according to ROUGE-L scores and the ranking list returned by our model for learning. We use top one probability and Cross Entropy to construct our objective function as:

$$\mathcal{L} = \sum\nolimits_{i=1}^{n} \left(-\sum\nolimits_{j=1}^{k} \left(\frac{\exp(y_j^{(i)})}{\sum_{t=1}^{k} \exp(y_t^{(i)})} \cdot \log(\frac{\exp(h_j^{(i)})}{\sum_{t=1}^{k} \exp(h_t^{(i)})}) \right) \right) \tag{12}$$

where n denotes the number of samples and k denotes the number of paragraphs for a question. $y_j^{(i)}$ represents the real ROUGE-L score. $h_j^{(i)}$ is the predicted score of the j-th paragraph for the i-th question.

4 Experiments

4.1 Dataset and Evaluation Metrics

To evaluate the performance of our method, we carried out experiments on DuReader, a large-scale real-world dataset for multi-passage MRC. DuReader has two versions. Compared to the first release which contains 200k questions, DuReader version 2.0 adds about 100K query-answers pairs with about 90K for training and another 10K for testing. ROUGE-L and BLEU-4 are used as official evaluation metrics and we follow this setting for meaningful comparison.

The questions of DuReader are sampled from real user queries. The paired documents are collected from the search results of Baidu search engine and Baidu Zhidao, a question answering community. Since it is computationally expensive to feed all paragraphs into the model, we select two paragraphs for each document according to the recall scores compared against the question and filter the samples without answers during training. The upper boundary of the candidate paragraphs on the DuReader development dataset is shown in Fig. 2. It can be seen that the best-matching paragraphs of Description questions which account for 62.76% in the dataset can achieve the ROUGE-L score of 70.0% while the worst-performing YesNo questions can obtain 56.7% ROUGE-L score. It supports our hypothesis that it is appropriate to select best-matching paragraphs to answer questions directly.

4.2 Experimental Settings

We use Glove [15] and sentences in DuReader to train 300-D embeddings. These pre-trained word embeddings are used in our model without update during training and out-of-vocabulary words are randomly initialized with the same dimension. Hidden vector size is set to 150 for all layers. We use the Adam [11] optimizer with a batch size of 16 and an initial learning rate of 0.0005, for 10 epochs. During training, the moving averages of all trainable parameters of the model are maintained with the exponential decay rate of 0.999.

Table 1. Performance of our method and competing models on the DuReader test set.

Model	DuReader v1.0		DuReader v2.0	
	ROUGE-L	BLEU-4	ROUGE-L	BLEU-4
Selected paragraph	30.20	16.40	32.85	19.16
Match-LSTM	39.20	31.90	42.79	35.88
BiDAF	39.00	31.80	43.36	38.50
PR+BiDAF	41.81	37.55	-	-
V-net	44.18	**40.97**	-	-
Our model	**47.72**	34.65	**51.59**	**44.36**
Human annotator	57.40	56.10	-	-

4.3   Baselines

Several baselines and state-of-arts on multi-passage MRC are used for empirical comparison. (1) The **Selected Paragraph** System directly selects the paragraph achieving the highest word-level recall score towards the given question as the answer. The (2) **BiDAF** and (3) **Match-LSTM** models implemented in [7] are provided as baseline systems too. These two methods are designed for single-passage MRC and can be applied to tackle multi-passage MRC by using a heuristic method to select several representative paragraphs and then concatenating all selected paragraphs as a single passage. (4) **PR + BiDAF** [24] combines a paragraph ranking model with BiDAF. (5) **V-net** proposed in [24] trains three different modules including answer boundary prediction, answer content modeling and answer verification jointly to find the final answer.

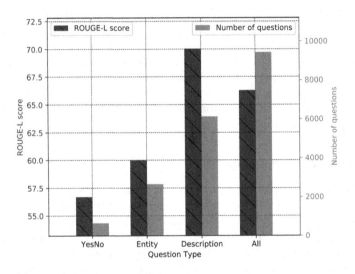

Fig. 2. The average ROUGE-L scores for the best-matching candidate paragraphs and the number of questions on various question types on the DuReader development dataset

4.4   Results and Analyses

We train and test our paragraph selecting model on both versions of DuReader. Besides, we train and test the BiDAF and Match-LSTM on the DuReader version 2.0 because there are only results on DuReader version 1.0 in [7]. Table 1 shows the overall performance of baselines and our model. It can be seen that our model outperforms all baselines on both versions by the ROUGE-L criterion, which shows the effectiveness of our model. Moreover, it is worth noting that our framework is based on BiDAF but the performance far exceeds it, which shows that selecting the best-matching paragraphs is helpful. On BLEU-4, the performance of our model is a little worse because it prefers to provide longer and informative answers compared to the extractive models but BLEU has brevity penalty.

To better understand the strengths and weaknesses of our model, we conduct some further analyses. First, we suspect that our model which can provide more complete contents is suitable for Description questions whose answers need more information and are longer than other question types. To verify this hypothesis, we examine ROUGE-L and BLEU-4 scores with respect to average answer length on various question types on the development dataset. The results are shown in Fig. 3. It can be seen that ROUGE-L and BLEU-4 scores are proportional to the answer length and Description questions obtain the highest ROUGE-L score.

From the perspective of ranking, top-1 effectiveness is the focus of our work and we evaluate it by recall and mean reciprocal rank (MRR). In calculating these two metrics, we treat paragraphs with the highest score as relevant and the others as irrelevant. Because the answers predicted by our competitive models may be text segments of several paragraphs, we cannot compare our method with them in these IR evaluation metrics, but we implement several IR methods including BM25 and Query Likelihood (QL) with Dirichlet smoothing. The results are shown in Table 2. We can see that our model is good at finding the best-matching paragraph from a group of candidates.

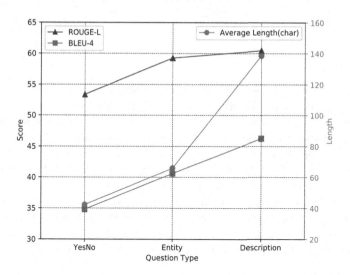

Fig. 3. Performance and average length of answers on various question types.

Table 2. Ranking accuracies on the development dataset

Model	MRR	Recall@1	Recall@3	Recall@5
BM25	0.329	0.122	0.361	0.576
QL	0.375	0.160	0.444	0.674
Our model	**0.602**	**0.407**	**0.729**	**0.894**

Table 3. Paragraphs selected by our model and their ROUGE-L scores.

Type	Question	Answer	Prediction	ROUGE-L
Description	黄磊是怎么9天瘦20斤的 How does Huang Lei lose 20 pounds in 9 days	运动加代餐。 Exercise with meal replacement.	在一篇文章介绍过，应该是运动加代餐。 It is introduced in an article that it should be exercise with meal replacement.	54.95
Entity	欢乐颂第二部什么时候上映 When will Ode to Joy II be released?	17年5月11日。 May 11, 17.	5月11日欢乐颂2首播 Ode to Joy II will premier on May 11	50.92
YesNo	行车记录仪有必要买双镜头吗 Is it necessary to buy a dual lens for the driving recorder?	这个意义不大，我们买记录仪主要目的之一是防碰瓷… It is of little significance. One of the main purposes to buy recorders is to prevent black-mail…	真心没必要，行车记录仪本身使命是记录前方现场画面… Really unnecessary. The mission of the driving recorder itself is to record the scene ahead…	19.52

4.5 Case Study

In order to analyze the performance of our model in a more intuitive way, we analyze a large number of examples for case study whose predictions' ROUGE-L scores are less than the average. To illustrate our point, we choose a representative example for each question type. The real ROUGE-L scores of these examples are listed in Table 3 and the average scores of the corresponding question types are shown in Fig. 3. For Description and Entity questions, we can see that the selected paragraphs both contain the correct and complete answer information although they have several redundant words. For the YesNo question, both the answer and prediction give the same suggestions with some differences in expression and reason. Therefore, some paragraphs selected by our model can be alternative answers for the given questions even though they get inferior ROUGE-L scores.

5 Conclusion and Future Work

In this paper, we studied the problem of combining a listwise approach to learning to rank with an attention-based neural network to solve multi-passage MRC task. Moreover, we proposed to adopt ROUGE-L as the ranking indicator of paragraph quality and to select the best-matching paragraph to answer a question directly. Experiments on a real-world dataset verify the effectiveness of our work in recommending high-quality paragraphs to answer questions.

Recently, there are some methods which incorporate Bidirectional Encoder Representations from Transformers (BERT) [6] into models and obtain promising results in MRC field. In future work, we will try to incorporate BERT into our framework and transfer our model to other datasets. Besides, we will look to examine possible improvements to our ranking model, such as combining some IR methods with our model and introducing external knowledge to help models to answer questions.

References

1. Cao, Z., Qin, T., Liu, T.Y., Tsai, M.F., Li, H.: Learning to rank: from pairwise approach to listwise approach. In: Proceedings of the 24th International Conference on Machine Learning, pp. 129–136. ICML 2007, ACM (2007)
2. Chen, D., Bolton, J., Manning, C.D.: A thorough examination of the CNN/daily mail reading comprehension task. In: Proceedings of the 54th Annual Meeting of the Association for Computational Linguistics. ACL 2016, vol. 1, pp. 2358–2367 (2016)
3. Chen, D., Fisch, A., Weston, J., Bordes, A.: Reading wikipedia to answer open-domain questions. In: Proceedings of the 55th Annual Meeting of the Association for Computational Linguistics (2017)
4. Cohen, D., Yang, L., Croft, W.B.: Wikipassageqa: a benchmark collection for research on non-factoid answer passage retrieval. In: The 41st International ACM SIGIR Conference on Research and Development in Information Retrieval, pp. 1165–1168. SIGIR 2018 (2018)
5. Das, R., Dhuliawala, S., Zaheer, M., McCallum, A.: Multi-step retriever-reader interaction for scalable open-domain question answering. In: The 7th International Conference on Learning Representations (2019)
6. Devlin, J., Chang, M.W., Lee, K., Toutanova, K.: Bert: pre-training of deep bidirectional transformers for language understanding. In: The 2019 Annual Conference of the North American Chapter of the Association for Computational Linguistics (2019)
7. He, W., et al.: Dureader: a chinese machine reading comprehension dataset from real-world applications. In: Proceedings of the Workshop on Machine Reading for Question Answering, pp. 37–46 (2018)
8. Hermann, K.M., et al.: Teaching machines to read and comprehend. In: Advances in Neural Information Processing Systems, pp. 1693–1701 (2015)
9. Hill, F., Bordes, A., Chopra, S., Weston, J.: The goldilocks principle: reading children's books with explicit memory representations. arXiv preprint arXiv:1511.02301 (2015)
10. Hu, M., Peng, Y., Huang, Z., Qiu, X., Wei, F., Zhou, M.: Reinforced mnemonic reader for machine reading comprehension. In: 27th International Joint Conference on Artificial Intelligence (IJCAI) (2018)
11. Kingma, D.P., Ba, J.: Adam: a method for stochastic optimization. arXiv preprint arXiv:1412.6980 (2014)
12. Lai, G., Xie, Q., Liu, H., Yang, Y., Hovy, E.: Race: large-scale reading comprehension dataset from examinations. In: Empirical Methods in Natural Language Processing, pp. 785–794 (2017)

13. Lin, Y., Ji, H., Liu, Z., Sun, M.: Denoising distantly supervised open-domain question answering. In: Proceedings of the 56th Annual Meeting of the Association for Computational Linguistics (vol. 1: Long Papers), pp. 1736–1745 (2018)
14. Nguyen, T., Rosenberg, M., Song, X., Gao, J., Tiwary, S., Majumder, R., Deng, L.: Ms marco: a human generated machine reading comprehension dataset. In: Proceedings of the Workshop on Cognitive Computation: Integrating Neural and Symbolic Approaches 2016 Colocated with the 30th Annual Conference on Neural Information Processing Systems (2016)
15. Pennington, J., Socher, R., Manning, C.: Glove: global vectors for word representation. In: Proceedings of the 2014 Conference on Empirical Methods in Natural Language Processing (EMNLP), pp. 1532–1543 (2014)
16. Rajpurkar, P., Zhang, J., Lopyrev, K., Liang, P.: Squad: 100,000+ questions for machine comprehension of text. In: Proceedings of the 2016 Conference on Empirical Methods in Natural Language Processing, pp. 2383–2392. EMNLP 2016 (2016)
17. Richardson, M., Burges, C.J., Renshaw, E.: Mctest: a challenge dataset for the open-domain machine comprehension of text. In: Proceedings of the 2013 Conference on Empirical Methods in Natural Language Processing, pp. 193–203 (2013)
18. Seo, M., Kembhavi, A., Farhadi, A., Hajishirzi, H.: Bidirectional attention flow for machine comprehension. In: Proceedings of the 5th International Conference on Learning Representations. ICLR 2017 (2017)
19. Tan, C., Wei, F., Yang, N., Du, B., Lv, W., Zhou, M.: S-net: from answer extraction to answer generation for machine reading comprehension. In: Proceedings of the 32nd AAAI Conference on Artificial Intelligence. AAAI 2018 (2018)
20. Vinyals, O., Fortunato, M., Jaitly, N.: Pointer networks. In: Advances in Neural Information Processing Systems, pp. 2692–2700 (2015)
21. Wang, S., Jiang, J.: Machine comprehension using match-lSTM and answer pointer. CoRR. arXiv:1608.07905 (2016)
22. Wang, S., et al.: R3: reinforced ranker-reader for open-domain question answering. In: Thirty-Second AAAI Conference on Artificial Intelligence (2018)
23. Wang, W., Yang, N., Wei, F., Chang, B., Zhou, M.: Gated self-matching networks for reading comprehension and question answering. In: Proceedings of the 55th Annual Meeting of the Association for Computational Linguistics (vol. 1: Long Papers). pp. 189–198 (2017)
24. Wang, Y., et al.: Multi-passage machine reading comprehension with cross-passage answer verification. In: Proceedings of the 56th Annual Meeting of the Association for Computational Linguistics. pp. 1918–1927. ACL 2018 (2018)
25. Yang, L., et al.: Beyond factoid QA: Effective methods for non-factoid answer sentence retrieval. In: European Conference on Information Retrieval. pp. 115–128. ECIR 2016 (2016)
26. Yulianti, E., Chen, R.C., Scholer, F., Croft, W.B., Sanderson, M.: Ranking documents by answer-passage quality. In: Proceedings of the 41st International ACM SIGIR Conference on Research & Development in Information Retrieval. SIGIR 2018 (2018)

Social Computing

Temporal Convolutional Networks for Popularity Prediction of Messages on Social Medias

Jiangli Shao[1,2(✉)], Huawei Shen[1], Qi Cao[1], and Xueqi Cheng[1]

[1] Institute of Computing Technology, Chinese Academy of Sciences, Beijing, China
{shenhuawei,caoqi,cxq}@ict.ac.cn
[2] University of Chinese Academy of Sciences, Beijing, China
shaojiangli15@mails.ucas.ac.cn

Abstract. Predicting the popularity of messages on social medias is an important problem that draws wide attention. The temporal information is the most effective one for predicting future popularity and has been widely used. Existing methods either extract various hand-crafted temporal features or utilize point process to modeling the temporal sequence. Unfortunately, the performance of the feature-based methods heavily depends on the quality of the heuristically hand-crafted features while the point process methods fail to characterize the longer observed sequence. To solve the problems mentioned above, in this paper, we propose to utilize Temporal Convolutional Networks (TCNs) for predicting the popularity of messages on social media. Specifically, TCN can automatically adopt the scales of observed time sequence without manual prior knowledge. Meanwhile, TCN can perform well with long sequences with its longer effective memory. The experimental results indicate that TCN outperforms all the baselines, including both feature-based and point-process-based methods.

Keywords: Popularity prediction · Temporal convolutional networks · Temporal sequence · Social medias

1 Introduction

Social media messages have caught much attention due to the significant role they play in our daily life. Individuals can express their feelings towards a specific message via retweet or comment behaviors, and the total number of these behaviors reflect the prevalence of a post, also known as the *popularity* of a message. With the large amount of messages on social media, predicting the popularity of a message in advance would allow discover hot information, help people out of information overload, and further be exploited in advertising [2,8], recommendation [19] and gossip monitoring [18]. Series studies indicate that it's effective to predict future popularity with early observed data of a message [16]. For example, by observing the reading volume of a news item for several hours,

© Springer Nature Switzerland AG 2019
Q. Zhang et al. (Eds.): CCIR 2019, LNCS 11772, pp. 135–147, 2019.
https://doi.org/10.1007/978-3-030-31624-2_11

we can predict whether it will receive widespread attention in the future. In this paper, we will also utilize these early temporal information to predict the future popularity of a message.

When faced with the problem of popularity prediction with early observation, typically there are two distinct solutions for us to choose: the feature driven approaches and the point process approaches. Feature driven approaches first extract an extensive set of features from observed sequences, and then leverage machine learning approaches to build a mapping function between extracted features and future popularity [17]. Various features, including total popularity and the popularity in each time interval [9], have been proved helpful in prediction tasks. Usually, results obtained from these methods can be well explained and the computational process is fast. However, the performance of the feature-based methods heavily depends on the quality of the hand-crafted features, which are generally extracted heuristically and require prior human knowledge.

The point process method regards serial user-behaviors as a counting process and models the time intervals between those actions as random variables. According to the mathematical theory of point process, different dynamic patterns in the sequential data can be well captured by different forms of intensity functions. In some scenarios, researchers have designed some specific forms of intensity functions like Reinforcement Poisson process [14] and Hawkes process [13]. Meanwhile, based on the observed input, the intensity function can also be estimated via Maximum Likelihood Estimation [17]. Once we find the intensity function, we are able to generate the following user-behavior sequences and finally give a prediction of future popularity. Supported by solid mathematical theory though, there still exist some limitations in point process methods. Usually, this approach makes strong assumptions about the variation trends of popularity when utilizing specific forms of intensity functions, while those assumptions might be inconsistent with reality. Although researchers proposed that we can model the intensity function by means of machine learning ways [5], such as RNN, to reduce those assumptions, the predicted accuracy declines as sequences become longer.

In this paper, we will adopt temporal convolutional networks(TCNs), whose basic idea is extracting features from sequences through machine learning approaches, to popularity prediction problems. This convolutional-based model, which is previously viewed as conducive to tackle grid data only [10], recently have been used to tackle sequential problems and have gained outstanding performance [1]. By introducing TCNs to popularity prediction problems, we expect to address the problems encountered in traditional feature extraction methods and point process method.

On the whole, our contributions in this paper can be briefly summarized as follows:

1. We make an attempt to innovatively apply TCNs to the problem of popularity prediction. This model, shown by our experimental results, outperforms the state-of-the-art approaches in popularity prediction fields, including the feature-based model and the point process based model.

2. By conducting a series of experiments on the real-world dataset, we give an explanation of the intrinsic reason for the performance improvement of TCN, especially the improvement on long-sequence problems. That is, TCN owns a longer effective memory and hence can capture more distant and comprehensive information in temporal sequences.
3. We show that TCNs can automatically adapt observation scales without prior knowledge. This characteristic is beneficial for avoiding the heuristical selection of observation scales suffered by feature-based methods.

2   Related Works

The following two types of methods are widely applied in popularity prediction fields. Our work is closely related to them.

2.1   Feature-Driven Method

In order to give a reliable prediction of future popularity, one feasible method is designing numerous hand-crafted rules by experienced experts to extract specific features of those temporal sequences. The totality of retweets in observing times, for instance, reveals the early influence of the source message and can be a serviceable indicator of future popularity [9]. Similarly, Szabo and Huberman discovered that the log-transformed early and future popularities are highly correlated, based on which they propose the simple but effective S-H model [15]. Pinto et al. divide the observing window into several intervals of the same size and regard the retweet number in each sampling interval as a feature to construct a multivariate liner(ML) model [12]. Furthermore, in order to characterize distinctive popularity patterns, they put forward the so-called MRBF model [12] by adding a feature measured by Radial Basis Functions (RBFs) to their initial ML model, which conceivably reduces predicted errors. However, this type of ways requires sufficient prior knowledge of given domains, which might be a considerable obstacle to extending a specialized model to different fields.

Compared with the previous hand-engineered feature extraction approaches, TCN is able to gain more expressive features and automatically adopt the observation scale, thus improving the accuracy of prediction.

2.2   Point Process Method

Unlike the traditional method which relies on different features, we can also describe ordinal user-behaviors with points on the timeline and the temporal information can be well captured by means of stochastic point process theory. In this theory, an important way to characterize point processes is via the conditional intensity function, which denotes the expected instantaneous rate of new behavior occurrence based on the history sequence. Researchers have designed some particular forms of intensity function to capture various dynamic patterns in sequences. For instance, the homogeneous Poisson process [11] assumes the intensity function is a constant and the inhomogeneous

Poisson process [14] choose polynomial as the intensity function. Both of them have been proved efficient in predicting popularity. Hawkes process [13], whose intensity function depends on the observing history, gain excellent performance in forecasting microblogs' forwardings [3]. Otherwise, self-correcting process and autoregressive conditional duration process are also common point process modeling approaches [5]. However, choosing specific forms of intensity functions may not works when facing more complex application scenarios. Du et al., to solve this problem, proposed an RNN-based method to obtain the intensity function expression, known as the RMTPP model [5]. They conduct experiments on various datasets and results indicated that, compared with models using specific intensity function, their machine learning based model is indeed better.

Powerful as it is, the limited memory length impedes the improvement of predicting accuracy when using RNN to model the intensity function. Although some advanced structures based on RNN are designed to overcome the disadvantage like LSTM, BRNN, and GRU, limitations still exist. The TCN structure, compared with these RNN-based structures, can effectively enlarge the memory length and get better performance.

3   Models

3.1   Problem Formulation

Firstly, we will introduce necessary definitions and then formulate the popularity prediction problems with two kinds of methods.

For a message i, we define the time sequence $S_i(T) = \{t_i^j\}$ as event sequence (e.g. the retweet sequence) up to time T. Here, T represents the whole observation times and $\{t_i^j\}$ is the timestamp when event j happens.

Feature Extraction Method: In this method, we will dissect the whole observation window T into a series of equal-sized intervals. Suppose the total number of these intervals is k. Then, the length of each time interval is $\Delta t = \frac{T}{k}$. Next, event volumes are added up within each interval, which forms the serialized input of the model. We define $N_m(\Delta t)$ as the event numbers in the m-th intervals:

$$N_m(\Delta t) = |S_i(m \cdot \Delta t)| - |S_i((m-1) \cdot \Delta t)| m = 1, 2...k \qquad (1)$$

Finally, the predicted value $N_i(t_{pre})$ is computed as follows:

$$N_i(t_{pre}) = \sum_{m=1}^{k} a_m \cdot N_m(\Delta t) + b \qquad (2)$$

where $a_m(m = 1, 2...k)$ and b are the model parameters.

Point Process Method: In this method, we use conditional intensity function to capture the temporal information in our input sequence. The conditional intensity function $\lambda^*(t)$ is defined as follows:

$$\lambda^*(t) = \frac{\mathbb{P}\{|S_i(t+dt)| - |S_i(t)| = 1|S_i(T)\}}{dt} \qquad (3)$$

$\lambda^*(t)$ represents the expected instantaneous rate of new event occurrence given the history sequence. Once we find the intensity function, the conditional density function $f^*(t)$ can be denoted as:

$$f^*(t) = \lambda^*(t)\exp(-\int_{t_n}^{t} \lambda^*(\tau)d\tau) \tag{4}$$

Finally, we could generate the following user-behavior sequences and added them up to give a prediction of future popularity.

3.2 Temporal Convolutional Networks

On the basis of the model put forward by Lea et al. [10], we display TCNs used in our tasks as follows.

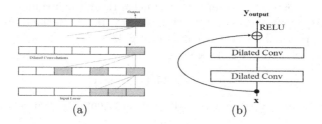

Fig. 1. The basic structure of TCNs (a) and the residual block (b)

As is depicted in Fig. 1(a), TCN is basically a hierarchical framework with a class of convolutions in each layer. As a feature extraction method, the input to this TCN is the time interval features which record popularity information in observing windows while the output is the predicted popularity. It is worth mentioning that in original structures, TCN will generate a sequence that has the same length with input data. According to our task, which merely requires the forecasting value at a specific prediction time in the future, we keep the last value in output sequence and leave out the others because the last value contains the most comprehensive information in the original sequence.

To obtain a wider range of information in input sequence, dilated convolutions [20] are employed in TCN structures, which enlarge the receptive field by skipping input values with a certain step. Formally, we define our input as a vector $X \in R^n$. Elements in X are denoted as $x_0, x_1......x_{n-1}$. The convolutional filter of size k is denoted as $f : \{0, 1, ...k-1\} \to R$. Then, the dilated convolution operation F on time t can be defined as:

$$F(t) = \sum_{i=0}^{k-1} f(i) \cdot x_{t-d \cdot i} \tag{5}$$

The parameter d in this formula represents the dilation factor, which controls the distance of two adjacent filter taps. Applying different factors will capture features at different ranges. When setting $d = 1$, dilated convolutions are equivalent to regular convolutions. In this paper, we set $d = 2^i$ at the i-th level. The configuration, for one thing, leads to an exponential receptive field growth. Therefore, a longer effective history can be achieved with identical layers, making TCN more powerful. For another, the setting above ensures an overall view of inputs, which means some top layer filters can hit each input elements. The filter size k, which shows the length of a filter, can also control the scale of the receptive field. But different from the impact of parameter d, which exponentially increases the receptive field, parameter k changes it linearly, making the adjustment of the receptive field more delicate.

The residual connection [6] is a kind of crucial technologies which are always utilized in large-scale neural networks. Residual connections effectively solve the degradation problem by adding an identity mapping to the original convolution operation. It enables us to train a deeper network and hence makes it possible for TCN to capture features of a longer period of time in initial data. The basic structure of a residual block is depicted in Fig. 1(b).

The output of a residual block is defined as:

$$y_{output} = RELU(F(\mathbf{x}) + \mathbf{x}) \tag{6}$$

where $\mathbf{x} \in R^n$ is the input vector and $F(x)$ represents the convolutional result of $\mathbf{x}$.

4   Experiment Setup

4.1   Datasets

In our experiments, we adopt the dataset in Sina Weibo, a popular Chinese social platform with over one hundred million registered users. Frequently, the lifespan of a message is about one or two days. Hence we collect the retweet information in 24 h since a message was initially posted [4].

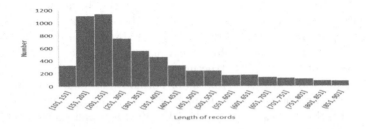

Fig. 2. The distribution of the length of message records

For a specific message, our dataset uses one record to write down the publishing time of it along with each forwarding time of this message in the next 24 h.

All of the records in our raw dataset are randomly gathered between June. 1st, 2016 and June. 9th, 2016. Then, considering the impact of the publishing time, We limit the release time of the message in the same hour in a day (randomly, this hour is set to be 20:00–21:00). We maintain the records whose publishing time is between 20:00 to 21:00. Also, we delete the records with less 100 forwards in 24 h and finally there are 6030 records left in our dataset. The length distribution of these records is shown in Fig. 2.

4.2   Baselines

We compare TCNs with the following three baselines. All of these methods are based on the temporal input only and other useful features like the network-structure information are invisible.

PINTO. This model is a representative of traditional feature extraction methods. It divides the whole observation window into a crowd of sampling intervals and regards repost numbers in each interval as a feature. Also, an RBF feature is added to measure the similarity between variation trends of popularity. These features are then combined through a simple multivariate linear model to finally give the predicted value [12].

LSTM. As a variant of RNN, LSTM owns a stronger ability in grasping the long-term information in sequences [7]. In popularity prediction fields, LSTM is used to model the intensity function and gains state-of-the-art results [5]. In this paper, we also apply LSTM in fitting the intensity function of input sequences. The predicted value is generated by intensity function we obtained.

PP-LSTM. Referring to the practice in [17], this model is composed of two LSTM. The first one will fit the conditional intensity function of input sequences and the other LSTM, which takes the timestamp of each retweet behavior together with the intensity value as input, will generate the predicted value. It is a kind of method based on point process theory. In the following passage, we abbreviate it as PP-LSTM (point-process-LSTM).

4.3   Experiment Setup

For our TCN model, there are still some details which deserve attention:

Firstly, TCN adopts causal convolutions as a result of the assumption that the predicted value at time t is just a function of values from time 1 to t. The prediction process is conducted without exploiting future information because that data is usually invisible in real-world problems.

Otherwise, dropout and normalization strategies are employed to alleviate the overfitting and gradient explosion phenomenon respectively.

As for the superparameter settings, we use Mini-Batch Gradient Descent optimizer with batch size 96 for all of these models. The dropout rate and learning rate are chosen through grid search. For TCNs, Kernel size k and TCN layers l are selected via grid search for the sake of an adequate receptive field.

Table 1. Optimal performance of different models (observing time $= 6$ h)

Models	MSLE	Relative gain
PINTO	0.8155	9.1%
LSTM	0.7815	5.1%
PP-LSTM	0.7802	5.0%
TCN	**0.7413**	—

As for PINTO model, we use Gaussian RBFs and set the width parameter σ to 130. For LSTM, we use a structure which has 3 layers. For PP-LSTM, we set LSTM layers to 2 and 3, respectively. For all of our four models, we train them for 1000 epochs to gain convergent results.

4.4 Evaluation Metrics

In order to measure the performance of different models, we calculate the mean square logarithm error (MSLE) between real values and predicted values. MSLE is defined as follows:

$$MSLE = \frac{1}{n} \sum_{i=1}^{n} [\log(y_{i_{pred}} + 1) - \log(y_{i_{true}} + 1)]^2 \qquad (7)$$

5   Experimental Results

In order to fully demonstrate the superiority of the TCN model, we conduct several experiments and show the corresponding results as follows.

5.1 Prediction Performance

Firstly, we make an overall comparison of the prediction performance among all of these models (We use 5-fold cross-validation). In this real-world task, the viewing-time is set to 6 h since a message was first published by users and we aim to provide a dependable forecasting number, which represents the popularity, after 24 h.

Following practices of Pinto et al. [12], we dissect the whole observation window into a series of equal-sized intervals. Then, repost volumes are added up within each interval, which forms the serialized input of the PINTO and TCN model. Based on the practical experience, we set the time intervals as 60 s, 90 s, 180 s, 300 s, 600 s, 900 s, 1080 s, 1200 s and 1800 s. The optimal results of PINTO and TCN among those intervals are listed in Table 1.

As for the LSTM and PP-LSTM, we directly use the timestamp as their input. Their performances are also listed in Table 1:

From Table 1, we can notice that TCNs can outperform the other three baselines, demonstrating the effectiveness of TCN framework in this prediction task. Contrasting the optimal outcomes among these models, TCN can decrease the predicting loss for about 9% over PINTO model and about 5% over LSTM or PP-LSTM.

To further understand the reason why the TCN structure can gain such an excellent performance, We analyze the relationships between the sequence length and the prediction performance, as well as the observation scale and the prediction performance.

5.2 Effecitive Memory Length

In this part, we intend to compare the effective memory length of each model. To achieve this goal, we vary the length of input temporal sequence. Specifically, we vary the observation time window from 1 h, 2 h, 3 h, 4 h, 5 h to 6 h. Meanwhile, in order to obtain sufficiently long input sequences, the time intervals of TCN and PINTO is restricted to 60 s, 90 s and 180 s. To maintain the parameters scale at the same level, we set the layers of TCNs to be 4 and the kernel size to be 5. Also, we record the best performance of these models respectively.

As depicted in Fig. 3, the predicted error of TCNs decreases with the observation time increasing. In general, longer observation sequences contain more information about variation trend of popularity. If these features are well extracted, the prediction errors will be effectively reduced, which is well reflected by experimental results of TCNs. As the sequence grows, the prediction error of TCN model on the data set decreases.

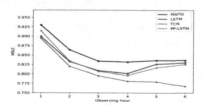

Fig. 3. Variation of predicted error with observation time

In contrast, the predicted error of PINTO model stabilized when observation time reaches 3 h. For both LSTM and PP-LSTM, the predicted error begins to rise after 4 h of observation. Meanwhile, the relative performance improvement between TCNs and other models is growing as observation windows getting larger. All of these results indicate that, with regard to the PINTO model, the LSTM model, or the PP-LSTM model, the length of input sequences has exceeded the length of models effective memory, thus the model cannot memorize the longer history and unable to capture more expressive features.

From the comparison above, we can come to the conclusion that the effective memory length of TCNs is much larger, which makes it possible to deal with longer temporal sequences.

Table 2. Prediction performance with different time intervals (observing time = 6 h)

Interval	PINTO	LSTM	PP-LSTM	TCN	Relative gain
60 s	0.8555	0.942	0.9374	**0.7413**	13.3%
90 s	0.8405	0.941	0.9272	0.7415	11.8%
180 s	0.8361	0.9271	0.8479	0.7427	11.2%
300 s	0.8219	0.808	0.8152	0.7441	7.9%
600 s	**0.8155**	0.7802	0.7809	0.7456	4.4%
900 s	0.8171	0.7733	0.7757	0.7463	3.5%
1080 s	0.8173	0.7724	**0.7702**	0.7506	2.5%
1200 s	0.8187	**0.7715**	0.7728	0.7571	1.9%
1800 s	0.8157	0.778	0.7782	0.7564	2.8%

Table 3. Superparametric K and L values of TCN for obtaining optimal results at different time intervals

Time	K	L	Time	K	L	Time	K	L
60 s	9	11	300 s	10	3	1080 s	7	6
90 s	14	6	600 s	12	4	1200 s	6	4
180 s	14	3	900 s	8	2	1800 s	5	4

5.3   Automatic Interval-Selection Characteristic of TCN

Moreover, our experiment results reveal another trait of TCNs which may attract great attention. Table 2 depicts the MSLE of PINTO, LSTM, PP-LSTM and TCN across different time intervals. (It is worth noting that, here, we use the repost number as the input of LSTM and PP-LSTM, which is different from their inputs in experiment 5.1.)

In general, some detailed information in sequences will be ignored if time intervals are too large while local noise data would reduce prediction accuracy when time intervals are too small. As a result, Some prior knowledge is needed to adjust the time interval parameters when applied PINTO, LSTM, or PP-LSTM model to real-world problems.

By contrast, TCNs gain the lowest MSLE when employing minimal time gaps. Here, to give a more detailed look, we list the hyper-parameters used in TCNs in Table 3:

We give a brief explanation that TCNs could aggregate local features of inputs to holistic features through its hierarchical framework and dilated convolutions. On the contrary, some features are left out if we adopt longer sections originally. Hence TCNs with tiny intervals performs better because more details are retained. This characteristic may serve as a meaningful instruction that we can choose the minimum observing gaps when facing a new problem since TCNs may assemble tiny features together to obtain an overall view of data and finally get long-term features which could be acquired when using larger intervals. The whole process seems like that TCNs automatically choose the proper partition ranges and all we need to do is to feed the most detailed data to it, which greatly reduces the training complexity of the model.

5.4 Efficiency Comparison

Finally, we compare the efficiency of each model, i.e., the training and predicting time. Firstly, each model is trained 1000 epochs with the superparametric values of its optimal results. Next, Under the same superparametric conditions, each model makes 1000 predictions on the whole test set (the whole test set contains 1206 pieces of records). During these two processes, the consumed time of each model is recorded respectively. Results are shown in Fig. 4. (The time consumption of LSTM and PP-LSTM is independent with time intervals):

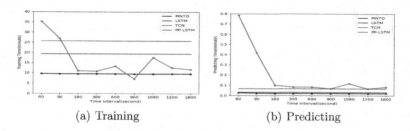

(a) Training   (b) Predicting

Fig. 4. The relationship between time-consuming and time intervals of each model

Taken together, we can find that the Pinto model takes the least amount of time in both training and prediction due to its simple structure and calculation process. However, the predicted error of Pinto model is also significantly high, which means it is not suitable for application scenarios where the prediction accuracy is pursued.

Compared with LSTM and PP-LSTM, TCN model has a lower training time cost when time interval is large. However, when choosing a small time interval, not only the training time but also the predicting time of TCNs become longer. Although the predicting time of TCN is several times larger than that of other baselines, TCNs can accomplish the task within one minute, which is affordable in reality.

From the above comparison, we can know that TCN model achieves a large performance improvement with a small amount of efficiency sacrifice and thus can be applied in practical problems.

6 Conclusion

In this paper, we apply a kind of convolutional architecture named Temporal Convolutional Network (TCN) to popularity prediction problems. Our experimental results show that TCN outperforms both the state-of-the-art feature-based methods and point process methods. TCN's excellent performance largely lies in its longer effective memory which not only advances the accuracy of prediction on datasets but also maintains the deviation at the same level as sequences lengthen. Additionally, our results also demonstrate that TCN is able to choose the observed scale automatically without prior manual knowledge. Future work can be done to fully explore the application of these characteristics of TCNs. Some other fields which need a relatively long observation, audio synthesis or document classification, for example, can take TCNs into consideration.

References

1. Bai, S., Kolter, J.Z., Koltun, V.: An empirical evaluation of generic convolutional and recurrent networks for sequence modeling. arXiv preprint arXiv:1803.01271 (2018)
2. Bakshy, E., Eckles, D., Yan, R., Rosenn, I.: Social influence in social advertising: evidence from field experiments. In: EC, pp. 146–161 (2012)
3. Bao, P., Shen, H.W., Jin, X., Cheng, X.Q.: Modeling and predicting popularity dynamics of microblogs using self-excited hawkes processes. In: WWW, pp. 9–10 (2015)
4. Cao, Q., Shen, H., Gao, H., Gao, J., Cheng, X.: Predicting the popularity of online content with group-specific models. In: WWW, pp. 765–766 (2017)
5. Du, N., Dai, H., Trivedi, R., Upadhyay, U., Gomez-Rodriguez, M., Song, L.: Recurrent marked temporal point processes: embedding event history to vector. In: SIGKDD, pp. 1555–1564 (2016)
6. He, K., Zhang, X., Ren, S., Sun, J.: Deep residual learning for image recognition. In: CVPR, pp. 770–778 (2016)
7. Hochreiter, S., Schmidhuber, J.: Long short-term memory. Neural Comput. **9**(8), 1735–1780 (1997)
8. Kim, H., Takaya, N., Sawada, H.: Tracking temporal dynamics of purchase decisions via hierarchical time-rescaling model. In: CIKM, pp. 1389–1398 (2014)
9. Kong, S., Mei, Q., Feng, L., Ye, F., Zhao, Z.: Predicting bursts and popularity of hashtags in real-time. In: SIGIR, pp. 927–930 (2014)
10. Lea, C., Flynn, M.D., Vidal, R., Reiter, A., Hager, G.D.: Temporal convolutional networks for action segmentation and detection. In: CVPR, pp. 1003–1012 (2017)
11. Malmgren, R.D., Stouffer, D.B., Motter, A.E., Amaral, L.A.N.: A poissonian explanation for heavy tails in e-mail communication. Proc. Nat. Acad. Sci. U.S.A. **105**(47), 18153–18158 (2008)
12. Pinto, H., Almeida, J.M., Gonçalves, M.A.: Using early view patterns to predict the popularity of youtube videos. In: WSDM, pp. 365–374 (2013)
13. Rizoiu, M.A., Lee, Y., Mishra, S., Xie, L.: A tutorial on Hawkes processes for events in social media, pp. 191–218 (2017)
14. Shen, H., Wang, D., Song, C., Barabási, A.L.: Modeling and predicting popularity dynamics via reinforced Poisson processes. In: AAAI, pp. 291–291 (2014)
15. Szabo, G., Huberman, B.A.: Predicting the popularity of online content. Commun. ACM **53**(8), 80–88 (2010)
16. Tatar, A., de Amorim, M.D., Fdida, S., Antoniadis, P.: A survey on predicting the popularity of web content. J. Internet Serv. Appl. **5**(1), 8 (2014)
17. Wu, Q., Yang, C., Zhang, H., Gao, X., Weng, P., Chen, G.: Adversarial training model unifying feature driven and point process perspectives for event popularity prediction. In: CIKM, pp. 517–526 (2018)

18. Wu, Q., Wang, T., Cai, Y., Tian, H., Chen, Y.: Rumor restraining based on propagation prediction with limited observations in large-scale social networks. In: ACSW, pp. 1:1–1:8 (2017)
19. Xiao, L., Min, Z., Yongfeng, Z., Yiqun, L., Shaoping, M.: Learning and transferring social and item visibilities for personalized recommendation. In: CIKM, pp. 337–346 (2017)
20. Yu, F., Koltun, V.: Multi-scale context aggregation by dilated convolutions. arXiv preprint arXiv:1511.07122 (2016)

A Method for User Avatar Authenticity Based on Multi-feature Fusion

Weinan Zhang[1], Lianhai Wang[1]([✉]), and Yongli Zan[2]

[1] Shandong Computer Science Center (National Supercomputer Center in Jinan),
Shandong Provincal Key Laboratory of Computer Networks, Qilu University
of Technology (Shandong Academy of Science), Jinan 250019, Shandong, China
wanglh@sdas.org
[2] School of Mathematics and Statistics, Qilu University of Technology
(Shandong Academy of Science), Jinan 250014, Shandong, China

Abstract. Social media provides users with a platform for information
sharing and communication. At the same time, there are a large proportion of users use a fake avatar. We attempt to automatically discriminate the authenticity of the user's uploaded person avatar based
on the machine learning method. In this paper, an avatar authenticity
discrimination method based on multi-feature fusion is proposed by combining user-based features, avatar features, and text-based features. We
use deep learning, image recognition and topic model techniques to process features. The method is verified on the Sina Weibo data set. The
experimental results show that the method can achieve 84.1% accuracy.

Keywords: Social media · User avatar · Machine learning

1 Intruction

Social media provides users with a platform for information sharing and communication. According to the 'China Internet Development Statistics Report'
in December 2018, Sina Weibo users reached 350 million, covered 42.3% of the
number of Chinese Internet users. Toutiao.com and wechat official accounts have
covered nearly 90% of netizens. However, the convenience of social media also
provides a powerful condition for criminals to carry out illegal advertisements,
fraud, and other activities. They created several accounts on the social media
platform to create malicious behaviors through fabricated personal information,
which seriously disrupted the internet environment and caused huge losses to
users. Therefore, it is very important to find these spam accounts in time to
maintain social media order and protect user rights. At present, many researchers
have studied the credibility evaluation and spammer detection. Many spammer
detection methods do not mention the user's avatar. At the same time, many
spammers simulate the real user's usage habits, by this to get rid of the automatic mechanism detection, so the traditional detection method can not detect
such spammers. To solve this problem. Our proposed methods can be roughly
divided into three aspects.

© Springer Nature Switzerland AG 2019
Q. Zhang et al. (Eds.): CCIR 2019, LNCS 11772, pp. 148–160, 2019.
https://doi.org/10.1007/978-3-030-31624-2_12

(1) Based on social network analysis [1], user credibility is evaluated by analyzing the account location in the social network structure.
(2) Based on user feature [2], user credibility evaluate through demographic information (such as gender, age, education level), dynamic statistics of the user's published content (such as repost number, number of comments).
(3) The combination of network features and user features [3].

Although these methods have achieved good results, there is not much consideration for the user's avatar authenticity. User avatars are often the first window to understand a user and the most intuitive way. Many criminals use a highly attractive avatar (such as a beauty lady) to entice a victim. Therefore, we attempt to automatically discriminate the authenticity of the user's uploaded avatar based on the machine learning method (which determines whether the character in the avatar is the user), and solve the problem of identifying the fake avatar account from a new perspective. By combining user-based features, avatar-based features, and text-based features, we propose a method for avatar authenticity discrimination based on supervised learning. The experimental results on the Sina Weibo dataset show that our method can achieve 84.1% accuracy.

2 Related Work

Social media has grown for 10 years. The prosperous development of social media has spawned research on user credibility evaluation and spammer detection. On the surface user's avatar authenticity judgment is different from the user credibility evaluation and the spammer detection, but most of the fake users use fake avatars, and the users who use the fake avatars are not all fake users. At the same time, there are many similarities between the spammer detection method and the avatar authenticity judgment method.

In terms of spammer detection, Gupta et al. [4] used the PageRank algorithm to calculate user trusted values. Liang et al. [5] established the user influence by user repost. Based on the community influence relationship, the author establishes a user community relationship to detect spammer. Kumar et al. [3] established a graph model between reviewers and reviewers to identify spammer. Laleh et al. [2] used user features to assess risk in social networks and detect spammers.

The above method of detecting spammer takes advantage of the unique connections on social networks. However, the text feature, such as emotions, are not taken into consideration, and this feature is usually implicit in the text. We study the text in order to expect more semantic features.

In the detection of fake reviews, Ott et al. [6] and Shojaee et al. [7] used the word features and text feature to obtain higher accuracy using support vector machines. Mukherjee et al. [8] detected fake reviews by release time and similar content.

In summary, most of the methods for spammer detection take into consideration the network structure, partially supplemented by user text features. In this paper, by combining the advantages of the two detection methods, user-based features, text-based features, and avatar-based features are used to determine the user's avatar authenticity.

3   Method

In this section, we will introduce our method, then introduce the features used in the method and give the symbol definition.

3.1   An Overview of Proposed Method

We propose features from three aspects: user-based features, avatar-based features, and text-based features. In order to reduce the imbalance data in the experiment, we use a variety of over-sampling and under-sampling methods to process the data. Then import data into a supervised machine learning model, such as a Support Vector Machine (SVM). The flowchart of the model is shown in Fig. 1.

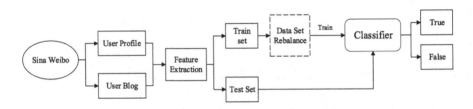

Fig. 1. An overview of our method

3.2   User-Based Feature

User Authority,User Attention and **User Fan**
($Authority\,(u)$,($Attention\,(u)$),$Fan\,(u)$): The size of $Authority\,(u)$ is proportional to the user real avatar. At the same time. Any user's follow behavior is the same, even if the fake user's follows are selected by humans. So, we propose $Attention\,(u)$. Sina Weibo has mutual follow, and mutual follow will affect the evaluation of user authority, and also increase the number of fans. In order to reduce the impact of mutual follow, we use user pure fan to describe user fan status. $Fan\,(u)$ is proportional to the pure fans.

$$Authority\,(u) = \frac{N_{fan}}{N_{fan} + N_{follow}}, \tag{1}$$

$$Attention\,(u) = \frac{N_{follow}}{N_{fan} + N_{follow}}, \tag{2}$$

$$Fan\,(u) = \frac{N_{follow} - N_{HF}}{N_{follow}}, \tag{3}$$

where, N_{follow} is the number of users' follows, and N_{fan} is the number of fans. If the number of fans and the number of users' attention are both 0, $Authority(u)$ is 0. N_{HF} is the number of mutual follow.

User Description ($Description(u)$): User description is convenient for users to introduce themselves in one sentence, and it is convenient for other users to understand themselves with a sentence. But the user description has multiple languages or expressions, we only judge whether the user description exists as a feature. For example, when the user description exist, $Description(u)=1$, when not exist, $Description(u)=0$.

User Verified ($Verified(u)$): There are official certification mechanisms on Sina Weibo and Twitter. Government and institutional certifications, called 'Blue V'. Personal certification called 'Orange V'. And if the user's blog has more than 10 million monthly reads, the user will upgrade from personal authentication to 'Gold V'. The value of $Verified(u)$ is shown in Table 1. The probability of authenticating users using real avatars is bigger than non-authenticated users

Table 1. $Verified(u)$ under different authentication conditions

Certification status	$Verified(u)$
Personal certification and head user (Gold V)	4
Personal certification (Orange V)	3
Government, Media, Agency Certification (Blue V)	2
No certification	1

User Rank ($Rank(u)$): The user rank is a comprehensive representation of the user's platform activity. In this part, we directly use the user rank as the user rank feature. $Rank(u)$ in the range of 1–48.

User Monthly Release ($Release(u)$): The monthly release represent the average number of blogs released per month.

$$Release(u) = \frac{Blog(u)}{N_{month}}, \tag{4}$$

where, $Blog(u)$ is number of blogs. N_{month} is the number of use.

3.3 Text-Based Feature

After our observation, real avatar users usually send high-quality blogs, fake avatar users' blog are usually low quality and even a lot of junk content. We will evaluate user blog quality in several ways.

Average Repost, Comment and Attitude Number
($Respost(u)$),$Comment(u)$,$Attitude(u)$): Repost is a function for user to transfers other users' blogs to their homepage. High quality blogs usually have a

lot of reposts. We defines the average number of reposts ($Respost\,(u)$). Comments are tools for user communication. High quality content makes it easier to get comments. We defines the average number of comments ($Comment\,(u)$). LIKE means endorsement of content. So we define the average number of likes ($Like\,(u)$). Those three features describes the quality of the user's blog.

$$Respost\,(u) = \frac{Number\ of\ Reposts}{Blog\,(u)}, \tag{5}$$

$$Comment\,(u) = \frac{Number\ of\ Commnets}{Blog\,(u)}, \tag{6}$$

$$Attitude\,(u) = \frac{Number\ of\ Likes}{Blog\,(u)} \tag{7}$$

Picture Blog ($Picture\,(u)$): Users can share pictures while posting a blog. This is the performance of user activity. Therefore, we define this feature ($Picture\,(u)$).

$$Picture\,(u) = \frac{Number\ of\ Picture\ Blogs}{Blog\,(u)} \tag{8}$$

User Positive and Negative Blog ($Positive\,(u)$,$Negative\,(u)$). User's emotions are ever-changing, and blog content is also an extension of user emotions. User blogs are emotionally inclined. Generally speaking, the real user's emotional distribution is uniform, and the fake user's emotional distribution is uneven. Optimistic personality reflects more positive blogs. Therefore, we define user positive blog and user negative blog.

$$Positive\,(u) = \frac{Number\ of\ Positive\ Blogs}{Blog\,(u)}, \tag{9}$$

$$Negative\,(u) = \frac{Number\ of\ Negative\ Blogs}{Blog\,(u)}, \tag{10}$$

In this part, we use a deep learning model based on BERT [9]. First, we mark the blog data as a train set. We choose three emotional extremes, positive, negative and neutral. Then use this model to predict all user blogs.

Blog Topic Distribution($Topic\,(u_K)$). The richness of the user's text indicates the average distribution of the blog topic. So, we propose a blog topic distribution. We use LDA [10] calculate the topic distribution of the user text, and then calculate the average of user blog topic distribution.

$$Topic\,(u_K) = \frac{\sum_{i=1}^{Blog(u)} P_i}{Blog\,(u)}, \tag{11}$$

where, $Topic\,(u_K)$ is the blog topic distribution of the $K-th$ topic. P_i is the $i-th$ topic.

User Geographic Position($Position\,(u_K)$). Geographic location as an important indicator of user activity, Many social media support users to insert geo-location information when posting blogs. Only real users have this activate. So we define the user's geographical position ($Position\,(u)$).

$$Position\,(u) = \frac{Number\ of\ Position\ Blogs}{Blog\,(u)} \qquad (12)$$

3.4 Avatar-Based Feature ($Gender\,(u)$)

We get all user avatars through the crawler. We use a deep learning model based on keras and cvlib to judge gender. In the user gender judgment part, we use a two-step operation, first use the cvlib tool to determine whether there is a face image in the avatar, then determine the gender attribute of the image. And compare with the gender in the user profile, if same $g\,(u)$=1, if not $g\,(u)$=0. $Gender\,(u)$ indicates the user's gender match.

3.5 Data Set Rebalance

In reality, users who use fake avatars are much smaller than users who use real avatars. In order to solve the data imbalance problem. We use Random Over Sampling (ROS), Random Under Sampling (RUS) and SMOTE Tomek (ST). Algorithm flow is shown in Algorithm 1.

Random Over Sampling (ROS). [11] ROS is a basic over sampling method. ROS help to achieve balance class distribution by random replicating minority class sampling. However, ROS may lead to over-fitting problems, which also increase the size of the training set

Random Under Sampling (RUS). [12] RUS is a basic under sampling method. RUS tries to rebalance class distribution through the random elimination of majority class sampling, but this method may remove some useful samples

SMOTE Tomek (ST). [13] ST achieves the rebalance sampling by generating new samples in minority samples with similar positions. Meanwhile the over-fitting problem can be solved in some extent

3.6 Normalized

To reduce the differences between the different features, we normalize all features.

$$x_{norm}^i = \frac{x^i - \min\,(x)}{\max\,(x) - \min\,(x)}, \qquad (13)$$

where, $\max\,(x)$ and $\min\,(x)$ are the maximum value and the minimum value of x over all users, respectively.

Algorithm 1. The Rebalance Process

Input: User train set d, Test set u.
Output: Class of sample u_i in u ($C(u_i)$)
  $D1$=ROS(d), $D2$=RUS(d), $D3$=ST(d)
  Train classifier C_1 using classifier with $D1$
  Train classifier C_2 using classifier with $D2$
  Train classifier C_3 using classifier with $D3$
  for $m = 1; m <= 3; m++$ **do**
    if $C_m(u_i) = 1$ **then**
      $U_{true} = U_{true} + 1$
    else
      $U_{false} = U_{false} + 1$
    end if
  end for
  if $U_{true} > U_{false}$ **then**
    $C(u_i)$ is *True user*
  else
    $C(u_i)$ is *Fake user*
  end if
  $C(u_i) = $ *Ture user* or *Fake user*

3.7 Summary

In the former section, we describe the user-based features we use, text-based features, avatar-based features, and text processing methods. We used a total of 17 features to verify the user's avatar authenticity. In order to obtain objective and accurate experimental results, we will use a variety of classifiers for experiments. Which are: support vector machine (SVM), logistic regression, random forest. And we will use cross-validation in our experiment.

4   Experiment

4.1   Data Set

The data we used was crawled on Sina Weibo. It is a service website launched by Sina.com.

We crawl user data by crawler. In order to reduce the cold start problem that newly registered users may bring, and in order to cover as many users as possible, we selectively crawl users who have registered for more than 4 years and have more than 400 blogs, and we only choose users who use the person's avatar as the user's avatar. After removing duplicates, according to statistics, we have climbed a total of 3,448 users. The number of user blogs is 5,015,998, with an average of more than 1,400 per user.

We use the BERT model to determine the emotional polarity of blogs. We manual mark the training set. And we chose two markers to give the same marked blog. After processing, we obtained 10,400 blog posts with good emotional polarity. We use these 10,000 of data as a training set and use the remaining 400 as a test set to verify accuracy.

Labeling follows the following criteria:

- Determine if the user is a person avatar.
- According to behavioral features: reposting a large number of advertisements, hype information, having obvious product intent or a large amount of low-quality text. If so, mark it as '0'.
- According to the user's photo album, observe that the user's daily pictures compared with the user's avatar. If they are the same, marked as '1', otherwise they marked as '0'.

After the tag is completed, we select the users whose two markers are marked as a same answer, and the non-same answer users are marked again by the third person. After this processing, we marked 2175 real avatar users and 1273 fake avatar users.

4.2   Evaluation Preparation

Parameter Set. In the LDA model, $\alpha=\frac{50}{K}$, $\beta=0.01$, which is a common value from Asuncion et al. [14]. Asuncion's experiment proves that the value of the hyper-parameters has little effect on the experimental results. The number of topics K we chose 5, 10, 20, 30 and 40 for test. We use JGibbsLDA [15] to calculate the blog's topic distribution.

For support vector machines, we choose LibSVM [16]. For the parameter settings of other classifiers, we use the default parameters in WEKA.

Evaluation Metrics. We use the common evaluation criteria in the field of information retrieval, which are accuracy, precision, recall, and F1-score.

$$P_{accuracy} = \frac{(TP+TN)}{\text{Total}}, \tag{14}$$

$$P_{precision} = \frac{TP}{(TP+FP)}, \tag{15}$$

$$P_{recall} = \frac{TP}{(TP+FN)}, \tag{16}$$

$$F_1 = \frac{2P_{recall}P_{precision}}{P_{recall}+P_{precision}}, \tag{17}$$

where TP is the correct number predicted in the positive class, TN is the number of prediction errors in the positive class, FP is the correct number predicted in the negative class, and FN is the number of prediction errors in the negative class.

4.3   Evaluation Result

LDA and BERT. In order to ensure the accuracy of the LDA model, we set the topic number are 5, 10, 20, 30 and 40. The tested by random forest classifier. The experimental results are shown in Table 2. To verify the accuracy of the emotion analysis, we validated the BERT model using 400 test set. The experimental results are shown in Table 3.

Table 2. Experimental results under different LDA topics

LDA topic	5	10	20	30	40
Accuracy	79.4%	80.4%	79.3%	79.2%	79.1%

Table 3. BERT model experiment results

Metrics	BERT model
Accuracy	87.3%
Recall	86.3%
F1-score	86.8%

In Table 2, The number of topics is 10 with the highest accuracy, we chose to set the number of topics to 10. According to Table 3, the accuracy of the model reached 87.3%, the recall rate reached 86.3%, and the F1-score reached 86.8%. Which it has a high experiment result. Based on this model, we predicted the emotional polarity of all blogs and calculated the user's emotional polarity features.

Result. In this section, the training set is composed of 1975 real avatar users and 1073 false avatar users. The test set consists of 200 real avatars and 200 fake avatar users. The experimental results are shown in Fig. 2 and Table 4.

Table 4. Our proposed method are compared with existing methods on balance and imbalanced data set

Classifier	Precision	Recall	F-score
Support Vector Machines	77.8% ± 0.3	77.6% ± 0.3	77.7 ± 0.2
Random forest	80.2% ± 0.1	80.1% ± 0.2	80.2% ± 0.1
Logistic regression	77.9% ± 0.4	78.0% ± 0.2	77.9% ± 0.2
Support Vector Machines with sampling	80.8% ± 0.2	80.6% ± 0.2	80.7% ± 0.2
Random forest with smapling	84.4% ± 0.2	84.1% ± 0.1	84.3% ± 0.1
Logistic regression with sampling	80.1% ± 0.1	80.0% ± 0.1	80.1% ± 0.1

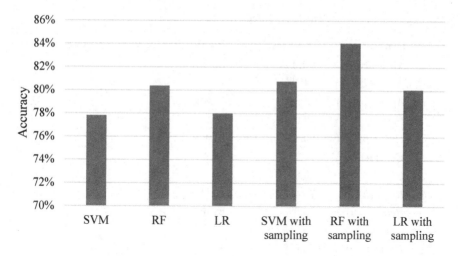

Fig. 2. The accuracy of our proposed method

According to the Fig. 2 and Table 4, the random forest has better accuracy than other classifiers. It maintaining a high recall rate and F-score. Based on the same data set, we found that the sampled data has a better experimental effect than the unsampled data. Compared to unsampled data, Random forest with sampling recall can reach 84.22%, which increased about 4%. Both precision and F1-score have improved. However, the proportion of the sampled data on the support vector machine and logistic regression is smaller than the random forest model.

In addition, we also tested the validity of each feature we used. Based on the previous experiment, we chose the model trained by random forest with sampling. Table 5 is the experimental result to verify each feature under the classifier. According to the results of the test. We found that $Respost(u)$, $Comment(u)$, $Like(u)$ have less impact on the experiment. In fact, many users with higher influence have higher activity and interaction rate, but they do not use a real avatar. In $Description(u)$, we found that nearly all of the users we crawled had description, and only a few users didn't have a description. The experimental results show that the effect is small. Other features have a bigger impact on the experimental results, indicating that the features we selected are valid.

In Table 6, we calculated the duration of training and testing. Although the random forest has a long train and prediction duration, but it has the highest accuracy. At the same time, the sampled data can reduce the calculation duration and improve the efficiency of the model.

According to Table 6, although the random forest has a long train and prediction duration, but it has the highest accuracy. At the same time, the sampled data can reduce the calculation duration and improve the efficiency of the model.

Table 5. Effectiveness of features

Feature	Random forests	Random forests with sampling
All Features	**80.4%**	**84.1%**
Authority (*u*)	74.5%	78.6%
Attention (*u*)	73.8%	79.8%
Fan (*u*)	73.0%	77.2%
Description (*u*)	80.4%	84.1%
Verified (*u*)	77.7%	80.9%
Blog (*u*)	76.8%	80.7%
Rank (*u*)	75.4%	80.2%
Release (*u*)	75.9%	81.6%
Gender (*u*)	70.2%	75.1%
Respost (*u*)	80.0%	83.7%
Comment (*u*)	80.2%	83.9%
Like (*u*)	79.8%	83.0%
Picture (*u*)	76.7%	80.9%
Positive (*u*)	75.0%	79.8%
Negative (*u*)	75.5%	79.2%
Topic (u_K)	75.7%	80.2%
Position (*u*)	75.3%	79.9%

Table 6. Duration of training and testing

Classifier	Train time	Test time
Support Vector Machines	14.3 s	0.66 s
Random forest	9.86 s	0.2 s
Logistic regression	2.22 s	0.05 s
Support Vector Machines with sampling	6.19 s	0.69 s
Random forest with smapling	8.81 s	0.31 s
Logistic regression with sampling	1.35 s	0.08 s

5   Conclusions and Future Work

In this paper, we present a detection method base on user, text, and avatar, and based on our research on user's avatar, we propose a variety of features. Considering the existence of the imbalance problem, RUS, ROS, and ST are used to deal with imbalanced data in the training process. Through analysis and comparison, our experiments can achieve better results than other classifiers. Our method can more effectively determine avatar authenticity. However, the method should require more complex calculations for avatar gender matching.

Our future work will focus on adding more avatar-based features. Increase the analysis of the user's photo album, and combine the photo album with the avatar to determine the avatar authenticity.

References

1. Ding, C., He, X., Husbands, P., Zha, H., Simon, H.: Pagerank, hits and a unified framework for link analysis. In: Proceedings of the 2003 SIAM International Conference on Data Mining, pp. 249–253. SIAM (2003)
2. Laleh, N., Carminati, B., Ferrari, E.: Risk assessment in social networks based on user anomalous behaviors. IEEE Trans. Dependable Secure Comput. **15**(2), 295–308 (2016)
3. Kumar, D., Shaalan, Y., Zhang, X., Chan, J.: Identifying singleton spammers via spammer group detection. In: Phung, D., Tseng, V.S., Webb, G.I., Ho, B., Ganji, M., Rashidi, L. (eds.) PAKDD 2018. LNCS (LNAI), vol. 10937, pp. 656–667. Springer, Cham (2018). https://doi.org/10.1007/978-3-319-93034-3_52
4. Gupta, P., Goel, A., Lin, J., Sharma, A., Wang, D., Zadeh, R.: WTF: the who to follow service at Twitter. In: Proceedings of the 22nd International Conference on World Wide Web, pp. 505–514. ACM (2013)
5. Liang, H., Lu, G., Xu, N.: Analyzing user influence of microblog. In: 2012 IEEE Fifth International Conference on Advanced Computational Intelligence (ICACI), pp. 15–22. IEEE (2012)
6. Ott, M., Cardie, C., Hancock, J.T.: Negative deceptive opinion spam. In: Proceedings of the 2013 Conference of the North American Chapter of the Association for Computational Linguistics: Human Language Technologies, pp. 497–501 (2013)
7. Shojaee, S., Murad, M.A.A., Azman, A.B., Sharef, N.M., Nadali, S.: Detecting deceptive reviews using lexical and syntactic features. In: 2013 13th International Conference on Intelligent Systems Design and Applications, pp. 53–58. IEEE (2013)
8. Mukherjee, A., Venkataraman, V., Liu, B., Glance, N.: What yelp fake review filter might be doing? In: Seventh International AAAI Conference on Weblogs and Social Media (2013)
9. Devlin, J., Chang, M.-W., Lee, K., Toutanova, K.: BERT: pre-training of deep bidirectional transformers for language understanding. arXiv preprint arXiv:1810.04805 (2018)
10. Blei, D.M., Ng, A.Y., Jordan, M.I.: Latent Dirichlet allocation. J. Mach. Learn. Res. **3**(Jan), 993–1022 (2003)
11. Kubat, M., Matwin, S., et al.: Addressing the curse of imbalanced training sets: one-sided selection. In: ICML, vol. 97, pp. 179–186, Nashville, USA (1997)
12. Mani, I., Zhang, I.: kNN approach to unbalanced data distributions: a case study involving information extraction. In: Proceedings of Workshop on Learning from Imbalanced Datasets, vol. 126 (2003)
13. Batista, G.E.A.P.A., Prati, R.C., Monard, M.C.: A study of the behavior of several methods for balancing machine learning training data. ACM SIGKDD Explor. Newsl. **6**(1), 20–29 (2004)
14. Asuncion, A., Welling, M., Smyth, P., Teh, Y.W.: On smoothing and inference for topic models. In: Proceedings of the Twenty-Fifth Conference on Uncertainty in Artificial Intelligence, pp. 27–34. AUAI Press (2009)

15. Phan, X.-H., Nguyen, L.-M., Horiguchi, S.: Learning to classify short and sparse text & web with hidden topics from large-scale data collections. In: Proceedings of the 17th International Conference on World Wide Web, pp. 91–100. ACM (2008)
16. Chang, C.-C., Lin, C.-J.: LIBSVM: a library for support vector machines. ACM Trans. Intell. Syst. Technol. 2, 27:1–27:27 (2011)

Multi-granularity Convolutional Neural Network with Feature Fusion and Refinement for User Profiling

Bo Xu[1,2], Michael M. Tadesse[1], Peng Fei[1], and Hongfei Lin[1(✉)]

[1] Dalian University of Technology, Dalian, People's Republic of China
hflin@dlut.edu.cn
[2] State Key Laboratory of Cognitive Intelligence,
iFLYTEK, Hefei, People's Republic of China

Abstract. User profiling is an important research topic in social media analysis, which has great value in research and industries. Existing research on user profiling has mostly focused on manually handcrafted features for user attribute prediction. However, the research has partly overlooked the social relation of users. To address the problem, we propose a multi-granularity convolutional neural network model with feature fusion and refinement. Our model leverages the convolution mechanism to automatically extract user latent semantic features with respect to their attributes from social texts. We also combine different machine learning methods using the stacking mechanism for feature refinement. The proposed model can capture the social relation of users by combining semantic context and social network information, and improve the performance of attribute classification. We evaluate our model based on the dataset from SMP CUP 2016 competition. The experimental results demonstrate that the proposed model is effective in automatic user attribute classification with a particular focus on fine-grained user information.

Keywords: User profiling · Feature fusion ·
Multi-granularity convolutional neural network · Feature refinement

1 Introduction

In recent years, online social media, such as Twitter, Facebook, and Sina Microblog, have developed rapidly. The amount of user data on social media increases accordingly. These user data, as an important resource, can accurately characterize social media users for user profiling. User profiling has thus become one of the hottest research topics in social media analysis, and has been applied to various domains, such as precision marketing, precision medical care, and financial risk forecasting. User attribute classification is a crucial problem in user profiling, which has significant commercial value in modern society. Since social media provide abundant user information for analyzing and inferring user attributes [1, 2], social media analysis based on user attribute classification has therefore become an effective way to discover potential business customers and generate intelligent marketing reports for different brands.

© Springer Nature Switzerland AG 2019
Q. Zhang et al. (Eds.): CCIR 2019, LNCS 11772, pp. 161–172, 2019.
https://doi.org/10.1007/978-3-030-31624-2_13

Previous research on user attribute classification has mostly focused on feature engineering [3–5]. Feature engineering generally requires much manual labor to design and extract task-specific features, which may partly limit the scalability of learned classification models. Different features are extracted for different attributes to achieve the ideal performance. Moreover, most studies using feature engineering were based on traditional machine learning classifiers [1, 6–8]. These studies may ignore semantic information in text and social information in user relationships.

In this paper, we propose a novel user profiling method for user attribute classification. Our method aims to capture the social and semantic information of users from fine-grained features. The proposed method makes the most of user-generated text and user social networks by combining text and social relation embedding in an end-to-end model. The learned model can automatically extract multi-granularity features for attribute classification tasks. We propose a multi-granularity convolution neural network to capture fine-grained user features using word embedding in the proposed model. We also combine difference machine learning classifiers for feature refinement. We conduct experiments to evaluate the effectiveness of our method on the dataset from the SMP CUP 2016 competition. Experimental results show that the proposed method can achieve the state-of-the-art performance for the user attribute classification task. The contributions of this paper are as follows.

- We extract abundant multi-granularity user features as model inputs based on the user generated contents and user social relationships. These features encode comprehensive user information for user profiling.
- We propose a multi-granularity neural network model based on the convolution mechanism to model social media users. The network integrates different types of features to capture more semantic information of users.
- We adopt the stacking mechanism to combine different types of machine learning classifiers, which model user preferences from different perspective. The outputs of stacked models refine the user features for more useful information.
- We conduct experiments to evaluate the effectiveness of the proposed method for the user attribute classification task. The experimental results show that the proposed model is effective in user profiling.

2   Related Work

Recently, the study of user attribute classification has attracted much attention in the research area of user profiling. Most early research focused on long text generated from social media platforms, such as blogs. For example, Schler et al. [13] built handcrafted feature sets to classify social media users in terms of age and gender by analyzing user writing styles differences and generating user contents for different ages and genders. Mukherjee et al. [14] combined feature selection methods and part-of-speech information to enhance the accuracy of blogger gender prediction.

With the development of short text based social media, many studies have focused on social data. User attribute classification has become one of the hottest research topics [4]. Burger et al. [15] extracted n-grams and other handcrafted features from microblog texts, user personal descriptions and user names. They modified the balance winnow algorithm with the extracted features to improve the performance of user gender classification. Miller et al. [16] combined the perceptron with the Bayes model using n-gram features for user gender classification. Their study implied that men paid more attention to technical celebrities, and women were more interested in family celebrities. Based on this information, they improved the performance of gender classification. Mueller et al. [17] used user names in Twitter to handcraft a variety of features based on word structures for user gender classification. These studies have indicated that information from social media can benefit user attribute classification with handcrafted features.

Existing studies have also focused on the extraction of different user attributes. For example, Bo et al. [18] incorporated information gain and the maximum entropy into feature selection for user geographical classification. Their method built a related geographical vocabulary to reduce feature dimensions for accelerating the classification. Ahmed et al. [19] applied the Chinese restaurant process to the recognition of geometrical name entities based on probability models and used the hierarchical relation information of each geographical location for geographical attribute extraction. Rahimi et al. [6] integrated the social relation information into extracting the information of the character '@' in microblogs, and they used the label propagation algorithm and the logistic regression model to improve the prediction of user geographical attributes. Another important research topic in user attribute classification is how to represent users as vectors for measuring user similarities based on representation learning techniques. Some recent studies have focused on this topic. For example, Peng et al. [20] proposed a new method to simultaneously identify the feature dimension of the learned subspace and learn the underlying subspace in the presence of Gaussian noise to boost classification accuracy, robustness and efficiency. They also bridged the gap between Frobenius-norm-based representation (FNR) and nuclear-norm-based representation (NNR) for providing new insights to understand FNR and NNR under a unified framework [21]. Word representation methods have also been used in user attribute classification tasks. Furthermore, Le et al. [22] represented sentences and documents as low-dimensional dense vectors to capture abundant semantic information. Some studies have also attempted to develop effective representations of nodes in large-scale graph. These methods have been successfully useful in many tasks, such as visualization, node classification, and link prediction.

3   Methodology

This section provides more details on the proposed model for user profiling. Our model first integrates abundant multi-granularity features of social media users as inputs. The input features are divided into two groups: text features and social features. Text features are extracted from microblogs of certain users, which can be further divided as microblog granularity features and user granularity features. Social features are extracted based on the social network of the users. We then use a feature fusion layer and a feature refinement layer to capture more effective information from input features. The feature fusion layer involves the convolutional neural network combined with multi-granularity features of users to take full advantage of the user generated contents. The feature refinement layer is designed to capture the useful information obtained from different models, because different models can construct the user profiles from different perspectives. We adopt seven machine learning models to refine user text features, and stack these multi-model results as outputs. Finally, we use an integrated output layer to combine the outputs of the feature fusion and feature refinement layers for ultimate user profiling. The overall framework of the proposed model is shown in Fig. 1.

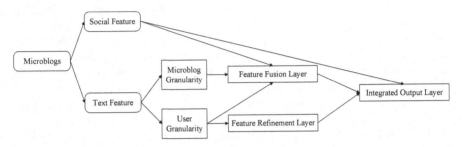

Fig. 1. The overall framework of the proposed model for user profiling

3.1   Multi-granularity User Feature Extraction

User generates large amounts of data by using social media in daily life, which involves abundant information for user profiling, such as the micorblog texts, user preferences, forwarding and temporal information. In our method, we extract multi-granularity features of users from the data, including text features and social features. We introduce these two groups of features as follows.

Text Feature. The microblog texts contain a large amount of information such as user habits, expressions, and topics of interest, which are critical in determining the attributes of users. In the existing research, microblogs of the user are investigated based on the bag-of-words model with n-gram features to predict the age and gender of certain users. However, this method may produce diverse prediction performance for users with different amounts of microblogs. To capture more comprehensive information of users, we consider two granularity feature representations of user's microblog texts: microblog granularity text features and user granularity text features.

a. Microblog granularity text features
   Different microblogs can always reflect user preferences from different perspectives, which contribute variously to user profiling. For example, some microblogs contain a lot of specific information, such as red envelopes, lottery, or phone charge. These microblogs tend to contain less useful information than those covering users' daily life, such as sunbathing and whining. The contents, quantity and proportion of different types of microblogs can reflect the user's own characteristics. Directly treating the microblog texts as bag of words may lose or dilute the useful information of users. In our method, the microblog granulariry text features first extract the TF-IDF features of each microblog, which reflects the independent

characteristics of each microblog. In order to better encode the semantic information of microblog, we introduce the pre-trained word embeddings to assign weights on the TF-IDF representations of microblogs, so as to obtain the embedded vector representation of each microblog for fine-grained text feature representation.

b. User granularity text features

User granularity text features aims to consider all the user generated texts as a whole to capture the user's overall presentation habits, writing style and other information. To extract user granularity text features, we calculate the TF-IDF features of each user's texts, which will then be taken as the inputs of the feature refinement layer. Since the TF-IDF feature of each user texts is high-dimensional and sparse, we adopt two methods to reduce the sparsity of user features for reduced user-level TF-IDF features. The first method uses singular value decomposition (SVD) to reduce the dimensionality of the TF-IDF feature representation. The second method uses average word embeddings weighted by TF-IDF for low-dimension user vector representations. We concatenate the two user vector representations by these two methods as the final user granularity text features

Social Features. In social media, user social behaviors are reflected by the characteristics of the relationship among users. To capture the social information of users, we extract social features from three respects: numerical statistical features, time statistical features and following statistical features. The numerical statistical features include the number of microblogs of each user, the number of comments, and the number of microblogs forwarded/commented. This type of features is used to obtain the online behavior characteristics and the degree of activity of users. For example, in general, young people tend to send more microblogs than the old-aged people. The time statistical features depict the number of login days of each user and the proportion of microblogs that are sent in each time period. This type of features can reflect the user's habit of publishing microblog. For example, people in different ages tend to update their microblogs at different time. Usually, people with older age like to browse microblogs during the day, while young people prefer to post and browse microblogs in the middle of the night or in the early hours of the morning. The following statistical features capture information such as the number of followers and the ratio of the number of comments to the number of followers. This type of features is used to reflect the user's level of attention and interaction. Usually, the phenomenon of mutual following among young people is more common, and more comments are forwarded to each other, while older users tend to comment less. Table 1 details these three types of features.

3.2 Feature Fusion Layer

The constructed multi-granularity features are vector representations of users from different perspectives, which is divided into fine-grained microblog text features and coarse-grained user text features. In order to better combine various feature representations, we propose a multi-granularity convolutional neural network model in feature fusion layer. Figure 2 shows the overall structure of the model.

The input of the model consists of three parts. The first part is the user granulariry text feature based on the TF-IDF feature of user microblog texts. The second part is the

Table 1. Three types of social features

Feature type	Specific features
Numerical statistical features	The number of microblogs, the number of deduplicated microblogs, the number of microblogs comments, the number of microblogs that have been forwarded, the number of microblogs with comments, the average number of microblogs, the average number of microblogs comments, and the microblogs comment rate (The number of commented microblogs/the total number of microblogs), the microblog forwarding rate (the number of microblogs with forwarding/the total number of microblogs), the number of microblogging sources, the total number of words in microblogs, the average number of words in microblogs, microblogs averaged word count, original microblog average word count, original microblog average word count
Time statistical features	Microblog login days, total active days (last day-first day), active days ratio (number of days to post microblogs/active days), number of daily microblogs, number of microblogs per day for each week, the number of login days per day in each week, the proportion of microblogs per day in each week, the number of microblogs on the workday/ proportion, and the number of microblogs/proportions in each time period (3 h and 6 h) are released according to the hourly statistics of each week. The number of microblogs, and normalized (7 * 24 dimensional features), according to the hourly statistics of the user, the number of microblogs, and normalized (24-dimensional features)
Following	Followers, microblog/comments/forwards vs. Followers, Follower Segmented by one-hot code

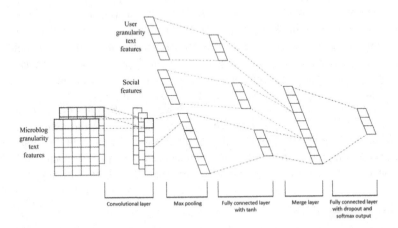

Fig. 2. Multi-granularity convolutional neural network model

social features including numerical statistical features and time statistical features. The third part is the microblog granularity text features including the weighted pre-trained the word vectors by TF-IDF values, and the SVD dimensionality reduced TF-IDF features. In order to distinguish the difference of semantic representations of different microblog users, we adopt the Convolutional Neural Network (CNN) to encode multiple microblog vectors. The local feature extraction ability of CNN network is used to highlight the latent semantics in text and social relationships. The microblog semantics, finally obtained by the maximum pooling layer and the fully connected layer, produce the final vector representations of users. This feature representation is concatenated with feature representations of multiple user granularities to form a final 300-dimensional user feature representation vector. Depending on the feature extraction ability of the network layer of different structures in the neural network, the model fuses multiple granularity features, and the obtained user vectors can well represent the characteristics of the users in terms of text semantics and user habits. User attributes can be predicted by classification via a Softmax layer.

Feature Refinement Layer. Microblog texts reflect the user topic of interest, word habits and other information. These types of information are closely related to the attribute of the users. One of the most widely used way in capturing the information is the classical model based on bag of words and TF-IDF weighting. Since this type of features are effective in many tasks, we adopt the stacking based fusion model to refine the features. The feature refinement layer is constructed by combining multiple machine learning models to make full use of the bag of word feature. The outputs of this layer are taken as the inputs of the integrated output layer. The structure of the feature refinement layer is shown in Fig. 3.

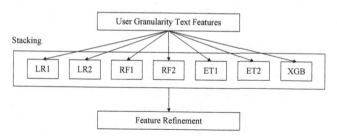

Fig. 3. Feature refinement layer

The user granularity text features are the combination of all text features of the microblogs of each user and the TF-IDF features calculated by the bag of word model. LR1 and LR2 represent logistic regression models with L1 penalty and L2 penalty, respectively. RF1 and RF2 represent two implementation versions of the random forest classification model with different parameters, respectively. RF1 is the CART tree based model with the Gini coefficient as the criterion, while RF2 is the CART tree based model with the information gain based on entropy as the criterion. Similarly, ET1 and ET2 represent two implementation versions of the extended random forest classification model [12] with the Gini coefficient and entropy as the criterion, respectively. XGB represents the XGBoost classifier with the linear mode. The above seven models are trained on the text features of the user granularity, and the outputted probabilities are combined by the stacking fusion method to obtain the 21-dimensional refined features, which is taken as inputs of the integrated output layer.

3.3   Integrated Output Layer

In our method, we first extract abundant social features based on microblog user behavior information. We then use the feature fusion layer to combine the user multi-granularity features as fused features. We also use a feature refinement layer to extract the refined feature to fully capture the useful information. Finally, we use the integrated output layer as the last layer of the framework to combine all the extracted features. The above three types of features are used as input features of the integrated output layer. Based on these features, eight XGBoost models are trained, and each model is selected to randomly train 80% of the training set to make a difference between the models. The main parameter settings of XGBoost are shown in Table 2. Finally, we adopt a plurality voting mechanism to obtain the final output of our method. The voting rules are shown as follows:

$$H(x) = c \underset{j}{\arg\max} \sum\nolimits_{i=1}^{8} h_i^j(x) \tag{1}$$

where h_i^j represents the output results of the ith XGBoost model on the label j.

Table 2. Parameters of XGBoost

Parameters	Values
objective	multi:softmax
booster	gbtree
max_depth	3
min_child_weight	1.5
subsample	0.7
gamma	2.5
eta	0.01
lambda	1
alpha	0

4   Experiments

4.1   Experimental Setup

We use the dataset from the SMP CUP 2016 competition[1] to evaluate the proposed method. The competition includes three subtasks in attribute classifications based on the same dataset. There are more than 350 teams participating in the competition. The dataset is constructed based on Sina Microblog, the largest social network website in China, which contains abundant information on social media users. The dataset contains three types of information, including social relations, microblogs and user

---

[1] https://biendata.com/competition/smpcup2016/.

attributes. Social relation information contains about 550 million followed relations of 25.67 million users. The followed relations are either one-directional or bi-directional. Microblogs provide the text information from 4.6 million users in the social network. User attributes include the age, gender and geographical attributes of about five thousand users from the above 4.6 million users with microblogs. These five thousand users are chosen by the organizer of the competition to compare the performance of different models. Readers can refer to the official website of the competition for more details. We provide the statistics of the used dataset in Table 3.

Table 3. Statistics of datasets

	#Users	#Microblogs	#Social users
Train	3200	241568	1561
Test	1240	95936	616
Total	4440	337504	2177

We examine the effectiveness of our models in three attribute classifications. The parameter values are empirically set in our model. Specifically, we pre-train 300 dimension word embeddings on a 5 GB Microblog dataset from SMP CUP 2016 with random initialization. We choose the dimension of word embedding following the existing models [9–11]. We tune the hyper parameters of our model using 10 percent of the training data as the development set. We switch the dimension of network embedding from 64 to 512 to obtain the optimal value. We observe that the accuracy tends to be higher with the dimension increase, but the cost on memory and time increases accordingly. We select the best configuration based on the performance on the development set.

4.2 Experimental Results

The competition used accuracy as the main evaluation metric, and we compare our method with the following baseline methods.

(1) LR1: LR1 model in the feature refinement layer;
(2) LR2: LR2 model in the feature refinement layer;
(3) RF1: RF1 model in the feature refinement layer;
(4) RF2: RF2 model in the feature refinement layer;
(5) ET1: ET1 model in the feature refinement layer;
(6) ET2: ET2 model in the feature refinement layer;
(7) XGB-Linear1: XGBoost model in the feature refinement layer;
(8) TCNN: Two-channel convolutional neural network in the feature fusion;
(9) XGB-Linear2: the model based solely on the feature refinement layer;
(10) MCNN: Multi-granularity CNN model used in feature fusion layer
(11) The proposed model: The integrated final model in the integrated output layer.

We report the comparisons of different models in Table 3. The reported performances are evaluated on the validation set and the test set, respectively (Table 4).

Table 4. Experimental result

Model	Validation set	Test set
LR1	53.63%	56.53%
LR2	56.53%	59.84%
RF1	58.13%	61.29%
RF2	58.94%	60.40%
ET1	58.38%	60.65%
ET2	59.28%	60.00%
XGB-Linear1	58.44%	60.48%
TCNN	**61.09%**	**63.15%**
XGB-Linear2	61.28%	63.15%
MCNN	**62.56%**	**65.00%**
The proposed model	**63.98%**	**67.98%**

From the table, we observe that in the feature refinement layer, only the accuracy of the logistic regression models LR1 and LR2 is relatively low, about 56%; while the performance of the other five models are comparable to each other on the validation set. On the test set, the accuracy rate has reached more than 60%. The reason may be that logistic regression is simply linearly combining different features, while the other five models use the principle of integrated learning so that better results can be obtained. Based on the models in the feature refinement layer, text features can help improve the accuracy on the validation set by 1.81%, and the accuracy of the test set is increased by 1.86%. This shows that text information capture more semantic information than the TF-IDF features in improving the overall performance. In the feature fusion layer, the accuracy of the MCNN model is 62.56% and 65.00%, respectively, which are higher than the XGB-Linear2 model using text features and social features. The results are also the best in all single models, which verifies the effectiveness of the proposed multi-granularity convolutional neural network model. In general, model fusion combines multiple models to give better prediction results than each single model. In the integrated output layer, we use the voting mechanism to obtain the final prediction results based on the stacking and fusing of features, which produces the best performance than other baseline models.

5   Conclusion and Future Work

This paper proposes a novel method based on neural networks and machine learning for microblog user profiling. Firstly, the multi-granularity features are extracted based on the division of microblog features. The features in the user's microblog data are divided into two categories, text features and social features. The text features continue to be refined into user granularity text features and microblog granularity. Based on this multi-granularity user feature extraction, we propose a multi-granularity feature fusion convolutional neural network model, which has achieved good results. In addition, based on the improved neural network model, in order to make full use of the multi-granularity features and social features of user microblog data, we propose to use multiple models to construct refined features combined with the integrated output of multiple model results. In this SMP CUP 2016 user profiling competition, we obtain the second place in the comprehensive score, and the highest accuracy of the age prediction subtask, which verified the effectiveness of the proposed method. In future research work, we will explore deeper information from social networks to better model social network users.

Acknowledgements. This work is partially supported by a grant from the Foundation of State Key Laboratory of Cognitive Intelligence, iFLYTEK, P.R. China (COGOS-20190001, Intelligent Medical Question Answering based on User Profiling and Knowledge Graph), the Natural Science Foundation of China (No. 61632011, 61572102,61702080) and the Fundamental Research Funds for the Central Universities (No. DUT18ZD102), Postdoctoral Science Foundation of China (2018M641691), the Ministry of Education Humanities and Social Science Project (No. 19YJCZH199).

References

1. Volkova, S., Bachrach, Y., Armstrong, M., et al.: Inferring latent user properties from texts published in social media. In: Twenty-Ninth AAAI Conference on Artificial Intelligence (2015)
2. Park, G., Schwartz, H.A., Eichstaedt, J.C., et al.: Automatic personality assessment through social media language. J. Pers. Soc. Psychol. **108**(6), 934 (2015)
3. Mueller, J., Stumme, G.: Gender inference using statistical name characteristics in Twitter. In: Proceedings of the 3rd Multidisciplinary International Social Networks Conference on SocialInformatics 2016, Data Science 2016, p. 47. ACM (2016)
4. Alowibdi, J.S., Buy, U.A., Yu, P.: Language independent gender classification on Twitter. In: Proceedings of the 2013 IEEE/ACM International Conference on Advances in Social Networks Analysis and Mining, pp. 739–743. ACM (2013)
5. Sloan, L., Morgan, J., Burnap, P., et al.: Who tweets? Deriving the demographic characteristics of age, occupation and social class from Twitter user meta-data. PLoS ONE **10**(3), e0115545 (2015)
6. Rahimi, A., Vu, D., Cohn, T., et al.: Exploiting text and network context for geolocation of social media users. arXiv preprint arXiv:1506.04803 (2015)
7. Ludu, P.S.: Inferring gender of a twitter user using celebrities it follows. arXiv preprint arXiv:1405.6667 (2014)
8. Sesa-Nogueras, E., Faundez-Zanuy, M., Roure-Alcobé, J.: Gender classification by means of online uppercase handwriting: a text-dependent allographic approach. Cogn. Comput. **8**(1), 15–29 (2016)
9. Chen, H., Sun, M., Tu, C., et al.: Neural sentiment classification with user and product attention. In: Proceedings of the 2016 Conference on Empirical Methods in Natural Language Processing, pp. 1650–1659 (2016)
10. Yang, Z., Yang, D., Dyer, C., et al.: Hierarchical attention networks for document classification. In: Proceedings of the 2016 Conference of the North American Chapter of the Association for Computational Linguistics: Human Language Technologies, pp. 1480–1489 (2016)
11. Cai, F., Chen, H.: A probabilistic model for information retrieval by mining user behaviors. Cogn. Comput. **8**(3), 494–504 (2016)

12. Peersman, C., Daelemans, W., Van Vaerenbergh, L.: Predicting age and gender in online social networks. In: Proceedings of the 3rd International Workshop on Search and Mining User-Generated Contents, pp. 37–44. ACM (2011)

13. Schler, J., Koppel, M., Argamon, S., et al.: Effects of age and gender on blogging. In: AAAI Spring Symposium: Computational Approaches to Analyzing Weblogs, pp. 199–205, June 2006

14. Mukherjee, A., Liu, B.: Improving gender classification of blog authors. In: Proceedings of the 2010 Conference on Empirical Methods in Natural Language Processing, pp. 207–217. Association for Computational Linguistics (2010)

15. Burger, J.D., Henderson, J., Kim, G., et al.: Discriminating gender on Twitter. In: Proceedings of the Conference on Empirical Methods in Natural Language Processing, pp. 1301–1309. Association for Computational Linguistics (2011)

16. Miller, Z., Dickinson, B., Hu, W.: Gender prediction on twitter using stream algorithms with n-gram character features. Int. J. Intell. Sci. 2(04), 143 (2012)

17. Mueller, J., Stumme, G.: Gender inference using statistical name characteristics in Twitter. In: Proceedings of the 3rd Multidisciplinary International Social Networks Conference on SocialInformatics 2016, Data Science 2016, pp. 47. ACM (2016)

18. Han, B., Cook, P., Baldwin, T.: Geolocation prediction in social media data by finding location indicative words. In: Proceedings of COLING 2012, pp. 1045–1062 (2012)

19. Ahmed, A., Hong, L., Smola, A.J.: Hierarchical geographical modeling of user locations from social media posts. In: Proceedings of the 22nd International Conference on World Wide Web, pp. 25–36. ACM (2013)

20. Peng, X., Lu, J., Yi, Z., et al.: Automatic subspace learning via principal coefficients embedding. IEEE Trans. Cybern. 47(11), 3583–3596 (2016)

21. Peng, X., Lu, C., Yi, Z., et al.: Connections between nuclear-norm and frobenius-norm-based representations. IEEE Trans. Neural Netw. Learn. Syst. 29(1), 218–224 (2016)

22. Le, Q., Mikolov, T.: Distributed representations of sentences and documents. In: International Conference on Machine Learning, pp. 1188–1196 (2014)

Author Index

Printed in the United States
By Bookmasters